CHILD ABUSE

OPPOSING VIEWPOINTS®

Other Books of Related Interest in the Opposing Viewpoints Series:

CHILD ABUSE

OPPOSING VIEWPOINTS®

David Bender & Bruno Leone, *Series Editors*

Katie de Koster, *Book Editor*
Karin L. Swisher, *Assistant Editor*

OPPOSING
VIEWPOINTS
SERIES®

Greenhaven Press, Inc.   PO Box 289009   San Diego, CA 92198-9009

Cover photo: Owen McGoldrick

Library of Congress Cataloging-in-Publication Data

Child abuse : opposing viewpoints / Katie de Koster, book editor : Karin L. Swisher, assistant editor.
        p.   cm. — (Opposing viewpoints series)
    Includes bibliographical references and index.
    Summary: Presents opposing viewpoints concerning issues related to child abuse, including what causes this form of abuse, and is it possible to justly prosecute it in the courts.
    ISBN 1-56510-056-5 (lib. : alk. paper) — ISBN 1-56510-055-7 (pbk. : alk. paper)
    1. Child abuse—United States.   2. Child abuse—Law and legislation—United States.   [1. Child abuse.]   I. de Koster, Katie 1948- . II. Swisher, Karin, 1966- . III. Series: Opposing viewpoints series (unnumbered).
HV6626.52.C55 1994
362.7'6—dc20   93-9240
                                                              CIP
                                                              AC

"Congress shall make no law . . . abridging the freedom of speech, or of the press."

First Amendment to the U.S. Constitution

The basic foundation of our democracy is the first amendment guarantee of freedom of expression. The Opposing Viewpoints Series is dedicated to the concept of this basic freedom and the idea that it is more important to practice it than to enshrine it.

Contents

Why Consider Opposing Viewpoints?

"The only way in which a human being can make some approach to knowing the whole of a subject is by hearing what can be said about it by persons of every variety of opinion and studying all modes in which it can be looked at by every character of mind. No wise man ever acquired his wisdom in any mode but this."

John Stuart Mill

In our media-intensive culture it is not difficult to find differing opinions. Thousands of newspapers and magazines and dozens of radio and television talk shows resound with differing points of view. The difficulty lies in deciding which opinion to agree with and which "experts" seem the most credible. The more inundated we become with differing opinions and claims, the more essential it is to hone critical reading and thinking skills to evaluate these ideas. Opposing Viewpoints books address this problem directly by presenting stimulating debates that can be used to enhance and teach these skills. The varied opinions contained in each book examine many different aspects of a single issue. While examining these conveniently edited opposing views, readers can develop critical thinking skills such as the ability to compare and contrast authors' credibility, facts, argumentation styles, use of persuasive techniques, and other stylistic tools. In short, the Opposing Viewpoints Series is an ideal way to attain the higher-level thinking and reading skills so essential in a culture of diverse and contradictory opinions.

In addition to providing a tool for critical thinking, Opposing Viewpoints books challenge readers to question their own strongly held opinions and assumptions. Most people form their opinions on the basis of upbringing, peer pressure, and personal, cultural, or professional bias. By reading carefully balanced opposing views, readers must directly confront new ideas as well as the opinions of those with whom they disagree. This is not to simplistically argue that everyone who reads opposing views will—or should—change his or her opinion. Instead, the series enhances readers' depth of understanding of their own views by encouraging confrontation with opposing ideas. Careful examination of others' views can lead to the readers' understanding of the logical inconsistencies in their own opinions, perspective on why they hold an opinion, and the consideration of the possibility that their opinion requires further evaluation.

Evaluating Other Opinions

To ensure that this type of examination occurs, Opposing Viewpoints books present all types of opinions. Prominent spokespeople on different sides of each issue as well as well-known professionals from many disciplines challenge the reader. An additional goal of the series is to provide a forum for other, less known, or even unpopular viewpoints. The opinion of an ordinary person who has had to make the decision to cut off life support from a terminally ill relative, for example, may be just as valuable and provide just as much insight as a medical ethicist's professional opinion. The editors have two additional purposes in including these less known views. One, the editors encourage readers to respect others' opinions—even when not enhanced by professional credibility. It is only by reading or listening to and objectively evaluating others' ideas that one can determine whether they are worthy of consideration. Two, the inclusion of such viewpoints encourages the important critical thinking skill of objectively evaluating an author's credentials and bias. This evaluation will illuminate an author's reasons for taking a particular stance on an issue and will aid in readers' evaluation of the author's ideas.

As series editors of the Opposing Viewpoints Series, it is our hope that these books will give readers a deeper understanding of the issues debated and an appreciation of the complexity of even seemingly simple issues when good and honest people disagree. This awareness is particularly important in a democratic society such as ours in which people enter into public debate to determine the common good. Those with whom one disagrees should not be regarded as enemies but rather as people whose views deserve careful examination and may shed light on one's own.

Thomas Jefferson once said that "difference of opinion leads to inquiry, and inquiry to truth." Jefferson, a broadly educated man, argued that "if a nation expects to be ignorant and free . . . it expects what never was and never will be." As individuals and as a nation, it is imperative that we consider the opinions of others and examine them with skill and discernment. The Opposing Viewpoints Series is intended to help readers achieve this goal.

David L. Bender & Bruno Leone,
Series Editors

Introduction

*"There is no more fundamental test of a society
than how it treats its children."*

Ronald Reagan

In the nineteenth century, American slaves were freed and animals were protected against cruelty while children were still considered their parents' chattel, to do with as they wished. Not until 1874 was the first court case of child abuse argued. The case, on behalf of a young girl named Mary Ellen, was brought by the American Society for the Prevention of Cruelty to Animals. The ASPCA successfully challenged the court to recognize that Mary Ellen was covered under laws barring inhuman treatment of animals. Society thus accepted a moral responsibility to protect children, even from their parents.

Eventually, many states responded to this moral responsibility by making child abuse illegal. Reporting child abuse, however, was still not required. Consequently, most child abuse remained unacknowledged. Finally, in 1974, Congress enacted the Child Abuse Prevention and Treatment Act. The act provided federal funds to fight child abuse for states that passed laws requiring certain professionals, such as teachers and health care personnel, to report suspected abuse. This financial incentive motivated every state to pass such a law. Now, many Americans had both a moral and a legal responsibility to report abuse.

That reports of child abuse now number in the millions annually is evidence that this responsibility is being taken seriously. However, although individuals may now be reporting abuse, the state does not always carry out its duty to protect the child once abuse has been reported. For example, for two years caseworkers for Wisconsin's Winnebago County Department of Social Services compiled careful records of the burns, bruises, and cuts that resulted in Joshua DeShaney's frequent hospitalization and his doctors' reports of suspected abuse. But the department left Joshua with his father. Joshua was not quite four when he was beaten into a coma and left permanently paralyzed and profoundly retarded. When Joshua was nine, the U.S. Supreme Court ruled that, even though county social workers had been aware of the abuse and had done little to stop it, Winnebago

County bore no constitutional responsibility for Joshua's fate. In commenting on the case, the editors of the *New Republic* noted, "Growing up free of physical abuse is not a constitutional guarantee. But preventing child abuse is nonetheless a vital function of the government, and the government seems to be failing at it."

Most observers would agree that the government ultimately must bear a large part of the responsibility for protecting children from abuse. For example, Article 19 of the United Nations Convention on the Rights of the Child directs that the state shall protect the child from all forms of maltreatment by parents or others responsible for his or her care. Giving the government this responsibility, however, can often produce unwanted consequences. Consider the case of Alicia Wade.

In San Diego in May 1989, eight-year-old Alicia was spirited away from her bed, raped and sodomized, then returned home before she was missed. Child Protective Services (CPS) decided, her protests to the contrary, that her father was the rapist and took the child from her family. For months, CPS workers and therapists worked at cracking the child's denial, finally persuading her to accuse her father. Just days before she was to be adopted into a new family (relatives of the CPS worker), two-year-old evidence surfaced that cleared her father and implicated a known molester who had committed a similar crime in the same neighborhood just five days after Alicia was attacked. Nearly two years and many thousands of dollars' worth of legal fees later, Alicia was reunited with her family.

In Joshua and Alicia's cases, egregious errors were made by the very government social workers responsible for protecting the children from abuse. Yet even well-intentioned, competent workers make mistakes because of the sheer volume of reports and the failures of the system. "Cases of real abuse go undetected and people are wrongly reported as possible abusers. The system fails everybody," charges Elizabeth Vorenberg, president of the National Coalition for Child Protection Reform. Clearly, while the government must be responsible in some way for helping abused children, measures are also needed to prevent the government from harming innocent families. The dilemma is summed up by social psychologist Carol Tavris: "Read only one case of a child being treated for gonorrhea of the throat . . . and you will feel a wave of nausea at what adults are capable of inflicting on children. Read only one false-accusation case, and you will feel misery and anger at what bureaucrats are capable of inflicting on parents."

How to handle the responsibility of protecting children from abuse is a common thread that runs through the subjects addressed in *Child Abuse: Opposing Viewpoints*. The authors examine the following questions: Is Child Abuse a Serious Problem?

What Causes Child Abuse? How Widespread Is Child Sexual Abuse? How Should the Legal System Respond to Child Abuse? How Can Child Abuse Be Reduced? As Debra Whitcomb writes in *When the Victim Is a Child*, "Public awareness has been aroused to unprecedented levels and with this heightened awareness has come political pressure to 'do something.'" It remains to be seen what that "something" will be.

Is Child Abuse
a Serious Problem?

Chapter Preface

A father doesn't notice his two-year-old has fallen into the swimming pool. A single mother on welfare goes out on a snowy night to buy medicine for her sick baby, leaving her three young children in an unheated apartment. An infant doesn't stop crying until his mother throws him against a wall. A man impregnates his daughter.

These incidents portray a wide range of behaviors, some of which are clearly abusive. But before the 1960s, few if any of the adults depicted in these incidents would have been charged with abuse. Abuse cases were only reported if they involved serious injury or death. As Susan Martin and Douglas Besharov write in *Police and Child Abuse*, "What happened in the family was regarded as largely a private matter." Then, in 1962, physician C. Henry Kempe described "the battered child syndrome" and suggested that doctors should report suspected abuse. In 1963, in large part due to the attention Kempe's article focused on the problem, 150,000 cases of maltreatment were reported; in 1991, the estimated number of abuse reports was 2.7 million. As the number mushroomed, child abuse, as Martin and Besharov put it, "came to be defined as a social problem needing social intervention and treatment."

Intervention—by individuals or government agencies—is imperative in some cases. In 1987, when six-year-old Lisa Steinberg was brutally beaten and left lying in a coma, the outcry that followed her death led many to insist that society be more vigilant and forceful in protecting its youngest members. However, as writer Robert P. Hey noted, "Some questions of abuse and neglect . . . involve the delicate relationship between the rights and responsibilities of family and government in the rearing of children."

Today, some Child Protective Services (CPS) personnel, haunted by failures to protect children like Lisa, act quickly when abuse is reported; they prefer the risk of family disruption to the risk of injury or death. Others prefer to try to preserve the family, using counseling, education, and social services. In both cases, though, authorities are intervening in family matters that once were considered private.

While experts debate where on the continuum of behavior we should draw the line—this is abuse and that is not; this concerns society as a whole, and that is the private concern of a family—children continue to be caught in the middle. The extent of child abuse and the degree of intervention society should provide are examined in the following chapter.

"Current rates of unfounded reports go beyond anything that is reasonably needed. Worse, they endanger children who are really abused."

The Extent of Child Abuse Is Exaggerated

Douglas J. Besharov

The number of reports of child abuse has increased significantly in recent years. In the following viewpoint, Douglas J. Besharov argues that many of these reports are inappropriate or unfounded. This glut of false reports, he says, makes it difficult for children who are abused to get help. Besharov, who was the first director of the National Center on Child Abuse and Neglect, is a legal scholar at the American Enterprise Institute for Public Policy Research, a conservative think tank in Washington, D.C.

As you read, consider the following questions:

1. What does Besharov think are the causes of the increased reporting of child abuse?
2. According to the author, what are some of the problems that are being inappropriately reported as child abuse or neglect? Why does he believe these reports are inappropriate?
3. What dangers result from the investigation of unfounded reports, according to Besharov?

News stories daily remind us that children are brutally maltreated by their parents—the very persons who should be giving them love and protection. Children are beaten until their bodies no longer heal, they are scalded with boiling water, they are starved and so dehydrated that their skin shrivels around their fragile bones, they are sexually assaulted and forced to perform all sorts of perverted acts, and they are locked in closets or tied to bed posts for days on end. Abused and neglected children are in urgent need of protection—protection that can be provided only if individual citizens are willing to help. . . .

Reporting suspected abuse and neglect is an indispensable first step in protecting endangered children.

Adults who are attacked or otherwise wronged can go to the authorities for protection and the redress of their grievances. But the victims of child abuse and neglect are usually too young or too frightened to obtain protection for themselves. Helpless children can be protected only if a concerned individual . . . recognizes the danger and reports it to the proper authorities.

Reporting begins the process of protection. . . .

Suspected Abuse Must Be Reported

Under threat of criminal and civil sanctions, all states now require a wide array of professionals—including physicians, nurses, dentists, mental health professionals, social workers, teachers (and other school officials), day care or child care workers, and law enforcement personnel—to report suspected child abuse and neglect. About twenty states require all citizens to report, regardless of their professional status or relation to the child. And, of course, all states *allow* any person to report. . . .

Unfortunately, professionals and lay persons alike often make the wrong decision—either in favor of a report when the child is not in danger or against a report when the child needs protection. . . .

Abused and neglected children are dying because they are not being reported to the authorities and because the wrong children are being reported. Thus, efforts to encourage more complete reporting must be joined with efforts to reduce the harmfully high rate of inappropriate and unfounded reports. Otherwise, increasing the number of reports will only increase the number and proportion of children who are ineffectually and harmfully processed through the system. . . .

Mandatory Reporting

Almost all states have laws that require the reporting of *all* forms of suspected child maltreatment, including physical abuse, sexual abuse and exploitation, physical neglect, and emotional maltreatment. Under a threat of civil and criminal penalties, these laws require most professionals who serve children to report suspected child abuse and neglect. About twenty states require all citizens to report. But in all states, any citizen is allowed to report.

Child Abuse and Neglect Reporting 1976-1991

Year	Number of Children Reported
1976	669,000
1977	838,000
1978	836,000
1979	988,000
1980	1,154,000
1981	1,225,000
1982	1,262,000
1983	1,477,000
1984	1,727,000
1985	1,919,000
1986	2,086,000
1987	2,157,000
1988	2,243,000
1989	2,407,000
1990	2,537,000
1991	2,694,000

These statistics, based on information supplied by the states to the American Humane Association (AHA), include "unfounded" reports, which are now an estimated 55 to 65 percent of all reports. In 1986, the American Association for Protecting Children of the AHA counted the total number of reported child victims (AAPC, 1988). This number is the base from which the 1987-1991 estimated numbers of reported child victims were derived by the National Committee for Prevention of Child Abuse (e.g., in 1987, the 2,157,000 estimate represents a 3 percent increase over 2,086,000). Figures for 1991 are based on 1989 census data.

These reporting laws and the associated public awareness campaigns have been strikingly effective. In 1963, about 150,000 children came to the attention of public authorities because of suspected abuse or neglect. By 1976, an estimated 669,000 children were reported annually. And, in 1987, almost 2.2 million children were reported—more than fourteen times the number reported in 1963. . . .

Most Reports "Unfounded"

At the same time that many seriously abused children go unreported, there is an equally serious problem that further undercuts efforts to prevent the maltreatment of children: The nation's child protective agencies are being inundated by "unfounded" reports. Although rules, procedures, and even terminology vary (some states use the phrase "unfounded," while others use "unsubstantiated" or "not indicated"), in essence, an "unfounded" report is one that is dismissed after an investigation finds insufficient evidence on which to proceed.

The emotionally charged desire to "do something" about child abuse, fanned by repeated and often sensational media coverage, has led to an understandable but counterproductive overreaction by professionals and citizens who report suspected child abuse. Depending on the community, as many as 65 percent of all reports are closed after an initial investigation reveals no evidence of maltreatment. This situation is in sharp contrast to 1975, when only about 35 percent of all reports were unfounded.

New York State has one of the highest rates of unfounded reports in the nation, and its experience illustrates how severe the problem has become. Between 1979 and 1983, while the number of reports received by the Department of Social Services increased by about 50 percent (from 51,836 to 74,120), the percentage of substantiated reports fell about 16 percent (from 42.8 percent to 35.8 percent). In fact, the *absolute number* of substantiated reports actually fell by about 100. Thus, almost 23,000 additional families were investigated, but fewer children were aided.

"Take No Chances"

These statistics should not be surprising. Potential reporters are frequently told to "take no chances" and to report any child for whom they have the slightest concern. There is a recent tendency to tell people to report children whose behavior suggests that they may have been abused—even in the absence of any other evidence of maltreatment. These "behavioral indicators" include, for example, children who are unusually withdrawn or shy, as well as children who are unusually friendly to strangers. However . . . only a small minority of children who exhibit such behaviors have actually been maltreated.

Years ago, when professionals were narrowly construing their reporting obligations to avoid taking action to protect endangered children, this approach may have been needed. Now, though, all it does is to ensure that child abuse hotlines will be flooded by inappropriate and unfounded reports. For example, a child has a minor bruise and, whether or not there is evidence of parental assault, he is reported as abused.

Many hotlines accept reports even when the caller cannot give a reason for suspecting that the child's condition is due to the parent's behavior. This writer observed one hotline accept a report that a seventeen-year-old boy was found in a drunken stupor. That the boy, and perhaps his family, might benefit from counseling is not disputable. But that hardly justifies the initiation of an involuntary child protective investigation. As Chris Mouzakits, a professor of social work, concluded: "Much of what is reported is not worthy of follow up."

"Child Protection" vs. "Child Welfare"

There is a deeper problem. Across the nation, child protective agencies are being pressed to accept categories of cases that traditionally have not been considered their responsibility and for which their skills do not seem appropriate. In community after community, the dearth of family-oriented social services is pushing child protective agencies to broaden their role from that of a highly focused service for children in serious danger to that of an all-encompassing child welfare service.

In essence, child protective agencies are paying the price for their past successes. People know that a report of possible maltreatment will result in action. As a result, child abuse hotlines are being barraged by reports that, at base, really involve the truancy, delinquency, school problems, and sexual acting out of adolescents—not abuse or neglect. Other inappropriate reports involve children who need specialized education or residential placement; parent-child conflicts with no indication of abuse or neglect; and chronic problems involving property, unemployment, inadequate housing, or poor money management. Many of these reports result in the family receiving much-needed services, but many do not. Either way, these additional, inappropriate calls to child abuse hotlines significantly increase the number of unsubstantiated cases, misdirect scarce investigative resources, and are an unjustified violation of parental rights.

Even "Unfounded" Reports Cause Trauma

The determination that a report is unfounded can be made only after an unavoidably traumatic investigation that is, inherently, a breach of parental and family privacy. To determine whether a particular child is in danger, caseworkers must inquire into the most intimate personal and family matters. Often, it is necessary to question friends, relatives, and neighbors, as well as schoolteachers, day care personnel, physicians, clergymen, and others who know the family.

Richard Wexler, a journalist in Rochester, New York, wrote about what happened to Kathy and Alan Heath (not their real names):

> Three times in as many years, someone—they suspect an "unstable" neighbor—has called in anonymous accusations of child abuse against them. All three times, those reports were determined to be "unfounded," but only after painful investi-

gations by workers. . . . The first time the family was accused, Mrs. Heath says, the worker "spent almost two hours in my house going over the allegations over and over again. . . . She went through everything from a strap to an iron, to everything that could cause bruises, asking me if I did those things. [After she left] I sat on the floor and cried my eyes out. I couldn't believe that anybody could do that to me." Two more such investigations followed.

The Heaths say that even after they were "proven innocent" three times, the county did nothing to help them restore their reputation among friends and neighbors who had been told, as potential "witnesses," that the Heaths were suspected of child abuse.

Laws against child abuse are an implicit recognition that family privacy must give way to the need to protect helpless children. But in seeking to protect children, it is all too easy to ignore the legitimate rights of parents. Each year, about 700,000 families are put through investigations of unfounded reports. This is a massive and unjustified violation of parental rights. . . .

Incidence of Reports, Not of Abuse, Is Increasing

State-by-state data on the number of child abuse cases known to the CPS [Child Protective Services] in each state have been gathered since 1976, but these statistics show the rate of intervention rather than incidence. The difference can be illustrated by the fact that the rate of sexually abused children known to CPS doubled from 1976 to 1977 and by 1985 was twenty-one times as great as in 1976. It is extremely unlikely that American children suddenly became so much more vulnerable to sexual abuse. The underlying incidence may even have decreased. Why then has the CPS rate increased? It is not unreasonable to suggest that it reflects a dramatic change in the willingness of the public and human services professionals to intervene and report sexual abuse. Thus, when the annual reported rates of child abuse are published each year and show yet another increase, it should be taken as an indication of progress in the fight to protect American children.

Murray A. Straus and David W. Moore in *Family Violence*, 1990.

Few unfounded reports are made maliciously. Studies of sexual abuse reports, for example, suggest that, at most, 4-10 percent of these reports are knowingly false. Many involve situations in which the person reporting, in a well-intentioned effort to protect a child, overreacts to a vague and often misleading possibility that the child may be maltreated. Others involve situations of poor child care that, although of legitimate concern, simply do not amount to child abuse or neglect. In fact, a substantial proportion of unfounded cases are referred to other agencies to provide needed services for the families.

Some "Unfounded" Reports Are Legitimate

Moreover, an unfounded report does not necessarily mean that the child was not actually abused or neglected. Evidence of child maltreatment is hard to obtain and may not be uncovered when agencies lack the time and resources to complete a thorough investigation or when inaccurate information is given to the investigator. Other cases are labeled unfounded when no services are available to help the family. Some cases must be closed because the child or family cannot be located.

A certain proportion of unfounded reports, therefore, is an inherent—and legitimate—aspect of reporting *suspected* child abuse or neglect and is necessary to ensure the adequate protection of children. Hundreds of thousands of strangers report their suspicions; they cannot all be right. But current rates of unfounded reports go beyond anything that is reasonably needed. Worse, they endanger children who are really abused.

Inappropriate Reporting Endangers Abused Children

The flood of unfounded reports is overwhelming the limited resources of child protective agencies. For fear of missing even one abused child, workers perform extensive investigations of vague and apparently unsupported reports. Even when a home visit in response to an anonymous report turns up no evidence of maltreatment, workers usually interview neighbors, schoolteachers, and day care personnel to make sure that the child is not abused. And, as illustrated by what happened to the Heaths, even repeated anonymous and unfounded reports do not prevent a further investigation. All this takes time.

As a result, children who are in real danger are getting lost in the press of inappropriate cases. Forced to allocate a substantial portion of their limited resources to unfounded reports, child protective agencies are less able to respond promptly and effectively when children are in serious danger. Some reports are left uninvestigated for a week and even two weeks after they are received. Investigations often miss key facts, as workers rush to clear cases, and dangerous home situations receive inadequate supervision, as workers ignore pending cases to investigate the new reports that arrive daily on their desks. Decision making also suffers. With so many cases of insubstantial or unproved risk to children, caseworkers are desensitized to the obvious warning signals of immediate and serious danger.

These nationwide conditions help explain why 25-50 percent

of the deaths from child abuse involve children who were previously known to the authorities. . . .

If child protective agencies are to function effectively, they must be relieved of the heavy burden of unfounded reports. To call for more careful reporting of child abuse is not to be coldly indifferent to the plight of endangered children. Rather, it is to be realistic about the limits to our ability to operate child protective systems.

"Most serious child abuse still escapes the attention of child protective authorities, despite their expanded efforts."

The Extent of Child Abuse Is Not Exaggerated

David Finkelhor

Although reports of child abuse have increased greatly over the past few years, David Finkelhor states in the following viewpoint, most serious cases of child abuse are not reported to child protection authorities. Finkelhor argues that the extent of child abuse requires greater support for reporting, investigating, and providing services to families in trouble. David Finkelhor is codirector of the Family Research Laboratory at the University of New Hampshire at Durham.

As you read, consider the following questions:

1. To what does Finkelhor attribute the rise in the rate of unsubstantiated reports of child abuse?
2. How does the author respond to the charge that the child protective system is being called upon for services that are outside its mandate?
3. Why does Finkelhor think unfounded reports may help children?

Excerpted from David Finkelhor, "Is Child Abuse Overreported?" *Public Welfare*, Winter 1990, vol. 48, no. 1, © 1990 The American Public Welfare Association. Reprinted with permission.

Between 1976 and 1987 reports of suspected child abuse and neglect rose nationally from an estimated 669,000 to 2,163,000, an average increase of more than 10 percent each year. Virtually no one has asserted that this was due to a recent epidemic of abuse. Most authorities think that a large reservoir of serious and previously undetected abuse is now being reported because both professionals and ordinary citizens have a greater awareness of the problem. A substantial amount of research backs up this idea.

Recently, however, a dissenting point of view has been advanced. Some people feel this large and ever increasing number of reports is evidence of an overreaction by professionals. The most visible advocate of this contention is Douglas Besharov, a legal scholar at the American Enterprise Institute. Besharov is knowledgeable and influential: he was the first director of the National Center on Child Abuse and Neglect and an architect of many of the early policy initiatives around child abuse. . . .

Unfortunately, the evidence suggests that Besharov's contentions are based not on an accurate assessment of child abuse statistics or a clear understanding of the child welfare system but rather on anecdote, stereotype, and misunderstanding. They simply do not hold up.

The fallacies break down into four claims:

• that there has been a "steady increase" in the percentage of unfounded reports (in other words, a decrease in the percentage of founded or substantiated reports), an indication of overzealous reporting;

• that a large and increasing proportion of what is reported as child abuse is not serious and not really child maltreatment;

• that when a report is unfounded or not substantiated, it involves "an unavoidably traumatic investigation which is, inherently, a breach of parental and family privacy";

• that the current level of unfounded cases is a serious social policy problem that requires a radical revision in current practice.

A Decreasing Rate of Substantiation?

Besharov often cites an allegedly dramatic drop in the rate of cases that are substantiated or founded. He uses a figure from 1976, when he claims the substantiation rate was 65 percent, and contrasts this with more recent data that show the rates to be much lower.

But Besharov is wrong. Although some states have seen a decline in the substantiation rate, the national rate, to the extent we can follow it, has not declined. Our best study to date in fact suggests that nationally the rate is increasing. . . .

Until recently, the only national trends in substantiation had to be pieced together from the data collected by the American Humane Association (AHA). The AHA data have many problems that make conclusions from them risky, but they have been the data to which Besharov himself has referred. . . . The figures from 1976 through 1986 . . . show a fluctuation between 40 percent and 49 percent with no strong pattern. AHA Director Patricia Schene told a national research symposium in 1986, "There was a consistent national rate of substantiation over time, around 40 percent.". . .

A more rigorous evaluation of recent national trends in substantiation rates is now finally available, thanks to the completion of the Second National Incidence Study (NIS) of Child Abuse and Neglect. In this study, researchers picked a random sample of counties in 1980 and 1986 and monitored all reports to child protective services (CPS) agencies using a standardized set of definitions and data collection procedures. This methodology was the best way to control for inconsistencies and changes in state child abuse counting systems. The NIS actually found an increase in the substantiation rate, up from 43 percent in 1980 to 53 percent in 1986. Because this is the only data set using completely equivalent definitions and sampling procedures at two different times, it is the most reliable indicator we have; and it contradicts Besharov's thesis. . . .

So Besharov's claim about a disturbing drop in substantiation cannot itself be substantiated. We cannot be completely sure what is happening to national substantiation rates. . . . The best evidence, however, points either to no dramatic change or even to some increase nationwide.

Nonserious Reports May Account for the Increase

Besharov also claims that most of what is now being identified, reported, and treated as child abuse consists of "minor situations that simply do not amount to child maltreatment."

The picture painted by critics of the child protection system is that after 15 years experience the system has already adequately mobilized to discover the serious forms of child maltreatment that are its primary targets. If reports continue to increase, the increase must be due to an overextension of the child abuse dragnet. According to this argument, overzealous child abuse professionals and the public are trying to use the child welfare system to correct minor kinds of bad parenting. Some critics who rely on Besharov's analysis have gone even further, charging that in an era when other welfare programs are being gutted, liberal social reformers have capitalized on child abuse concerns to sneak services to disadvantaged—but not truly abusive—families by shunting them into the child welfare system under the rubric of child abuse.

Here again, the available evidence mostly contradicts the revisionist thesis. For example, the type of abuse whose reports and cases have been growing fastest in recent years is sexual abuse. Constituting only 7 percent of all cases in the late 1970s, by 1986 sexual abuse made up almost 16 percent. According to the NIS, while all known abuse cases were increasing 66 percent between 1980 and 1986, sexual abuse cases were more than tripling. No serious child welfare authority, including Besharov, has suggested that sexual abuse is a minor type of abuse or that the rise in sexual abuse cases is a devious attempt to expand the definition of child abuse. So here is one major increase that surely is warranted.

But overall, Besharov's approach to child abuse statistics seems callous. He minimizes 80 percent of all substantiated cases as "excessive corporal punishment, minor physical neglect, educational neglect or emotional maltreatment" by claiming without any detailed analysis that they "pose no serious physical danger." In this category he lumps all emotional abuse, which can include children locked for weeks or months in their rooms, children threatened with death, and children driven to suicide attempts. He also excludes any physical neglect where no serious physical injury occurs: for example, the mother who abandons her 3-month-old child in an alley or the mother who regularly leaves three unsupervised children under age 6 for the day in a squalid, rat-infested tenement—as long as these children are fortunate enough to be rescued before any actual physical injury occurs. He rules out nine-tenths of all physical abuse victims because according to the strict NIS criteria they did not suffer an injury severe enough to require professional care; this would exclude, for example, a child who had been shot at by his father, as long as the father missed. His claim that most substantiated child abuse is "minor" is based entirely on unsupported inferences from the NIS data.

Much Serious Abuse Is Still Not Reported

At the same time, Besharov ignores perhaps the most important conclusion from that study. Even using his own definition of seriousness, NIS data indicate that most serious child abuse still escapes the attention of child protective authorities, despite their expanded efforts.

One of the main functions of the NIS was to look at cases of child abuse that were known to professionals but were not getting into the CPS system. . . . The results show that a large proportion of serious abuse known to other professionals is not reported or identified by state child protection agencies. In 1986, only 40 percent of all maltreatment and 35 percent of the most serious cases known to professionals—cases involving children who had a fatal or serious injury or impairment as a result of abuse and neglect—were getting into the CPS system. There is an enormous reservoir of serious child abuse that CPS is still not discovering in spite of the increased reporting.

Nor is it true that an increasing portion of child protection work is monopolized by so-called minor cases. Here again evidence from the NIS data is clear. . . . According to NIS Director Andrea Sedlak, "Very little of CPS time and resources are being expended on the low priority, but . . . more than half of the very serious cases of child maltreatment still fail to come to the official attention of CPS."

The overall portrait one gets from the available data is not of a system that is casting an increasingly large net by diluting the meaning of child abuse or deviously trying to bring into its scope other tangential social problems. Rather the picture is of large numbers of seriously abused children, whose families and abusers have managed in past years to successfully evade detection, now finally being discovered by professionals and community members who have been sensitized to the problem. . . .

There is a great deal of confusion about what is involved when a child welfare agency declares a case unsubstantiated or unfounded. In his writing . . . Besharov's portrayal of child abuse investigations can be highly emotional and one-sided. The following is how he argues his case:

> The intrusive nature of some investigations is illustrated in the case of E.Z. v. Coler, where the parents claimed that the male caseworker completely undressed their two-year-old daughter in the presence of her four-year-old brother and a neighbor. They further claimed that he held her up to a light, spreadeagled, for visual inspection of her vaginal area. He then placed her on a couch and lifted her legs over his head to make a visual inspection of her anus.

If this incident actually occurred, it of course would be a terrible violation of a child's privacy. But Besharov admits in a footnote that "the court's opinion suggests that there is reason to question the accuracy of this claim." (It was made as part of a parent's suit against a child protection agency—which the court dismissed.) It is possible that violations of this sort have occurred, but they certainly are extreme cases. No one seriously believes them to be illustrative of child abuse investigations.

There is simply no evidence to back up the assertion that child protection investigations are "unavoidably traumatic." Moreover, there is some evidence to suggest that they are not.

In some child abuse reports that are classified as "unsubstantiated" the family is never contacted, let alone harassed. . . . A . . . recent study in 12 counties in five states found that 42 percent of all allegations of maltreatment were "screened out" by CPS agencies without any investigation at all: many because no injury was reported or the allegation was vague, some because the event happened too long ago or the perpetrator was not a caretaker, others because the child was no longer at risk (for example, was living somewhere else), and still others because the family could not be located or had left the CPS jurisdiction. Unfortunately, many people continue to equate an unsubstantiated case with a false allegation. In reality, unsubstantiated cases frequently mean that, for reasons of time or jurisdiction, no investigation was made.

Contact Is Not Necessarily Traumatic

Even when some contact with the family is made, this contact is not "unavoidably traumatic." According to talks with child protection officials, in the typical unsubstantiated investigation, a worker goes out to visit a family, talks with the parent about the incident, talks with the child about the incident, and, on the basis of the explanation given (say, for a bruise or an injury) and the demeanor of the child, decides that the report has no basis. . . .

Besharov's arguments that investigations are a "breach of . . . family privacy" and "coercive state intervention into family life" ignore the fact that the family is not the proper unit of analysis. Children and parents have different interests at stake in these matters. What may be intrusion for parents may be rescue for a child. Even in cases where abuse is not substantiated, the investigation may result in an improvement in conditions for a child by alerting parents to the potential for intervention or informing parents about the availability of services. The face-off in child protection is not simply, as Besharov portrays it, the state versus families.

"Unsubstantiated" Cases May Involve Abuse

Overall, child abuse reports have maintained a steady growth between 1985 and 1991 with an average increase of about 6% each year. . . .

The debate over how to estimate the national substantiation rate is almost as intense as the debate over how to interpret this statistic. . . .

Debate also centers on what "substantiation" means. Some take the inverse of this rate and conclude that this is the "unfounded" rate or the percentage of cases where no maltreatment occurred (Besharov, 1990). While some number of reports are indeed inappropriate, research suggests that some proportion of the unsubstantiated cases involve maltreatment or potential maltreatment. For example, the 1986 National Incidence Study noted that 9% of the cases determined to be unfounded by child protective service workers did indeed involve mistreatment that resulted in physical harm to the child. This figure represents a significant increase over a similar study conducted in 1980 in which only 3% of the unfounded cases were found to constitute maltreatment.

Deborah Daro, *Current Trends in Child Abuse Reporting and Fatalities: The Results of the 1991 Annual Fifty State Survey*, April 1992.

Besharov's argument might make more sense if all the parties involved in unsubstantiated investigations were innocent. Any intrusion would then clearly seem unjust. But this is not the case. In many unsubstantiated investigations, workers were simply unable to make firm determinations. Some of these children were being abused and will later be reported again. According to a recent study, approximately 25 percent of unsubstantiated cases will be reported again within a four-year period. As some states have learned all too painfully, in a few of these unsubstantiated cases the next report will involve a dead child.

In other situations, a case is unsubstantiated as a negotiated settlement with the child protection authorities in the same way that a criminal conviction may be plea-bargained. In some agen-

31

cies, if parents admit to the maltreatment and agree to a course of action, workers may declare the case unsubstantiated in return. Child protective investigations should be as unintrusive as possible, but one cannot simply judge any intrusion that occurs in an unsubstantiated case as a gross violation of the rights of innocent people.

So the strongest argument left to Besharov is that the intrusiveness of child abuse investigations is currently unknown and that isolated violative incidents have been reported. . . .

Society's Values Require Some Inefficiency

One of Besharov's points is sound. Large numbers of reports of child abuse are not substantiated. He puts this figure at 750,000 per year. At the very least, this appears inefficient. And even if only a small percentage of these cases involve unwarranted intrusion into families, this problem merits attention.

But Besharov deals these large numbers into an analytical void and claims that they are proof of a serious problem in the system. This is not the case. Like any other social enterprise, child abuse detection is a process that sometimes achieves its goal and sometimes does not. . . . The key question is whether the costs of the failures are somehow disproportionate to the social value of the successes. By such a standard, in fact, the child abuse reporting and investigation system is surprisingly cost-beneficial. . . .

Policy makers are willing to implement and the public is willing to tolerate very inefficient social control systems that sometimes entail serious invasions of privacy when the objective is important enough. People are frightened about crime; they do not want fellow citizens cheating on their tax returns; and they are afraid of airplane hijackings.

By comparison, the child welfare system is more efficient at rooting out problematic behavior than is the criminal justice system—and probably the tax audit system as well. It is also arguably less invasive under most conditions for those unfairly targeted. But the key issue highlighted by this comparison is that the degree of inefficiency and intrusion tolerated by the public is a function of the importance of the objective. Ultimately, Besharov's argument reduces to the premise that child abuse is not worth it: child abuse detection and the cases that are uncovered are not important enough to tolerate 750,000 unsubstantiated cases a year.

Besharov is clearly out of step with the American public. In national public opinion surveys, the public has urged again and again that more be done about the problem of child abuse. In the one recent national survey, respondents specifically endorsed the idea that "public child welfare agencies should investigate all reports of child abuse regardless of the seriousness of the charge" (67 percent) over a proposal that "parents should be reported as child abusers only when there is clear evidence of serious harm or injury to a child" (30 percent).

The goals of making the child protection system more efficient, effective, and fair are laudable. The system has many problems and many faults. Besharov's criticisms point to some key issues. . . .

But two of the major needs of the child protection system run exactly counter to Besharov's analysis. First, the system needs more trained staff to respond to reports, conduct investigations, and provide services to families. By almost everyone's analysis, the increase in serious child abuse cases coming to CPS attention has not been matched by commensurate increases in staff and budget to deal with these cases. This lack of staff has been one of the primary obstacles to effective action.

Second, the system needs greater public and professional confidence and esteem. Child welfare work needs to be honored and welcomed. The public clearly wants to combat child abuse. People need to be educated that this means accepting a modest level of outside scrutiny into the affairs of families. They also need to recognize that this sometimes entails difficult moral choices between family, neighborhood, and professional loyalties, on the one hand, and the welfare of children, on the other.

"Child abuse and neglect in the United States now represents a national emergency."

Child Abuse Requires Increased Government Intervention

U.S. Advisory Board on Child Abuse and Neglect

The U.S. Advisory Board on Child Abuse and Neglect was established under the Child Abuse Prevention and Treatment Act to evaluate efforts to treat and prevent child abuse and recommend ways to improve those efforts. In the following viewpoint, excerpted from the board's first report, the authors declare that child abuse is an emergency that threatens the integrity of the nation as well as abused children. While government has responded to the crisis to some degree, the response has been too little, too late—a situation, the board says, that is a moral disaster.

As you read, consider the following questions:

1. Why does the board believe that billions of dollars' worth of programs such as foster care and treatment of adolescent pregnancy are likely to fail?
2. Why do the authors argue that it is important to society as a whole for children to be protected from abuse?
3. What are some of the long-term problems the board foresees from the failure to prevent child abuse?

From *Child Abuse and Neglect: Critical First Steps in Response to a National Emergency* by the U.S. Advisory Board on Child Abuse and Neglect, the Department of Health and Human Services.

"It was the best of times, it was the worst of times,
it was the age of wisdom, it was the age of foolishness,
it was the epoch of belief, it was the epoch of incredulity,
it was the season of Light, it was the season of Darkness,
it was the spring of hope, it was the winter of despair,
we had everything before us, we had nothing before us,
we were all going direct to Heaven,
we were all going direct the other way."
                 Charles Dickens, A Tale of Two Cities

Dickens's characterization of life in 18th century Europe is valid today as a description of how America's children are faring. The health and potential longevity of most of the nation's children are greater than at any other time in American history. Neonatal and infant mortality rates have improved significantly over the last fifty years, and many fatal or crippling diseases such as poliomyelitis, diphtheria, and tetanus have virtually disappeared.

Yet in the midst of this picture of healthy children is a subpopulation for whom these are the worst of times. They are America's abused and neglected children. What renowned pediatrician Dr. C. Henry Kempe estimated to be a problem affecting 302 hospitalized "battered children" in 1961 has grown to a problem reflected by reports of 2.4 million abused and neglected children in 1989. . . .

For twenty-five years the nation has become more aware of the magnitude of child abuse and neglect. When the nation thought there were only 302 cases, the problem seemed manageable. With over two million reports, the nation is in very serious trouble, and, as Dickens says: ". . . going direct the other way."

The U.S. Advisory Board on Child Abuse and Neglect (the Board) has concluded that child abuse and neglect in the United States now represents a national emergency. . . .

Chronic System Failure

The board finds that, in spite of the nation's avowed aim of protecting its children, each year hundreds of thousands of them are still being starved and abandoned, burned and severely beaten, raped and sodomized, berated and belittled. The consequences of this maltreatment will remain with them throughout their lives. For some, those lives will be tragically short because many children die as a result of their maltreatment.

The Board further finds that the system the nation has devised to respond to child abuse and neglect is failing. It is not a question of acute failure of a single element of the system; there is chronic and critical multiple organ failure. In such a context, the safety of children cannot be ensured. Indeed, the system itself can at times be abusive to children.

MARGULIES
©1982 THE JOURNAL
ROTHCO

SOCIAL SERVICES

Monday's child was cruelly beat,
Tuesday's child had zero to eat,
Wednesday's child was badly burned,
Thursday's child's scars have returned,
Friday's child was forced into bed,
Saturday's child has more tears to shed,
But the child abused on Sabbath day
has nightmares which simply won't go away.

© Margulies/Rothco. Reprinted with permission.

Moreover, the Board estimates that the United States spends billions of dollars on programs that deal with the results of the nation's failure to prevent and treat child abuse and neglect. Billions are spent on law enforcement, juvenile and criminal courts, foster care and residential facilities, and the treatment of adults who themselves were maltreated in a prior generation. Billions more are spent on efforts to prevent substance abuse, eating disorders, adolescent pregnancy, suicide, juvenile delinquency, prostitution, pornography, and violent crime—all of which have substantial roots in childhood abuse and neglect. Programs (and dollars) that address these outcomes and do not address and recognize the relationship of abuse and neglect to them are not likely to succeed. . . .

A Moral Disaster

Child abuse is wrong. Not only is child abuse wrong, but the nation's lack of an effective response to it is also wrong. Neither can be tolerated. Together they constitute a moral disaster.

Children are in a dependent position because of their inability to care for themselves, or because the law and social custom have established that children are unable to act on their own behalf. Society has decided that healthy socialization demands that parents—and other adults charged with caring for children outside the home—should have great control over children's lives. It is especially cruel when such control, intended for children's own benefit, instead is used to degrade or exploit them.

Beating children, chronically belittling them, using them for sexual gratification, or depriving them of the basic necessities of life are repellent acts and cannot be permitted in a civilized society. Tolerating child abuse denies the worth of children as human beings and makes a mockery of the American principle of respect for the rights and needs of each individual.

Child neglect is also wrong.

Children must be given the basic necessities of life—food, shelter, clothing, health care, education, emotional nurturance—so that they do not suffer needless pain. If children are to become full participants in the community, then they must be given basic sustenance so that they will then be in a position to develop their own personality and point of view. Children are not in a position to obtain such sustenance on their own. When those who have assumed responsibility for providing the necessary resources for children (usually parents) fail to do so, it is wrong. When parents and other caretakers have the psychological capacity to care for their children adequately but lack the economic resources to do so, *society itself is derelict* when it fails to provide assistance.

Society Must Protect Children

All Americans share an ethical duty to ensure the safety of children.

The nation recognizes and enforces children's dependency upon adults. In such a context, Americans should ensure, at a minimum, that children are protected from harm. With the adoption in November 1989 of the Convention on the Rights of the Child, the United Nations General Assembly recognized such protection for children as a basic human right essential to their dignity.

Protection of children from harm is not just an ethical duty: it is a matter of national survival.

It is bad enough—simply immoral—that the nation permits assaults on the integrity of children as persons. To make matters worse, such negligence also threatens the integrity of a nation that shares a sense of community, that regards individuals as worthy of respect, that reveres family life, and that is competent in economic competition.

Although some children recover from maltreatment without serious consequences, the evidence is clear that maltreatment often has deleterious effects on children's mental health and development, both short- and long-term.

Maltreated children are more likely than their peers to have significant depression. They also are more apt to engage in violent behavior, especially if they have been subjected to physical abuse, and their social and moral judgments often are impaired. Maltreated children also tend to lag behind their peers in acquiring new cognitive and social skills, so that their academic achievement is chronically delayed.

An Endless List of Horrors

Family violence is a simple phrase, but it encompasses a horrifying list of abusive behaviors, both physical and psychological, inflicted by one family member on another.

Family violence refers to people who are beaten, slapped, punched, shaken, kicked, burned, raped, sodomized, starved, abandoned, thrown down stairs, stabbed, shot, bludgeoned, choked, grabbed, shoved and killed.

It covers people who are subjected to verbal abuse, threats against themselves and those they love, abuse of pets, destruction of property and forced isolation. People who are denied access to money, food, transportation, medical care and other necessities of life. Who are deprived of rights. Who are forced to watch or listen as others in their families are abused.

The list is endless. There is seemingly no end to the horrors some human beings can inflict on those whom this society calls their "loved ones."

Flora Johnson Skelly, *American Medical News*, January 6, 1992.

Often these effects are long-lasting and even intergenerational. For example, the rate of depression among adult women who report having been sexually abused as children is quite high. Adult survivors of sexual abuse also are especially likely to report concerns about their sexual adequacy. Similarly, aggressiveness is a remarkably persistent personality trait in abused boys and often is part of a pattern of continuing antisocial behavior. Although most maltreated children do not become maltreating parents, the risk of their doing so is markedly greater than if they had not been abused themselves.

Infants or young children are at greater risk of serious physical harm as a result of abuse or neglect. For evidence, one need only look at the costs accrued in intensive care units when infants are shaken or beaten, when young children suffer serious injuries when they are left unsupervised, and when infants "fail to thrive," and their survival and development are threatened by a lack of weight gain and emotional nurturance as a result of neglect.

Although most victims of serious and fatal child abuse are very young, to regard older children and adolescents as invulnerable to the severe consequences of abuse and neglect is a mistake. . . .

Incidence of Abuse

Some may question whether the incidence of child abuse and neglect amounts to an emergency. . . . The figures for abuse are approximate because there has been no consistent national effort to collect accurate data. Nevertheless, available information indicates that in 1989, 2.4 million reports of suspected child maltreatment were filed in the United States, of which more than 900,000 cases were officially substantiated. It has been estimated that 2.5 percent of American children are abused or neglected each year.

The increase in the number of reports of child maltreatment in recent years has been astronomical. When the "battered child syndrome" was first identified, C. Henry Kempe et al. estimated it to be a problem affecting 302 hospitalized children. In 1974, there were about 60,000 cases reported, a number that rose to 1.1 million in 1980 and more than doubled during the 1980's.

Experts do not know whether the increase in reports is primarily the result of a change in public awareness or whether it largely reflects actual increases in the incidence of some forms of child maltreatment. In either case, the number of substantiated cases of which the nation is now aware undeniably represents an extremely serious social problem requiring a major societal response.

Experts do know that the magnitude of the increase in reports is not the product of widespread vindictive, careless, or overanxious reporting. While such errors in judgment do occur occasionally, the proportion of substantiated cases (nearly one-half of all reports) has varied little since mandated reporting laws were enacted in the late 1960's. Accordingly, the absolute number of unsubstantiated cases has increased at a rate as shocking as the increase in the number of reported cases.

The number of substantiated cases of child maltreatment is almost too great to imagine, but there are reasons to believe that even that number is just a fraction of the actual incidence of child abuse and neglect. Surveys of professionals working with children consistently show that large proportions of cases of suspected child maltreatment remain unreported, despite the requirements of law. Moreover, some cases that are reported but not substantiated do in fact involve child maltreatment, but the evidence is inadequate to prove the cases. . . .

Massive Response Required

To say that the governmental response to date has not adequately served the interests of society in protecting its children from abuse and neglect is not to say that government at all levels has done nothing. To the contrary, government has done much.

Those actions, however, are dwarfed by the magnitude and complexity of the child protection crisis. Throughout the nation, resources remain insufficient to reduce child abuse and neglect significantly. There are not enough staff, funds, training programs, services to special populations, or prevention and treatment services to make a serious reduction of child abuse and neglect a reality.

Beginning in the 1970's—but certainly no later than the early 1980's—it might have been possible to design and implement a new strategy for protecting children with relatively little difficulty. Now, however, because of the towering crisis currently faced by the child protection system, the barriers to its fundamental restructuring are immense. Crisis remediation must precede the implementation of a new strategy.

America *must* and *can* begin *now* to establish a caring community for those of its children who are vulnerable to abuse and neglect.

4

"Abuse and neglect threaten children . . . by furnishing a pretext for extensive government intrusion into the family home."

Government Intervention Can Be Harmful

Family Research Council

While child abuse and neglect are serious problems worthy of our attention, the Family Research Council believes that government efforts to prevent child abuse have led to excessive intervention into family life. In the following viewpoint, the council argues that the government's response to child abuse has been overbroad. This too-enthusiastic reaction may result in the abuse of the family and, thus, harm the very children people are trying to protect. The Family Research Council, a nonprofit advocacy organization promoting traditional family values, is located in Washington, D.C.

As you read, consider the following questions:

1. What objections does the council have to the federal mandatory reporting system for child abuse?
2. Why does the council believe that the "nominally state-level" programs to deal with child abuse are actually a federal program?
3. What threats to constitutional rights does the council find in the present system?

From "Threats to Children: A Generation Under Siege," in *Free to Be Family* by the Family Research Council, Washington, D.C. Copyright 1992 by the Family Research Council. Reprinted with permission.

Truly caring about children can only begin properly by viewing them in their rightful context: their families. In light of the trend toward viewing children as separate from their parents, as potential clients or customers in commerce, and as a potential, separate client class even of government, this cannot be said too often or too forcefully.

The well-being of children is largely determined by individual choices made within their individual families. These are behavioral issues outside the reach of government action and bureaucratic programs. . . .

Parents, doing their best to guide their children through the shoals of increasing maturity, have in this generation confronted a growing obstacle: the intrusion of "experts" who claim superior knowledge in the arenas that are traditionally, and naturally, parental domain—both intellectual and moral education, sexual guidance, health questions, even parenting itself.

Most parents navigate around this intrusive obstacle, working hard to inculcate their own values in their children. Tragically other, external, threats remain. These threats are ones against which parents feel increasingly powerless to protect their children. . . .

Intervention Efforts Have Backfired

One [threat] frequently takes parents by surprise—very few parents expect to be harassed by a system that was set up to help children: the state child protective services. Nor are most parents aware of how few legal rights they have if they are accused of any wrongdoing by the child protective system. One mother found this out too late and spent a year battling with her local Department of Social Services to get her daughter back after being accused of sexually abusing her daughter. She had simply called with questions about breastfeeding. The night after her call, she was in jail and her daughter in foster care.

How can this happen? In response to the very serious problem of child abuse, massive federal and state education and intervention efforts have been put in place. An entire bureaucracy has sprung up to combat child abuse. Unfortunately, some of these efforts have backfired, seriously injuring the very children they were designed to protect. Besides being a grave threat to children in their own right, abuse and neglect threaten children in yet another way: by furnishing a pretext for extensive government intrusion into the family home, resulting frequently in traumatic disruption of viable families. Very simply, the child protective system is one that does not have the appropriate checks and balances required in the American judicial system.

In June 1990, the U.S. Advisory Board on Child Abuse and Neglect declared that the "abuse and neglect of children constitutes a national emergency." Calling the increase "astronomical," the Board reported that child abuse cases now top 2.4 million, a 200 percent increase since 1977.

The fact masked by the numbers is that "reported child abuse cases" are not necessarily actual cases of child abuse. 60 percent of the cases reported are dismissed as "unfounded reports" after an initial investigation. This is an unacceptably high percentage of wasted—and precious—investigation time. When flooded with reports of child abuse cases, state agencies cannot follow up quickly or even respond to all of them. The truly abused children may never receive care.

Child Abuse Allegations Suspend Rights of Accused

In many of our supposedly free states, the mere allegation of "child abuse" is now sufficient completely to suspend the constitutional rights of any parent unlucky enough to be so charged. An anonymous phone call is often all it takes to set social services in motion, and in many scenarios the accused is never allowed to face the accuser. The state's inquisition of experts takes over, at times extracting "evidence" from confused children via cruel brainwashing techniques and dragging families through the dungeons of a psychological hell, regardless whether they are really guilty, merely misunderstood, or entirely innocent.

C. Winsor Wheeler, *Chronicles*, March 1992.

Additionally, the range of maltreatment deemed to justify intrusive government action has been broadened to include "neglect," an imprecisely defined word. Approximately 80 percent of "child maltreatment" cases involve emotional or developmental dangers to children, but not a serious physical threat. Educational, emotional and physical neglect are difficult problems, but they do not fall into the same category with physical abuse that results in injury or death. Nor do they require the same urgent, emergency attention. Child abuse should be defined with care, and with due regard for a judicious diversity among child-rearing techniques.

A Hair-Trigger Child Protection System

As a result of the continued reporting to the public of the numbers of alleged cases of child abuse and neglect—and not reporting the numbers that are discarded as unfounded—it is now an accepted truism that child abuse is on the increase in America. To deal with it, over the past thirty years our nation has put into place a system that operates outside the criminal justice system, and is subject to far fewer constitutional restrictions on its methods.

State social services bureaucracies, in response to an unsupported, even anonymous, allegation of child abuse or neglect, are allowed to do the following:

• Make a "home visit," at any time, which may include an extensive search;

• Ask questions, which may have severe consequences, without informing the parent of the right to remain silent and to have an attorney—this is because in this situation, there is no right to remain silent or to have an attorney;

• Interview a child, outside the parents' hearing, about their child-rearing practices;

• Take children into protective custody;

• Charge the parents for the costs of such custody;

• Initiate proceedings for termination of parental rights; such termination requires a hearing, but at such hearings, indigent parents have no right to appointed counsel, and the burden the state must meet is "clear and convincing evidence"—a lower standard than "beyond a reasonable doubt."

If there were a high threshold for such intervention, so that no one was subjected to it unless there was solid evidence that they had done something harmful to their children, this system would be far less objectionable. But in fact, the system operates with a hair-trigger.

The hair-trigger is set up by the federal statute that provides the incentive structure for all the nominally state-level child abuse and neglect programs. (The programs are maintained by the states, and usually delegated by them to the counties, but they are federally funded, and the statute under which this funding is authorized sets forth detailed requirements for them. States are free to go their own way, but none wants to forego the federal dollars. In effect, this is a federal program masquerading as a state one.)

Mandatory Reporting

One of the requirements of the federal statute is that the state must maintain a system of *mandatory reporting* of child abuse and neglect. All health professionals, and many others besides—including teachers—are mandatory reporters of child abuse and neglect.

The mandatory reporting system is overbroad in three respects:

First, in some states, it takes in too many categories of professionals. Physicians should of course be included, but it is far from clear, for example, that teachers have the necessary expertise to diagnose abuse or neglect. Where teachers are conscripted into this system, the reason is not their professional expertise in child abuse, but their extensive access to information about children and their families. Extending mandatory reporter status to non-medical personnel without guarantees that adequate expertise is present to minimize or eliminate false reports will inevitably undermine the welfare of at least some children.

False Accusations: Carefully Molded Fantasy

"Child abuse" is a charge which easily sets the emotions going. Who would not be revolted by alleged actions against the smallest and most innocent in our society, who have no way to defend themselves?

What is less known, however, is how often charges of child abuse, launched against parents and others providing the care and keeping of our children unconsciously implanted by those who were interrogating them, and asking them questions the implications of which they did not understand, turn out to be figments of a child's imagination. A child's real and fantasy worlds are often indistinguishable in the child's mind. In case after case the accusations have turned out to be carefully molded by social agency authorities whose program has both anti-family, anti-parental and pro-socialization intent.

Eric Brodin, *Conservative Review*, January 1992.

Second, and far more seriously, the mandatory system requires the designated professionals to report not only known abuse or neglect, but also *suspected* abuse or neglect. In theory, this deprives the reporters of leeway in which to form their own professional judgment as to whether government intervention is required or not. (One must hope that many mandatory reporters exercise such discretion notwithstanding.)

And third, in many states, mandatory reporters are subject to civil and criminal penalties for failure to report; at the same time, the parent reported is barred from learning the identity of the reporter. Given this incentive structure, it is not surprising that false reports are rampant.

Costs of False Reports

False reports are costly: They harm abused children by wasting valuable resources and they harm non-abused children by putting them in a tug-of-war between the state and their parents. Additionally, they are a severe trauma to the parents, and they intrude on constitutionally protected privacy interests. It is no wonder that families who are aware of this system often defer excursions outside the home when a child has a skinned knee or an innocently incurred bruise.

A recent article in *State Legislatures* magazine notes that:

> . . . all children are traumatized by separation from their families. Even if removed in severe circumstances, the child suffers emotional damage that may be underestimated. Typically, children don't understand why they must move in with strangers, and they blame themselves for loss of their family.

It is encouraging that the social policy community is beginning to become aware of this problem; yet it is distressing that such commonsense observations could have stayed so long submerged beneath reassuring bromides about "the best interests of the child."

An Overzealous Bureaucracy Leads to False Convictions

An even greater horror than an unjust accusation of child abuse for parents and children is the false conviction. In Florida, a 1989 review of child abuse records over a six-month period found that 92 percent of those who appealed child abuse convictions were falsely accused. For example, in one California case, a young girl who had been raped by a burglar was separated from her parents for two years after her father was accused of incest. The social services bureaucracy simply refused to believe the young girl's rape story.

In Minnesota, a report from the attorney general found that:

> In many instances, parents were arrested and charged with abusing their children even though these children denied the abuse through several weeks of interrogation and separation from their parents. In some cases, these children were told that reunification with their families would be facilitated by "admissions" of sex abuse by their parents and other adults. . . .

Child abuse and neglect are serious problems. However, other crimes in our society are serious problems too, yet we do not allow searches without probable cause, or imprisonment without either counsel or a trial in which the state must prove its case beyond a reasonable doubt. It is time to take a critical look at the child abuse system.

The System Needs Reform

Reform is needed along three lines: to ensure that abused children receive the immediate, emergency protection to which they are entitled—and are not returned into abusive homes; to make it less likely that non-abusive, non-neglectful parents will be forced into contact with a system whose services are unwanted and unneeded and whose resources could be spent in much more productive ways; and to provide a higher level of due process protection for families and children that do come into contact with the system. . . .

Nothing in this summary should be construed to imply that child abuse and neglect are not horrifying problems. The system we have now is not an adequate way to deal with the severity of child abuse. Not only do false reporting and unmerited investigation occur, but real abuse and neglect also go undetected and uncorrected. The system is simultaneously over- and under-corrective. The best way to help children who are suffering from abuse is to unclog the system so that help can reach them.

"Numerous are the examples of innocent accused fathers who liken their experience to the Salem witch-hunts."

Divorcing Parents Are Often Unfairly Accused of Child Sexual Abuse

Robert Sheridan

Child abuse is horrifying, but especially so when a parent is accused of molesting his or her own child. In the following viewpoint, San Francisco attorney Robert Sheridan argues that false accusations of child abuse have become the weapon of choice in the angry wars that may accompany divorce. The emotionalism caused by allegations of child abuse often prohibits a rational examination of the facts, the author believes. The result, he concludes, is that many parents—usually fathers—are unjustly branded as child abusers and deprived of contact with their children. Sheridan, a criminal defense lawyer and former deputy district attorney in San Francisco, writes on relationships between social beliefs and child molestation issues.

As you read, consider the following questions:

1. What parallels does Sheridan draw between the Salem witchcraft cases and accusations of child abuse in divorce cases?
2. What processes may be factors in the development of false accusations of abuse in custody battles, according to Sheridan?
3. How can opposing facts be used to support accusations of child sexual abuse, according to the author?

From Robert Sheridan, "The False Child Molestation Outbreak of the 1980s: An Explanation of the Cases Arising in the Divorce Context," *Issues in Child Abuse Accusations*, Summer 1990. Reprinted with permission.

In 1981, Congress enacted legislation to deal with actual cases of child abuse by requiring the states, as a condition for the funding of state programs, to enact mandatory reporting laws. California's statute requires all child care custodians, medical, and nonmedical practitioners, defined to include teachers, nurses, and dental hygienists, among others, to report suspected cases of child abuse—sexual, physical, and emotional. . . .

Behavioral indicators of child abuse, according to the prosecutor's handbook put out by the National Center for the Prosecution of Child Abuse, of Alexandria, Virginia, a subsidiary of the National District Attorneys Association, may include overly submissive behavior, aggressive acting out or incorrigible behavior, school related excesses, sleep disturbances, bed-wetting and "clingingness." Such broadly defined so-called indicators have a grave potential for contributing to a false accusation, because children who have not been sexually molested may exhibit such behavior.

There are other error factors which either cause false reports to be made or contribute to the failure to recognize a false report.

In the divorce context, this may be seen when an overly suspicious mother tells the child protection intake workers that she suspects the father for some reason, such as vaginal redness. The young child, under the mother's questioning, may acknowledge the father touched her "there" during weekend visitation. The worker interrogates the child and develops the story. A report is written and submitted to a court which cuts the father off from the child, who remains with the mother. Criminal proceedings may result based on the uncorroborated word of children as young as three. Fathers have been bankrupted, emotionally wrenched, and deprived wrongly of their children based on circumstances such as this. Some may have been erroneously convicted as well.

Why?

I would ascribe it to a failure of reason in the context of an emotional situation.

The Salem Witch-Hunt

There have been notorious examples of rational failure in the past. The Salem, Massachusetts, witch-hunt of 1692 is the classic irrational child molestation case of all time, with eleven girls ages eight through seventeen instrumental in causing twenty executions and 130 condemnations to death on the charge of witchcraft.

More precisely, the Salem children's parents and the surrounding adults were responsible for the outbreak, not the children. The adults were acting as child advocates, working for the best interests of the children. . . .

When Dr. Griggs was called to examine children who had adopted "odd postures," "foolish, ridiculous speeches," "distempers," and "fits," he diagnosed the "Evil Hand" or malefic witchcraft. Perhaps, believing in the devil, he expected to find his presence.

Overreaction in Custody Cases

There are so many allegations. A perfect example are the divorce cases, where you have Mom and Dad conflicting over the child, family courts becoming involved, because now they're going to have to decide about custody. It's common for us to get a case where the child has spent the weekend with the dad and all of a sudden, she's been molested. And then you bring the kid in and the kid says, "Well, he was giving me a bath and he did touch my vaginal area." Oh. Now everyone overreacts. You've got CPS saying, "Oh, he's a pervert!" you know? And then I say to them, "Well, wait a minute! I gave my daughter a bath and she's 3 years old; am I a pervert?"

Lawrence Daly in *The Child Sexual Abuse War*, 1988.

The household of the Rev. Samuel Parris, in which the first witchcraft accusations were developed, was irritated and disturbed. Parris was at war with his congregation and his town and felt betrayed by their failure to pay his salary, which included corn and firewood, essential to withstanding the winter.

The context may be likened to that of a divorcing family, a microcosm coming to an end, with attendant fear and anxiety, marked by bitterness and ever increasing ruthlessness in fighting, with the children used as weapons. Had Dr. Griggs, and the real experts, the ministers, objectivity and sufficient distance from the problem they might have looked for the cause of the children's behavior, and subsequent allegations, in the context of what preceded them.

From the distance of three centuries, it seems more clear.

The children, according to Paul S. Boyer and Stephen Nissenbaum (*Salem Possessed*, Harvard U. Press, 1974), were experimenting with fortune telling on the subject of their future status, including love and marriage. . . .

Questioned by Puritan elders, they at first resisted answering, one supposes because of the sexual content of the imaginings being probed. . . .

A Puritan elder's interrogation might be a frightening thing to a child, just as any child might be apprehensive in admitting a sexual curiosity to a strict adult who professed against such things as being sinful.

Rumors began going around and, although resistant at first, the girls, "under the pressure of adult questioning, had finally named as their tormenters" three women who were accused as witches. . . .

Unless one believes in witches, and the confessions of witchcraft extracted under some pressure by interrogators, the twentieth century rational analysis of such cases would require looking to other causes, and treating the children's testimony not as direct evidence of their claim of molestation by a witch, but as circumstantial evidence that something very disturbing had occurred in their lives. This would require some investigation to determine that the case had nothing to do with witches.

I think *we* would focus on what was disturbing in the children's lives. . . .

We might also look to the misinterpretation placed by the adults on the unfamiliar behavior of children.

Finally, we would look to the interrogation process by which the allegations themselves were first developed by adults, to see whether the statements of the children had been contaminated by the expressions of the adults.

I suggest that this would be a rational approach to understanding both Salem's, and today's experiences with uncorroborated molestation charges developed by adults from the mouths of children, following some not-clearly-understood behavior or appearance.

Emotional Response Prevents a Rational Approach

Child abuse cases are peculiarly difficult for those in authority to deal with rationally for a number of reasons. The underlying causes of difficulty are the emotions such cases engender, together with the pressure to "do something" right away to "protect the child" from the imagined abuse. The result, in the false cases, may be characterized as an order amounting to a judicial kidnap, the taking of the child away from an innocent parent, usually the father, and delivering the child into the arms of a wrongdoing mother, who is strongly motivated to support the newly established status quo. . . .

In child abuse cases the amount of proof required to remove a child temporarily from a parent is trivial. The mere reported statement of the child is often sufficient, particularly when the reporting party is a person wearing the mantle of the flimsiest authority or competency, such as a so-called child-advocate or social worker.

The rational approach requires that no adverse action be taken on insufficient proof, and that reasonable objections must be shown not to exist before adverse action can justifiably be taken.

The misinterpretation of a young child's account of an overnight visit with the father is the most common cause of a false report. . . .

Devastating Charges

While it is clearly unpopular to "advocate" the rights of child molesters, and political suicide to be perceived in that posture, there is a serious problem attendant to the crime of child molestation. That problem results from the reality that such charges are easily made, with no need for corroboration or objective evidence. Once made, such charges have the potential for devastation to the innocent accused, with no realistic prospect of punishment as a deterrent to the false and malicious accuser.

Joel Erik Thompson, *Issues in Child Abuse Accusations*, Summer 1992.

The misinterpretation of the child's account of a visit with father is the result of observer bias, ineptitude, frustration, and the like. The riskiest area involves improper questioning technique. Questioning is improper when it supplies new words or concepts which may elevate the child's level of sexual sophistication, or suggest details the child hadn't uttered.

Reinforcement by Manipulation

The reinforcement of selected responses by reacting positively or negatively to the child's statements and the projection of the questioner's own emotions, fears and concerns, gives several messages to the child. She learns that these things are expected and it is okay to say them. She experiences that she will be rewarded with love, sympathy, and protection, on a personal level. She is told that she will be helping daddy get needed "help" to prevent him from molesting again. . . .

The critical factors comprising this risky scenario include the domination by one in a superior position over a weaker person who is dependent on the superior person for continued unpunished existence, and the essentials of life, such as food, shelter, clothing, and emotional peace, particularly the latter. Indoctrination through confrontive, suggestive questioning in a hostile and fearful context provides the necessary information. This information is later repeated, orally or through drawings, dolls, or "play therapy"—devices used to entice a child into reiterating what it is she is supposed to know. . . .

Peaceful intact families, where each parent supports the other in the role of loving parent and protects the child's sense of emotional security, rarely produce children who falsely accuse of sexual molestation. This is seen most often in warring families where one parent vies for the child's attention and love, and may use the child as a lever for the destruction of the other parent.

In a divorce, the elements of dependence, isolation, hostile context, bitterness, increasingly ruthless fighting, motivation, indoctrination, and time to take effect, are present along with the child's need to accommodate for the sake of emotional peace. If the price of peace is the destruction of the father, it is not too high for a child disturbed from living in such an anxious, conflicted state, particularly where the mother represents the hope of refuge.

One would think that anything the child says in such a context would be treated as . . . brainwashed, coerced, not the product of free will, suspect, subject to confirmation by independent, dependable evidence before being accepted. No corroboration, no faith.

This is not the invariable response. Numerous are the examples of innocent accused fathers who liken their experience to the Salem witch-hunts, with good reason.

What stopped the Salem executions was the fact that the newly arrived governor's wife, Lady Phips, having expressed sympathy for the condemned, found herself accused by the children, following which her husband abolished the special court he had established to handle the outbreak of cases. This effectively put a stop to the prosecutions which were increasingly being questioned as more and more people, mostly women, were being condemned.

In the outbreak we see today, the governor's wife has yet to be falsely accused. . . .

Weapons of Choice in the Divorce Wars

In the divorce wars, each on the field of combat has a weapon of choice.

First I should note that I have never heard of a case in which a father sexually abused his child to get back at his ex-wife. Incest is a differently motivated pathology entirely. The typical male response to the provocation, frustration, and rage of divorce, is to drink or use violence against his wife, perhaps in the presence of the children, or both.

The wife's weapon of choice is not violence, but the child. She gets back at the husband by depriving him of the only thing out of the broken marriage he dearly loves, the child. The child is her leverage to insure cooperation and punishment for a recalcitrant and deserving husband. If she can point out to the child examples of his misbehavior, she is well on her way toward succeeding in the alienation process.

The role of the mother in developing a false accusation may

have causative factors in addition to her own hatred, spite, and desire for revenge. She may feel guilty for some part she played in the breakup of the family. She also may achieve three positive emotional gains by succeeding in developing an accusation out of the child's mouth:

First, she secures the "buying-in" of the child to her hostile view of the father.

Second, in the eyes of herself, the child, her family and friends, the mother goes up a peg and the father goes way down, because even if the accusation is not formally acted upon, the stigma becomes part of the family lore, and the father is always seen in some degree as being tainted. I see this as an attempt to achieve a "status exchange."

Third, what do we naturally do when we feel guilty about something bad we've done? We relieve the guilt by shifting the blame. We point out someone who is even more blameworthy.

No matter what misconduct a woman is guilty of, from sex, to drugs, to child neglect, it is not as bad as child sexual molestation perpetrated by the father. Guilt transference is the first resort of the scoundrel.

Mental Abnormality Is Another Factor

A hysterical mother, obsessed with the thought that her children may be victimized sexually by the hated father, is apt to go looking for signs where none exist, and find them anyway. Experienced child protective service workers have come to expect mothers to bring young daughters in on Mondays following visitation, with redness, rash, or itching precisely because fathers sometimes avoid cleansing the child's vaginal area thoroughly because of a reluctance to touch there. . . .

The myth current in Salem, Massachusetts, 1692, was that there was a devil who tormented children through adult intermediaries who were in league with him as witches. Today's equally malefic myth is that repeated in the brochure of San Francisco General Hospital's child abuse intake unit termed CASARC, for Child-Adolescent Sexual Assault Resource Center. SFGH is the publicly funded county hospital. Its brochure states:

"Always believe the child who discloses sexual abuse. Children NEVER lie about this problem" (Emphasis in original). . . .

Only truth deserves to be believed, and neither the children nor their advocates have a monopoly on it. Nonsense to the contrary contributes to the failure to detect falsity even where there is a willingness to look competently, which is rare. . . .

How bad are the rational failures of inept child-advocates? I call it the trick mirror approach. I see it in the arguments over the validity of cases. The false premise is that the facts support the truth of the child's uncorroborated accusation, but if the facts are otherwise, the accusation is still true.

Examples:

(1) *Consistency* in the repetition of the story indicates truthfulness, whereas *inconsistency* also indicates truthfulness, because the child is disturbed over having been molested.

(2) *Timeliness* in reporting the distressing event indicates truthfulness, whereas *delay* also indicates truthfulness, because the child is disturbed and thus reluctant to talk about the unpleasant event.

(3) The presence of *graphic details* indicates truthfulness, whereas the *absence of details* also indicates truthfulness, for the same reason.

(4) That the child *sticks to the story* indicates truthfulness, whereas if the child *recants*, this also indicates truthfulness, because of the disturbing consequences of relating the traumatic experience.

On this latter point, I suspect that some children would sometimes like to extricate themselves from having made a false report, but are not permitted to do so.

(5) If the father *confesses*, the accusation is true; if he *denies* guilt, it is also true, because admitting guilt is too shameful in these cases.

The Governor's Wife

Many people acknowledge wrongdoing, including men who have molested children. There is no reliable study concluding that there is a greater reluctance in these cases than others. You would expect an innocent man to deny wrongdoing. That is what *you* would do if you were falsely accused of anything. . . .

Not the least of the rational problem areas is the tendency, perhaps unintentionally, *to shift the burden of proof to the accused father* and to expect him to explain how the mother could have induced the child to so testify, while at the same time not permitting him competent access to the child or the mother. . . . In divorce cases, undue influence should be presumed until eliminated factually. . . .

There is the tendency *to lower the burden of proof* to mere nothingness, to have intake workers testify as to what they think they recall the child was saying, in order to spare the supposedly molested child the "additional" trauma of testifying in court, or confronting the person she accuses.

Until these problems are effectively dealt with, we'll see many more false cases before the Governor's wife is accused and a stop is put to the child molestation witch-hunts that crop up with increasing frequency.

"Protection of the accused now operates at the expense of vulnerable child victims."

Divorcing Parents Underreport Child Sexual Abuse

Meredith Sherman Fahn

A basic tenet of American society is the assumption that parents will act in the best interests of their children. Because accusations of intrafamily child sexual abuse contradict this assumption, Meredith Sherman Fahn argues in the following viewpoint, they are inherently difficult to believe. This reluctance to credit allegations of abuse operates with special force in cases of divorce and contested custody, she maintains, resulting in a system that is unable to adequately protect child victims. Although the media have fostered a belief that false accusations are widespread, the opposite is true, Fahn asserts: Parents are reluctant to accuse their spouses of abuse because they fear a judicial backlash will cost them custody of their children. Fahn is a litigator with the law firm of Bryant, Clohan, Ott, and Baruh in Palo Alto, California.

As you read, consider the following questions:

1. According to Fahn, how can an accusation of child abuse threaten the accusing parent?
2. What effect have the media had on accusations of parental sexual abuse, according to the author?
3. What connections does Fahn find between the breakup of the family and accusations of sexual abuse?

From Meredith Sherman Fahn, "Allegations of Child Sexual Abuse in Custody Disputes: Getting to the Truth of the Matter," *Family Law Quarterly*, Summer 1991. Copyright 1991, the American Bar Association. Reprinted with permission.

In the last decade, American society has grown in its awareness of intrafamily child sexual abuse. Although the exact rate of incidence is unknown, it is well established that many children are sexually abused by adult family members. While any given case of alleged intrafamily sexual abuse is inherently unbelievable, it is especially difficult to believe that any parents would seek gratification by exploiting their own children. The legal presumption that the parent acts in the best interest of the child reflects our societal view of reality; this belief is reinforced by the deeply rooted taboo against incest. In addition, most cases of child sexual abuse cannot be proven with absolute certainty because there are no witnesses other than the child and the abuser. The truth seems especially hard to determine when the allegations arise in the context of a custody dispute. The adversarial setting muddies the facts, and one wonders whether the accuser is trying to protect the child or to throw dirt on an ex-spouse.

A child who is sexually abused by a parent may be the most vulnerable of all victims. Most children are dependent on their parents for virtually all physical and emotional sustenance. Furthermore, they are subject to their parents' authority and control. A child is ill-equipped to defend himself from a parent's sexual abuse; therefore, the society and legal system outside the home must provide adequate protection. . . .

Burden of Proof

When parties litigate a custody dispute and an allegation of child sexual abuse is raised, the burden of proof is on the accuser. Because intrafamily child sexual abuse is so difficult to prove, many investigations result in unsubstantiated findings. Thus, if neither party offers conclusive proof, the result is a finding of no abuse.

Contrary to the popular assumption that accusers have nothing to lose by raising false allegations, a mother who fails to meet a stringent standard of proof faces the risk of losing custody. This threat is especially strong in a case involving a very young child, where the mother would ordinarily get primary custody. The court may view her assertions of abuse as indicative that she will be uncooperative toward the father when he exercises his right to visitation. In the past, courts have transferred custody to the father to ensure that each parent will have the opportunity to visit and maintain a relationship with the child.

The System Fails to Protect Children

Generally, it is a mistake to apply this reasoning to cases involving allegations of child sexual abuse. Even where a court finds the evidence insufficient to conclude that the allegations are true, the alleged abuse may have actually occurred. The tug of war over the rights to the child subsumes the child's right to be free from abuse. The effect of sending the child who actually has been abused to a less protective situation becomes merely incidental to the court's decision.

Many parents who have raised allegations of child sexual abuse were met by the disbelief of the judicial system, and then ordered to make the child available for visitation with the alleged abuser. As the current situation stands, many separated or divorced mothers cannot be confident that reporting to the system is the best way to protect her child. . . .

"Unproved" Does Not Mean "Untrue"

When a judge is faced with the issue of whether a parent has sexually abused a child, that judge is influenced by the outcome of any investigations conducted by others working within the legal system. Many of these investigations yield findings that the allegations were "unsubstantiated," a state-of-the-art term that is frequently misconstrued by judges and other legal professionals. To accurately understand an investigator's evaluation, one must know the meaning of the term and how an investigation might end up with that result.

Basically, "unsubstantiated" refers to cases in which the evidence was insufficient to affirmatively conclude that the child was sexually abused by the alleged abuser. In some jurisdictions, even when it is clear that the child was abused, a case may be unsubstantiated if the identity of the abuser cannot be conclusively established. . . .

Truth Can Be Elusive

When a question arises as to whether a family member has sexually abused the child, an investigation begins at the child protective services agency. Although the procedures vary in different jurisdictions, usually, a team of professionals interviews the child and the parents to evaluate the home environment and family dynamics.

The need to resolve the case quickly in order to minimize the strain on the family sometimes prevents an evaluator from taking the time necessary for a thorough investigation. Furthermore, in some jurisdictions, caseworkers are overburdened with enormous caseloads. Another problem is the lack of uniformity regarding the assessment skills and interviewing techniques of different caseworkers, and the opportunity for increased supervision or review is similarly limited. A finding that the allegations were unsubstantiated may be attributable to the time constraints rather than the merits of the particular case. In such instances, the caseworker has little choice but to label the allegations "unsubstantiated." In other words, the investigation was not extensive enough to affirmatively substantiate the allegations of abuse.

Even where the caseworker was afforded the opportunity to make a full investigation, with several interviews of each family member individually as well as together, the question of whether the child has been sexually abused simply cannot be answered. In virtually every case of intrafamily child sexual abuse, the only witnesses are the abuser and the child victim. And there is always blanket denial: the abusive parent practically never admits it, the child is often intimidated into silence, and other family members allow themselves to remain comfortably unaware. In general, incest is a family secret. Therefore, a given case of intrafamily child sexual abuse is extremely difficult to prove.

False Allegations Are Rare

The potential for false allegations of sexual abuse in divorce and custody cases, where a parent's vindictiveness may lead to prompting a child to lie about sexual abuse by the other parent, has become a growing concern. No evidence has appeared so far, however, that false reports are more likely in this context. Josephine S. Bulkley mentions recent surveys of domestic court personnel that indicate that false allegations, while they do exist, are exceedingly rare.

Margaret Rieser, *Child Welfare*, November/December 1991.

Another reason why caseworkers often conclude that the allegations of sexual abuse are unsubstantiated is that they are not expected to make a definitive finding of fact. In the social work setting, a caseworker does not give a verdict like a jury or a judge. The caseworker is oriented toward evaluating the family relationships rather than delivering judgments.

Except for the most extreme and obvious case, the caseworker couches his findings as to the "likelihood" of abuse without making an absolute conclusion. In some jurisdictions, this determination frequently constitutes one portion of an overall finding that the charges of abuse were not substantiated. . . .

Accusations Are Automatically Suspect

In the context of a custody dispute with unsubstantiated allegations, there is a tendency to suspect that the person who raised the allegations—usually the mother—deliberately made a false accusation in a vengeful attack against her husband, towards whom she is bitter. The prevalence of this assumption is attributed to the media explosion in which reports of supposedly false allegations have been overpublicized.

The appropriate term for deliberately false allegations of child sexual abuse is "fictitious allegations." Experts disagree as to the specific percentage of allegations that are fictitious, but most acknowledge that this occurs rarely.

It should be emphasized that unsubstantiated does not mean that the allegations of abuse are untrue. Distinctions should be made between unsubstantiated allegations and affirmative findings that there was no abuse.

The adversarial nature of the legal system impedes the ability of a court to protect children in cases with unsubstantiated findings. The standard of proof in a civil suit is that of a preponderance of the evidence. But realistically, the inflammatory character of a charge of child sexual abuse, as well as the fact that the parent's right to maintain a relationship with his child is at stake, renders the actual standard to be more like that of a criminal case. If the accuser fails to meet her burden of proof, the alleged abuser is presumed to be innocent of the civil charges. Because burdens of proof are merely shifted, a failure to prove is similar to an unsubstantiated allegation, but operates more like a vindication of the charge. Consequently, the court relinquishes the father's right to custody or visitation, and in so doing fails to protect some children from further sexual abuse.

The legal system should recognize that its current mechanisms cannot and do not adequately protect children from intrafamily sexual abuse. . . .

A Popular Misconception

The mass media has popularized an image of the mother in a custody dispute who raises allegations of child sexual abuse in order to hurt the father rather than out of a legitimate need to protect the child. Such a mother is perceived as hysterical or crazy. At other times she is depicted as an angry, bitter woman who will stop at nothing to avenge the wrongs of her fallen marriage. In addition, she is viewed as a bad mother for exploiting the child to prevail in the adversary proceeding.

In this way, the media sends a message that a mother who accuses her ex-husband of sexually abusing their child has made up a terrible and fantastic tale in a desperate attempt to deny him access to their child, perhaps as a vengeful ploy. This view promotes an inherent disbelief in practically any case. Despite this spread of disbelief, individuals and groups who advocate the rights of accused parents insist that the legal system is biased against them. . . .

The child frequently confirms the truth of the allegations. But children's allegations of sexual abuse are often met with skepticism from adults. This additional incredibility factor of the child as an unreliable source seems to double when a parent is accused and to triple when the allegations arise amidst a custody battle. Defendants and advocates for accused parents virtually always attribute the falseness of the charges to the fact that they arose in a custody suit; in addition, they attribute the child's confirmation to fantasy or to brainwashing by the mother. . . .

Associations Between Family Breakup and Child Abuse

When a parent raises an allegation of child sexual abuse in a custody proceeding, the natural inquiry is whether the charges are false. But it is incorrect to assume that an allegation is less reliable just because it arises during a custody dispute. The public forum has entertained much speculation as to why a mother or child would fabricate such a story, but little attention has been paid to the reasons why actual abuse would be exposed at that time.

One reason is that a sexually abusive relationship is more likely to develop right after the parents separate. The abusive parent is lonely for emotional and sexual companionship, and the child is vulnerable and accessible.

In instances where the abuse was ongoing while the family was intact, the separation creates an opportunity for disclosure. The dynamics of intrafamily sexual abuses are such that the passive parent typically refuses to face the occurrence of abuses while the family is together. Upon separation, however, the parent has reason to become aware and not continue to selectively perceive what has been going on. A sexually abused child frequently is intimidated into silence by threats, including the abuser's warnings that no one would believe her. The child may feel more free to speak up when she senses that she will be believed.

In addition, children who are sexually abused sometimes experience a sense of responsibility for keeping the family together and feel obliged to endure their roles in the family dynamics. This pressure dissipates when the family splits. The extended absences of the abusive parent enable the child to feel more free to confide in the other parent.

Even though a child is harmed by sexual abuse, he may feel torn by loyalty toward his abuser. The child still desires affection from the parent and may comply with abuse even though it is unwanted. Again, the separation of the parents is conducive to disclosure because the original scenario of abuse is disrupted. When the child is removed from the abuse and away from the abuser, his emotional conflict is less looming.

Because children face a conflict over whether to tell when

61

they are sexually abused by a family member, they sometimes later retract their allegations. This phenomenon is known as the child sexual abuse accommodation syndrome. . . .

The Judicial Bias Against Allegations of Abuse

When a judge is confronted with a custody dispute involving allegations of child sexual abuse, he has to make a difficult judgment. Child sexual abuse is perpetrated in private; if other members of the house suspect abuse, they usually react with denial. Thus, there are no other witnesses and the dispute boils down to the alleged abuser's word against that of the other spouse. By the nature of the problem, absolute proof cannot be established.

Abuse Allegations in Divorce Cases on the Rise

We often hear that child abuse allegations are false, because they arrive in divorce cases. However, the study done by the American Bar Association in conjunction with the National Legal Research Center for Child Advocacy and Protection and the Association of Family and Conciliatory Courts, states that these are a rarity and that 95 percent of these cases are not unfounded allegations.

In our organization [Mothers Against Raping Children], the calls of these cases across the country are on the increase.

Denise Gooch, testimony before the Senate Judiciary Committee, May 16, 1989.

The deeply embedded taboo against incest negatively affects the unbelievability of an actual case. The average member of our society is shocked and repelled upon hearing the details of a particular instance of intrafamily sexual abuse. Although our society has demonstrated a growing awareness of the existence of child sexual abuse, it is difficult to believe allegations in an individual case, particularly if the alleged abuser is the child's parent. Judges, too, are at least somewhat reluctant to believe that a child has been sexually abused.

When the alleged abuser is a middle- or upper-class man and a respected professional, other similarly situated people may identify with him and feel defensive on his behalf. They may think that this is a decent, hardworking member of society who has a normal love and affection for his children. The father conveys to the judge that he cares deeply about his children's welfare and would never harm them. On the surface, it is indeed hard to believe that this man could do such a terrible thing to his child.

Like everyone else, outside the courtroom the judge is exposed to the overpublicized image of mothers maliciously raising fictitious allegations. The thought arises that the allegations were raised in the context of a custody dispute and therefore should be considered suspect. Finally, even a subconscious identification with the father would arouse the judge's anger toward the mother for stooping so low to accuse him of such an awful thing.

It is submitted that in many cases, a judicial bias operates against the accusing mother and the child. This is one explanation for the occurrence of unreasonable decisions favoring defendant fathers. In other cases, a judge may not harbor a bias, but may still hesitate to pin a finding of abuse on a father where the facts cannot be proven with certainty. The standard of proof is that of a preponderance of the evidence, but realistically, the strong stigma that attaches to a charge of child sexual abuse probably influences many judges to impose a standard akin to that of proof beyond a reasonable doubt. . . .

The Legal System Should Protect the Child

The legal precept that one is innocent until charges are proven is designed to protect the accused. Usually, the possibility of a defendant being cleared of charges presents minimal threat to society; no specific foreseeable victim exists. The value of protecting the accused is worth the cost to society because the cost is small and unidentifiable.

But in the case of actual intrafamily child sexual abuse, a failure to satisfy the burden of proof inevitably results in continued abuse for the child. Protection of the accused now operates at the expense of vulnerable child victims. For this reason, in custody disputes involving allegations of child sexual abuse, the alleged abuser should have to bear a burden of proof equal to that of the accuser to establish a judicial finding of no abuse.

"Many women don't have memories, and some never get memories. This doesn't mean they weren't abused."

Repressed Memories of Abuse Prove That Abuse Is Widespread

Ellen Bass and Laura Davis

Sexual abuse of children is only beginning to emerge from the shadows, in part because children are at a disadvantage as witnesses. Recently many adults in therapy have remembered abuse they had repressed, sometimes for decades. This discovery may mean that many more people have been abused than statistics show, and that sexual abuse of children is widespread. The bible of the repressed memory movement is *The Courage to Heal*, by Ellen Bass and Laura Davis, from which the following viewpoint is excerpted. Bass is a counselor and lecturer who has worked with survivors of child sexual abuse since 1974. Davis is an author and workshop leader who specializes in helping others recover from child sexual abuse.

As you read, consider the following questions:

1. How is recovering repressed memories different from remembering with the conscious mind, according to Bass and Davis?
2. What are some of the ways the authors suggest repressed memories may be triggered?
3. Why are specific memories of abuse not necessary to accepting that abuse occurred, according to the authors?

Ellen Bass: I first heard that children were abused in 1974, when a young woman in my creative writing workshop pulled a crumpled half-sheet of paper out of her jeans pocket. Her writing was so vague, so tentative, that I wasn't sure what she was trying to say, but I sensed that it was important. Gently, I encouraged her to write more. Slowly she revealed her story. In pieces, on bits of paper, she shared the pain of her father's assaults, and I listened.

Shortly afterward, another woman told me her story. And then another. And another. There were no groups for survivors of child sexual abuse then. The word "survivor" was not yet in our vocabulary. But as they sensed that I could understand their stories, more and more women shared them with me. The psychologist Carl Rogers once said that when he worked through an issue in his life, it was as if telegrams were sent to his clients informing them that they could now bring that subject to therapy. Once I became aware of child sexual abuse, it was as if women knew that I was safe to talk to.

I was stunned by the number of women who had been sexually abused. I was deeply moved by the anguish they had endured. And I was equally impressed by their integrity, their ability to love and create through such devastation. I wanted people to know about this, about their strength and their beauty. . . .

Survivors of Abuse

Bass and Davis: For many survivors, remembering is the first step in healing. To begin with, you may have to remember that you *were* abused at all. Second come specific memories. (If you think you were abused but don't have any memory of it, see the section titled "But I Don't Have Any Memories.") The third kind of remembering is the recovery of the feelings you had at the time the abuse took place. Many women have always remembered the physical details of what happened but have forgotten the emotions that went with it. One survivor explained, "I could rattle off the facts of my abuse like a grocery list, but remembering the fear and terror and pain was another matter entirely."

Remembering is different for every survivor. If, as a young woman, you turned your abuser in to the police and testified against him in court, there's not much chance you forgot. Likewise, if you had to raise your abuser's child, or abort it, you've probably always remembered. Or the abuse may have been so present in the daily texture of your life that there was no way to forget. . . .

You may not have forgotten entirely, but coped by having selective memories. . . . There is no right or wrong when it comes to remembering. You may have multiple memories. Or you may just have one. Years of abuse are sometimes telescoped into a single recollection. When you begin to remember, you might have new images every day for weeks on end. Or you may experience your memories in clumps, three or four of them coming in a matter of days, then not again for months. Sometimes survivors remember one abuser, or a specific kind of abuse, only to remember, years later, a second abuser or a different form of abuse.

There are many women who show signs of having been abused without having any memories. You may have only a vague feeling that something happened but be unable to remember what it was. There are reasons for this, and to understand them, we have to first look at the way early memories are stored.

About Memories

The process of storing memories is complex. We store different experiences in the right and left halves of our brain. The left brain stores sequential, logical, language-oriented experience; the right stores perceptual, spatial experiences. When we try to retrieve right-brain information through left-brain techniques, such as logic and language, we sometimes hit a blank. There are some experiences that we are simply not going to remember in an orderly, precise way.

If you were abused when you were preverbal, or just as you were learning to talk, you had no way of making sense of what was happening to you. Babies don't know the difference between touching someone's penis and touching someone's leg. If a penis is put in their mouth, they will suck it, much as they would a breast or a bottle. Young children are aware of sensations but cannot come up with a name or a concept—like "sexual abuse"—for what is being done to them.

Another thing that makes remembering difficult is the simple fact that you are trying to remember details of something that happened a long time ago. If you ask friends who weren't abused, you will find that most of them also don't remember a great number of details from their childhood. It is even more difficult to remember the times when we were hurt, humiliated, or otherwise violated.

If the abuse happened only once, or if it was an abuse that is hard to name (inappropriate boundaries, lewd looks, subtler forms of abuse), it can be even harder to remember. For others, the constancy of the abuse prevents detailed naming. As one survivor put it, "Do you remember every time you sat down to eat? What you had for dinner the Tuesday you turned six? I remember the flavor. It was a constant, like eating. It was always there."

Recovering occluded memories (those blocked from the surface) is not like remembering with the conscious mind. Often the memories are vague and dreamlike, as if they're being seen from far away.

> The actual rape memories for me are like from the end of a tunnel. That's because I literally left my body at the scene. So I remember it from that perspective—there's some physical distance between me and what's going on. Those memories aren't as sharp in focus. It's like they happened in another dimension.

Other times, memories come in bits and pieces.

> I'd be driving home from my therapist's office, and I'd start having flashes of things—just segments, like bloody sheets, or taking a bath, or throwing away my nightgown. For a long time, I remembered all the things around being raped, but not the rape itself.

If memories come to you in fragments, you may find it hard to place them in any kind of chronological order. You may not know exactly when the abuse began, how old you were, or when and why it stopped. The process of understanding the fragments is a lot like putting together a jigsaw puzzle or being a detective. . . .

Memory Is Extremely Credible

"By and large, long-term memory is extremely credible," maintains Jill Otey, a Portland, Ore., attorney whose office receives five calls a week from women saying they have suddenly remembered childhood abuse. "I find it highly unlikely that someone who can remember what pattern was on the wallpaper and that a duck was quacking outside the bedroom window where she was molested by her father when she was four years old is making it up. Why in the hell would your mind do this?" Reflecting that faith, at least a dozen states since 1988 have amended their statute of limitations for bringing charges to allow for delayed discovery of childhood sexual abuse.

Anastasia Toufexis, *Time*, October 28, 1991.

Flashbacks. In a flashback, you reexperience the original abuse. Flashbacks may be accompanied by the feelings you felt at the time, or they may be stark and detached, like watching a movie about somebody else's life.

Frequently flashbacks are visual: "I saw this penis coming toward me," or "I couldn't see his face, just the big black belt he always wore." First-time visual memories can be very dramatic. . . .

But not everyone is visual. One woman was upset that she couldn't get any pictures. Her father had held her at knifepoint in the car, face down in the dark, and raped her. She had never seen anything. But she had heard him. And when she began to write the scene in Spanish, her native language, it all came back to her—his threats, his brutality, his violation.

Regression. Another way to regain memory is through regression. Under the guidance of a trustworthy therapist, it is possible to go back to earlier times. Or you may find yourself going back on such a journey on your own, with only the prompting of your own unconscious. . . .

Sense memory. Often it is a particular touch, smell, or sound that triggers a memory. You might remember when you return to the town, to the house, to the room, where the abuse took place. Or when you smell a certain aftershave the abuser wore.

Thirty-five-year-old Ella says, "It's all real tactile, sensory things that have brought memories back. Textures. Sounds. The smell of my father's house. The smell of vodka on somebody.". . .

Touch can also reopen memories. Women have had images come up while they were being massaged. You may freeze up and see pictures when you're making love. Your lover breathes in your ear just as your abuser once did, and it all comes spilling back. . . .

The body remembers what the mind chooses to forget. It is also possible to remember only feelings. Memories are stored in our bodies, and it is possible to physically reexperience the terror of the abuse. Your body may clutch tight, or you may feel the screams you could not scream as a child. Or you may feel that you are suffocating and cannot breathe.

> I would get body memories that would have no pictures to them at all. I would just start screaming and feel that something was coming out of my body that I had no control over. And I would usually get them right after making love or in the middle of making love, or right in the middle of a fight. When my passion was aroused in some way, I would remember in my body, although I wouldn't have a conscious picture, just this screaming coming out of me.

Memories come up under many different circumstances. You might remember because you're finally in a relationship that feels safe. Or because you've just been through a divorce and everything in your life is unraveling. Women often remember childhood abuse when they are raped or attacked in adult life.

How Memories Surface

Memories don't always surface in such dramatic ways. While talking with her friend, one woman suddenly heard herself saying something she didn't realize she knew. "It's as though I always knew it," she explained. "It's just that I hadn't thought about it in twenty or thirty years. Up until that moment, I'd forgotten."

You may remember seemingly out of the blue. Or because you're having persistent nightmares that reach up through sleep to tell you:

> I'd always had a dream about my brother assaulting me. It was a foggy dream, and I had it over and over again. I'd wake up thinking it was really disgusting because I was enjoying it in the dream. I'd think, "You're sick. Why are you having this dream? Is that what you want?" I'd give myself all those kinds of guilt messages, 'cause it was still a dream. It wasn't history yet.

> Then, six months ago, I was sitting in a training meeting for working with sexual assault prevention. I don't even remember what the trainer said, but all of a sudden, I realized that it wasn't a dream, and that it had really happened. I can't tell you anything about the rest of the meeting. I was just in shock.

The fact that this woman remembered in the middle of a training session for sexual assault is significant. As the media focus on sexual abuse has increased, more and more women have had their memories triggered.

Media Coverage of Sexual Abuse

Jennierose, who remembered in her mid-forties, was sitting with her lover one night, watching a TV program about sexual offenders in prison. The therapist running the group encouraged the offenders to get very emotional, at which time they'd remember the traumatic events in their own childhoods.

In the middle of the program, Jennierose turned to her lover and said, "I wish there was a therapist like that I could go to, because I know there's something I'm not remembering." As soon as she said that, Jennierose had a vision of the first time her father sodomized her, when she was four and a half and her mother had gone to the hospital to have another baby. "It was a totally detailed vision, to the point of seeing the rose-colored curtains blowing in the window."

Sobbing, Jennierose said to her lover, "I think I'm making something up." Her lover simply said, "Look at yourself! Look at yourself! Tell me you're making it up." And Jennierose couldn't. She knew she was telling the truth.

This kind of memory is common. Often women become very uncomfortable (nauseated, dizzy, unable to concentrate, emotional) when they hear another survivor's story and realize that what's being described happened to them too.

When you break an addiction. Many survivors remember their abuse once they get sober, quit drugs, or stop eating compul-

sively. These and other addictions can effectively block any recollection of the abuse, but once you stop, the memories often
surface. . . .

Record Numbers of Adults Seek Help

A tremendous amount of media coverage on childhood sexual
abuse . . . has encouraged a growing public awareness of the
problem and has resulted in record numbers of adults who were
molested as children to now seek help.

If you have ever had reason to suspect that you may have been
sexually abused, even if you have no explicit memory of it, the
chances are very high that you were. It is not something you
would *choose* to suspect or "make up." Many of my clients describe having a vague "feeling" that they were abused as children. I believe these "hunches" are correct, because I trust my
clients' perceptions, probably far more than they do. In fifteen
years of practicing as a psychotherapist, I have never worked
with a client who initially suspected she was sexually abused but
later discovered she had not been.

Beverly Engel, *The Right to Innocence,* 1989.

When you become a mother. Mothers often remember their
own abuse when they see their children's vulnerability, or
when their children reach the age they were when their own
abuse began. Sometimes they remember because their child is
being abused. Dana was court-ordered to go for therapy when
her three-year-old daughter, Christy, was molested. Dana first
remembered when she unconsciously substituted her own
name for her daughter's:

> I was in therapy talking about Christy, and instead of saying
> "Christy," I said "I." And I didn't even catch it. My therapist
> did. She had always suspected that I was abused too, but she
> hadn't said anything to me.
>
> She told me what I had said, and I said, "I did? I said 'I?'" I
> hadn't even heard myself. It was really eerie.
>
> What came out was that I was really dealing with Christy's
> molestation on a level of my own. The things that I was out-
> raged at and that hurt me the most were things that had hap-
> pened to me, not things that had happened to Christy. Part of
> the reason I fell apart and so much came back to me when I
> found out about Christy was because my husband was doing
> the same things to her that my father had done with me.

After a significant death. Many women are too scared to remember while their abusers are still alive. One woman said, "I

couldn't afford to remember until both my parents were dead, until there was nobody left to hurt me." A forty-seven-year-old woman first remembered a year and a half after her mother died: "Then I could no longer hurt my mother by telling her.". . .

Letting Memories In

Few survivors feel they have control over their memories. Most feel the memories have control of them, that they do not choose the time and place a new memory will emerge. You may be able to fight them off for a time, but the price—headaches, nightmares, exhaustion—is not worth staving off what is inevitable.

Not everyone will know a memory is coming, but many survivors do get warnings, a certain feeling or series of feelings, that clue them in. Your stomach may get tight. You may sleep poorly, have frightening dreams. Or you may be warned in other ways:

> I always know when they're coming. I get very tense. I get very scared. I get snappy at things that ordinarily wouldn't make me angry. I get sad. Usually it's anger and anxiety and fear that come first. And I have a choice. It's a real conscious choice. It's either I want it or I don't want it. And I said "I don't want it" a lot. And when I did that, I would just get sicker and sicker. I'd get more depressed. I'd get angry irrationally.

> Now I don't say I don't want it. It's not worth it. My body seems to need to release it. The more I heal, the more I see these memories are literally stored in my body, and they've got to get out. Otherwise I'm going to carry them forever. . . .

"But I Don't Have Any Memories"

If you don't remember your abuse, you are not alone. Many women don't have memories, and some never get memories. This doesn't mean they weren't abused.

If you don't have any memory of it, it can be hard to believe the abuse really happened. You may feel insecure about trusting your intuition and want "proof" of your abuse. This is a very natural desire, but it is not always one that can be met. The unconscious has its own way of unfolding that does not always meet your demands or your timetable.

One thirty-eight-year-old survivor described her relationship with her father as "emotionally incestuous." She has never had specific memories of any physical contact between them, and for a long time she was haunted by the fact that she couldn't come up with solid data. Over time, though, she's come to terms with her lack of memories. Her story is a good model if you don't have specific pictures to draw from:

71

Do I want to know if something physical happened between my father and me? Really, I think you have to be strong enough to know. I think that our minds are wonderful in the way they protect us, and I think that when I'm strong enough to know, I'll know.

I obsessed for about a year on trying to remember, and then I got tired of sitting around talking about what I couldn't remember. I thought, "All right, let's act as if." It's like you come home and your home has been robbed, and everything has been thrown in the middle of the room, and the window is open and the curtain is blowing in the wind, and the cat is gone. You know somebody robbed you, but you're never going to know who. So what are you going to do? Sit there and try to figure it out while your stuff lies around? No, you start to clean it up. You put bars on the windows. You assume somebody was there. Somebody could come along and say, "Now how do you know someone was there?" You don't know.

That's how I acted. I had the symptoms. Every incest group I went to I completely empathized. It rang bells all the time. I felt like there was something I just couldn't get to, that I couldn't remember yet. And my healing was blocked there.

Part of my wanting to get specific memories was guilt that I could be accusing this man of something so heinous, and what if he didn't do it? How horrible for me to accuse him! That's why I wanted the memories. I wanted to be sure. Societally, women have always been accused of crying rape.

But I had to ask myself, "Why would I be feeling all of this? Why would I be feeling all this anxiety if something didn't happen?" If the specifics are not available to you, then go with what you've got.

I'm left with the damage. And that's why I relate to that story of the burglar. I'm owning the damage. I want to get better. I've been very ill as a result of the damage, and at some point I realized, "I'm thirty-eight years old. What am I going to do—wait twenty more years for a memory?" I'd rather get better.

And then maybe the stronger I am, the more the memories will come back. Maybe I'm putting the cart before the horse. Maybe I've remembered as much as I'm able to remember without breaking down. I don't want to go insane. I want to be out in the world. Maybe I should go with that sense of protection. There is a survivor in here and she's pretty smart. So I'm going with the circumstantial evidence, and I'm working on healing myself. I go to these incest groups, and I tell people, "I don't have any pictures," and then I go on and talk all about my father, and nobody ever says, "You don't belong here."

*"The memories that result from such therapy
sessions . . . must be regarded as highly suspect."*

Many Memories of Childhood Sexual Abuse Are False

Richard Ofshe and Ethan Watters

In the following viewpoint, Richard Ofshe and Ethan Watters examine the relatively new field of repressed memory psychotherapy and find it lacking in scientific validity. Ofshe and Watters
assert that the widespread claims of child sexual abuse that supposedly occurred years or even decades ago are, in many instances, therapist-induced fantasies. The patients are victims,
Ofshe and Watters agree—but of their therapists, not of their alleged abusers. Ofshe, a professor of sociology at the University
of California at Berkeley, was awarded a Pulitzer prize in 1979.
Watters, a free-lance journalist, has written about accused satanic molesters and the induction of false memories of abuse for
Mother Jones, a bimonthly magazine of liberal opinion.

As you read, consider the following questions:

1. What procedures do therapists employ to recover repressed
   memories, according to Ofshe and Watters?
2. According to the authors, how do therapists identify patients
   who have repressed memories of abuse?
3. Who is harmed by false memory therapy, in the authors' view?

Practitioners on the fringes of the mental health professions periodically develop new miracle cures. Most of these therapies lean toward drama, if not theatricality, and are often marketed through pop-psych books and talk shows. . . .

Recently, a new miracle "cure" has been promoted by some mental health professionals—recovered memory therapy. This treatment leads clients to see their parents as monsters who sexually abused them as children. Parents have to witness their adult children turn into monsters trying to destroy their reputations and lives. In less than ten years' time this therapy, in its various forms, has devastated thousands of lives. It has become a nationwide phenomenon—one that is becoming entrenched in our culture and the mental health professions with enormous speed.

The Magic Key

The modus operandi of recovered memory therapy lies in uncovering supposed repressed memories from the client's past in order to cure their mental problems. According to practitioners, hundreds of thousands of adults, primarily women, suffer from the debilitating consequences of sexual abuse endured in childhood. Clients are told they have no knowledge of their abuse because their memories have been repressed. But full awareness of unrecognized abuse is the magic key to the client's return to mental health.

Practitioners of this type of therapy believe repression is a powerful psychological defense that causes one to lose all awareness of physically or sexually terrifying events. Not only is the event repressed but so are memories of the trauma's social context—that is, everything preceding and following it that would suggest to the victim that some trauma has occurred. According to the theory, virtually any mental disorder or symptom can result from repressed childhood abuse. Clients who respond to this therapy become convinced that they were ignorant of abuse which may have gone on for a decade or more. They may remain unaware of the trauma for perhaps thirty years, until they enter treatment where they discover their repressed memories. Once these memories are dredged up and accepted as real, practitioners encourage their clients to publicly accuse, confront, and perhaps sue those they believe to have been the perpetrators. These often turn out to be parents, siblings, grandparents, or sometimes groups of unidentified strangers. The inevitable result is the destruction of the families involved. Therapists feel obligated to do whatever is necessary to uncover their client's hidden traumatic history. The methods employed have generated profound controversies. Critics charge the therapy does not unearth real memories at all. Rather their origin is iatrogenic—therapist induced. Clients are essentially being tricked into believing that they are remembering events that never happened. . . .

Is Repression Valid?

Can the mind repress memories in the way these therapists claim? If repression is a valid concept, clients could be recovering long hidden memories of abuse. If invalid, repression is nothing more than a pseudo-scientific smoke screen for treatment techniques that create false memories. The concept of repression has been used in different ways in the mental health community for a hundred years. Freud employed the term to describe the mind's conscious and unconscious avoidance of unpleasant wishes, thoughts, or memories. Even under this conservative definition, the existence of repression has never been empirically demonstrated. Sixty years of experiments that would demonstrate the phenomenon have failed to produce any evidence of its existence. . . .

In recovered memory therapy, repression is the essential mechanism and the only acceptable explanation for a client's sudden report of abuse. Practitioners of the therapy have developed repression into a psychological phenomenon far more powerful than was ever suspected by Freud or anyone else until recently. Since 1980, the operational meaning of repression has been pumped up beyond all recognition.

In accordance with this robust repression concept, a person could, for example, banish awareness of the experience of having been brutally raped one or a hundred times during childhood. . . . The memories might not be "recovered" until years later under the influence of therapy. The only evidence supporting this concept is circumstantial and only comes out of the therapy sessions.

Modern memory research has demonstrated that normal recall of distant or even relatively recent events is subject to information loss and error for details. Recovered memory therapy's fundamental conception of how memory functions assumes that the human mind records and stores everything perceived. Under this assumption, it is reasonable to presume that minutely detailed recollections of the remote past are feasible. . . .

Scientific studies have revealed memory to be much more malleable than any recorder/playback analogy would suggest. Memory behaves in a reconstructionist fashion. Memories not only change over time but are influenced by the circumstances under which they are recalled. Memory is malleable for details, even for events that actually happened. . . .

To recover repressed memories, therapists employ various procedures such as hypnosis, guided fantasy, automatic writing, strategic use of support groups, suggestion, interpersonal pressure and old fashioned propaganda, that is, directing clients to seemingly authoritative books in which the therapist's theory is advertised. Recovered memory therapy is an example of the maxim that those who ignore history are doomed to repeat it. Early in his career Freud used some of the same techniques modern-day recovered memory therapists employ—specifically, hypnosis, interpersonal pressure, leading, and suggestion. He too produced accounts of early childhood sexual abuse. Patients never spontaneously told such tales nor did they ever tell complete stories without strong pressuring. In Freud's words, he could obtain these stories only "under the most energetic pressure of the analytical procedure, and against an enormous resistance." Almost perversely, Freud's confidence in the accounts grew in direct proportion to the amount of pressure he had to apply before patients provided him with tales of sexual abuse during the first years of their lives. . . .

The Big Bang That Will Rock Therapy

A minimally trained therapist reads somewhere that obesity or anorexia is a symptom of childhood sexual abuse, and a light clicks on. One woman told me that within five minutes after her first session started, the therapist announced: "You're obese and that means you were sexually abused as a child—so let's talk about that."

This is crazy. There's no other way to describe it. . . .

This issue of false accusations will be the Big Bang that will rock therapy in the 1990s. . . . I think eventually malpractice lawsuits will be filed against some of these therapists when their patients figure out what's been done to them.

Darrell Sifford, *Philadelphia Inquirer*, March 15, 1992.

It is quite likely that Freud communicated his strongly held assumptions and expectations about instinctual drives to his patients through questioning and interacting and that he unknowingly introduced and shaped the sexual contents of their fantasies. He was then correct to conclude that all of his patients were producing some fantasy material, but he failed to understand that his assumptions about human nature and the role of sex were causing the particular contents of their confabulated accounts of sexual abuse.

Freud's initial mistake of classifying pseudo-memories as factual accounts is chillingly similar to what is happening today in recovered memory therapy. Fortunately, examining the mechanisms of a contemporary phenomenon is much easier than conducting a retrospective analysis of Freud's techniques. Descriptions of the therapy's procedures are published in practitioners' books, articles, training tapes, and lectures on recovered memory therapy. In addition to the therapists' revelations, interviews with clients fill in important details of the picture of what transpires during treatment sessions and the pressures to which the clients are subjected. Therapists must first convince clients that they are in need of therapy. Early in the treatment they establish their special ability to identify the stigmata signaling repressed memories, which include classic symptoms of mental illness as well as a variety of commonplace physical symptoms, certain attitudes, and certain behaviors. In addition to obvious signs of major mental illness, "warning signs" of hidden abuse can include physical symptoms such as headaches, stomach pain, asthma, dizziness, and pelvic pain.

Lists of attitudes and behaviors that imply repressed memories are usually long and contain some quite exceptional statements, such as having a phobia about closing stall doors in bathrooms or awakening from sleep and attacking one's bed partner. Symptoms also include indications so general that they could apply to almost anyone—difficulty in maintaining a relationship, general feelings of dissatisfaction, liking sex too much, lack of career success, and fear of dentists. The presence of only a few symptoms is enough for someone to be considered a candidate for the therapy.

Disbelief Is Confirmation of Abuse

The first step in the cure is getting the trusting, unaware but possibly resistant, client to agree that brutalization probably did occur—most likely by a relative. Any shock or disbelief the client may express only confirms the reality of the abuse, the therapist tells them. The therapist's expectations predict the direction of the treatment. The client responds to techniques that encourage guesses, speculation, and confabulation. What starts as a guess about what type of abuse might have caused their present emotional problems, grows into guessing which relative committed the abuse. Repetitive retelling and reshaping of this account can transform a "perhaps" into a "for sure" and can thereby create a sense of certainty. The process may culminate in elaborate fantasies about schemes by parents, neighbors, teachers, or any other adults who were around during the client's childhood. It is now commonplace for clients to eventually arrive at the belief that they have repressed involvement in a satanic cult's rituals, involving murder of infants and cannibalism. Some therapists estimate that more than 15 percent of repressed memory therapy clients remember such brutal scenes. This estimate may well be very conservative.

Clients begin therapy with no awareness of the abuse that is supposedly at the root of their disorders. They are blank canvasses on which the therapists paint, using the techniques of the therapy. Studies have shown that people are most susceptible to suggestion when unsure about the matter at issue. New clients, being completely ignorant of what repressed memories their minds might contain, are exceedingly vulnerable to influence. Studies show that memories of details of actual events, even quite recent ones, are subject to gross distortion when pressure or subtle suggestion is used to change perceptions. Research also documents that entirely false memories can be created with minimal pressure or suggestion. For instance, subjects have "remembered" events from childhood that were made up by the researchers. Research into interrogations of crime suspects also shows that it is possible to lead psychiatrically normal suspects to "remember" committing a murder they did not commit. In both laboratory and field settings, once test subjects accept the premise that an event occurred, many confabulate appropriate details that make the memory seem real. . . .

Hypnosis Produces Fantasies

Hypnotic procedures arm the therapist with a powerful tool for influencing perceptions and beliefs, procedures that play an important part in recovered memory therapy. Hypnotic trance can be accomplished either through formal induction procedures, which are obvious, or via indirect methods, such as guided visualization or relaxation. Hypnosis has even greater dramatic power to create false memories than social influence. But like social influence, hypnosis induces subjects to confabulate additional details to fill in the gaps in their memory. Hypnosis can accomplish exceptional degrees of cognitive influence. The scientific literature documents that hypnotized subjects routinely accept as memories scenes that have been suggested and visualized in a state of trance. These pseudo-memories help subjects develop confidence that these hypnotically generated fantasies are real. . . .

The memories that result from such therapy sessions differ dramatically in quality and texture from normal recollections of long ago events and therefore must be regarded as highly suspect. The attributes of recovered memories match those of hypnotically induced pseudo-memories which can be so powerful and engaging that subjects sometimes volunteer that visualizing these scenes is "like watching a movie." With time and retelling, these visions tend to become highly detailed, in vivid color, and crystal clear. Details may include what people were wearing, what someone smelled like and specific dialogue. Therapists take such vividness and detail as proof of the accuracy of the memory when it actually implies the opposite.

Recovered memory therapy seems to have been produced by a series of mistakes. Most obviously, practitioners manage to ignore research showing that their principal techniques, social influence and hypnosis, cause false or grossly inaccurate memories. They refuse to acknowledge that three generations of researchers have tried and failed to confirm the existence of the repression phenomenon, in even its most conservative form. They ignore the fact that no evidence has been found to suggest that the human mind is capable of hiding from itself the kind of traumatic events elicited from clients in recovered memory therapy. Their assumptions about the way the human mind operates is known by specialists in memory to be nothing but pre-scientific folklore and myth. In short, these therapists are out of touch with modern research on the subjects on which the miracle cure depends. No one can doubt that recovered memory therapy is producing something quite significant—agreement with the therapist's expectations.

To a growing number of knowledgeable academic and clinical specialists in hypnosis, social influence, memory, clinical psychology, and psychiatry, it is obvious that the practitioners of repressed memory are misusing therapeutic techniques. Repressed memory therapy is a triumph of misapplied influence in which practitioners are demonstrating the power of their methods to create beliefs. Doubtless recovered memory clients are victims—victims not of their parents or their past, but of their therapists. While the outcome of the therapist's influence on the client is not always certain and many clients reject the suggestions, it has worked frequently enough to warrant recognition of its manipulative power and of the fact that [the] recovered memory movement is evolving into one of the century's most intriguing quackeries masquerading as psychotherapy. . . .

A Reckless Therapy Becomes Institutionalized

A therapy's success in developing an institutional basis ultimately depends on the political trends that contributed to its rise. Broad concerns about child protection and feminist thought have contributed to the interest in these therapeutic innovations and their ready acceptance. Unfortunately, movements promoting social change face the danger, if not the inevitability, of stimulating opportunistic, zealous, and simpleminded spin-offs.

The constituencies created by the larger social concerns provide the muscle behind the institutionalization of repression theory and the therapy's procedures. The most startling example of this institutionalization is legislation and/or recent court decisions in fifteen states that now permit litigation based on recently recovered repressed memories. The unsubstantiated repression hypothesis is thus elevated to the status of fact. The new laws are tantamount to official certification that the phenomenon exists.

False Memory Syndrome

Unfounded accusations of childhood sexual abuse are tearing apart families all over North America, Pamela Freyd [executive director of the False Memory Syndrome Foundation] says. . . .

Freyd says that while many reports of incest and sexual abuse "are surely true, these delayed memories are too often the result of false memory syndrome caused by a disastrous 'therapeutic' program.

"Some of these so-called therapists are doing brain surgery with a knife and fork," she says. . . .

"Do I believe children are sometimes abused by their parents? Absolutely. But to the degree that we are being asked to accept? Absolutely not."

Bill Taylor, *Toronto Star*, May 18, 1992.

The potential impact is staggering since it opens the door to thousands of civil and criminal complaints. By alleging negligence on the part of a non-perpetrator parent, it is possible to involve homeowner's insurance policies and create deep pockets for people of modest means. At least 300 such lawsuits are known to have been initiated on the basis of recovered repressed memories. Widespread attorney interest is predictable. . . .

In recent months the mass media has begun to report the other side of the repressed memory story, notably criticism by professionals and outrage by those who say they were falsely accused. If the media continues balanced coverage the most likely result is that therapists practicing the cure will become convinced that the world has misunderstood and rejected them. The elements of such a reaction are already evident.

In 1992 a grass roots organization, the False Memory Syndrome (FMS) Foundation, was formed in Philadelphia. It represents members of over 2,400 families who protest that they have been falsely accused. In the recovered memory movement the formation of FMS is classified as merely part of the backlash against women and children. Some leaders of the movement seem to regard anyone who questions their therapy as anti-female, anti-child, probably stupid, or worse. Worse is that critics are, to use Dr. Cory Hammond's description, "dirty"—meaning they are part of the satanist conspiracy. Many professionals who have voiced criticism of the movement have at one time or another been accused of being satanists or agents of satanists.

These responses signal the collective paranoia of a social movement turning inward. The steps to isolation include rejection of the opinions of non-believers and increased reliance on only those who validate the ideology and claims of persecution. Once people become committed to an ideology, even one that masquerades as a testable scientific theory, the fact that it has failed is not necessarily perceived or it is often discounted. . . .

As long as practitioners are not accountable for what they lead their clients to believe and what they encourage them to do, they will remain reckless. They have no need to notice the power of their techniques and will continue to believe the damage they are causing is of benefit to their clients and the suffering they cause parents is a just punishment. Their refusal to acknowledge what the scientific literature demonstrates about their methods and to face the possibility that they are dreadfully wrong may be thought of as a defense mechanism that has deep psychological, professional, and economic meaning—it functions to protect therapists from full awareness of what they are doing. In the parlance of recovered memory therapy, they are in denial.

Periodical Bibliography

The following articles have been selected to supplement the diverse views presented in this chapter.

Eric Brodin	"Child Abuse Cases: An Open Invitation to Government Coercion," *Conservative Review*, January 1992. Available from 6861 Elm St., Suite 4H, McLean, VA 22101.
Christine A. Courtois	"The Memory Retrieval Process in Incest Survivor Therapy," *Journal of Child Sexual Abuse*, vol. 1 (1), 1992. Available from Haworth Press, 10 Alice St., Binghamton, NY 13904-9981.
Nina Darnton	"The Pain of the Last Taboo," *Newsweek*, October 7, 1991.
Family Therapy Networker	"Incest: The Darkest Secret," special section, May/June 1992. Available from 7705 13th St. NW, Washington, DC 20012.
Daniel Goleman	"Childhood Trauma: Memory or Invention?" *The New York Times*, July 21, 1992.
Christine Gorman	"Incest Comes Out of the Dark," *Time*, October 7, 1991.
William Norman Grigg	"The Politics of Child Abuse," *The New American*, September 7, 1992. Available from 770 Westhill Blvd., Appleton, WI 54915.
George K. Hong and Lawrence K. Hong	"Comparative Perspectives on Child Abuse and Neglect: Chinese Versus Hispanics and Whites," *Child Welfare*, July/August 1991.
Karen L. Schaefer	"Children Should Be Seen and Heard and Believed," *Children's Voice*, Winter 1993. Available from Child Welfare League of America, 440 First St. NW, Suite 330, Washington, DC 20001-2085.
Jean Seligman	"Horror Story or Big Hoax?" *Newsweek*, September 21, 1992.
Teena Sorenson and Barbara Snow	"How Children Tell: The Process of Disclosure in Child Sexual Abuse," *Child Welfare*, January/February 1991.
Thomas Sowell	"Long on Claims, Short on Evidence," *Forbes*, November 23, 1992.
Carol Tavris	"Beware the Incest-Survivor Machine," *The New York Times Book Review*, January 1, 1993.
Anastasia Toufexis	"When Can Memories Be Trusted?" *Time*, October 28, 1991.
Paul Waller	"The Politics of Child Abuse," *Society*, September/October 1991.

What Causes Child Abuse?

Chapter Preface

Determining what causes child abuse is a complex and difficult task. Many of the factors that experts say contribute to child abuse, such as stress or emotional problems, are common to most families. Since most parents do not abuse their children, isolating just what factors cause parents to become abusers remains puzzling.

In general, though, experts have grouped the factors that influence whether abuse will happen into two categories—internal and external. Internal problems include biological, psychological, or emotional difficulties. Some of these may be as common as low intelligence or as rare as severe personality disorders such as schizophrenia. As psychologists Joel S. Milner and Chinni Chilamkurti state, "Neuropsychological difficulties [mental health problems] are believed to increase the likelihood of inappropriate parental behavior, including physical child abuse."

External problems that affect potential abuse include economic hardship, lack of social support, and chemical dependency. For example, a 1991 survey of child abuse done by the National Center for Child Abuse Prevention Research showed that drug or alcohol abuse was one of two top causes of child abuse in 61 percent of the states. Another factor, a family history of abuse, remains the most significant and most studied predictor of child abuse. Studies done in the late 1980s indicate that about one-third of abused children go on to abuse their own children.

While many of the internal and external problems associated with child abuse are common to almost all American families, most parents do not abuse their children. What, then, is it that pushes some parents into abuse? Some experts hypothesize that in abusive situations many problems overlap and combine to create a more stressful, threatening environment that causes parents to lose control. According to the survey by the National Center on Child Abuse Prevention Research, "Families reported for child maltreatment often display a number of problems which can contribute to their likelihood for engaging in abusive behavior."

Because so many factors can cause parents to abuse their children, identifying potential abusers is difficult. The authors in the following chapters debate the various social, cultural, emotional, and psychological causes of child abuse.

"*Overburdened foster care systems face an army of neglected and physically and sexually abused children, the majority of them victims of drug-using parents.*"

Drug Addiction Causes Child Abuse

Ron Harris

Addiction to drugs is one of the leading causes of child abuse, according to *Los Angeles Times* staff writer Ron Harris. In the following viewpoint, Harris contends that addiction to cocaine, alcohol, heroin, and other drugs by parents makes them less responsible for and more violent toward their children, causing both physical and emotional damage.

As you read, consider the following questions:

1. How have drugs affected the economic situations and stability of many families, according to Harris?
2. What happens to abused and neglected children when the government agencies charged with protecting them remove them from the abusive situation, according to the author?
3. According to the author, what effects besides child abuse has drug addiction had on many children?

The unseen victims behind statistics on adult drug abuse are children.

Theirs are the hidden faces behind the news reports of drug arrests and record cocaine seizures, behind the public policy debates on treatment versus punishment.

And in America there are hundreds of thousands of them.

They are youngsters like Ryan Carlson, 10, and his brother Kristofer, 8, whose mother shot cocaine into her veins for longer than her sons have been alive. Consequently, the two St. Paul boys endured an early childhood of uncertainty and neglect. Unkempt and underfed, they were shuffled from home to home until Kristofer eventually was admitted to a medical facility to be treated for homicidal and suicidal tendencies.

They are children like Deann Shorter, 12, and her siblings, Twoana, 10, James, 8, and Dashalla, 2, who have spent the last two years in St. Paul foster homes after being taken from their mother, an addict who neglected them so severely that she lost all parental rights.

They are like Terri, 12, a Maryland girl who watched in horror one night as her family wrestled a doped-up uncle to the floor to keep him from leaping through a window of their 20th-floor apartment in the belief that he could fly.

They are like twins Susan and Shonda, 13, whose father's drug use in Newark, N.J., transformed him into a violent, abusive husband. Eventually, their family was torn apart and their mother fled the state with her children.

They are adoptees Rene and Taralyn Ankrum, two California children who are among the nation's estimated 300,000 drug babies. Because of their mothers' prenatal drug use, they were born with neurological and psychological damage so severe that they face a possible lifetime of developmental disorders.

The Legacy of Drug Abuse

While the nation struggles to bring narcotics use under control, a legacy of adult drug abuse is being etched into the lives of the next generation—children who will carry its scars even if they never smoke a joint, pop a pill or snort a line of cocaine.

Teachers, counselors, social workers, psychologists and children themselves say that for many youngsters today, growing up in America means maneuvering through an obstacle course of drugs and drug-related activity.

"In one way or another, whether they are bystanders or active participants, rich or poor, black or white, whether they are urban, suburban or rural, children cannot escape being affected by the increased use of drugs in our society," said Nancy Peterson, spokeswoman for the Chicago-based National Committee for the Prevention of Child Abuse. "It's permeated about every facet of life. It's part of the fabric of our society these days."

Across the nation, those who deal with social trends paint a dismal picture of drugs' impact on the innocent:

—Schools and welfare agencies must deal with growing numbers of children whose two-parent families have been shattered by drug use.

—Overburdened foster care systems face an army of neglected and physically and sexually abused children, the majority of them victims of drug-using parents.

—Children have become one of the fastest growing segments of the homeless population, and officials say many belong to addicted parents who have been forced onto the street after spending their money on narcotics.

—Thousands of children drift from guardian to guardian as they await the return of parents—particularly mothers—who are increasingly serving time in jails and prisons for drug-related offenses. Since 1983, the number of women in prison has grown at a rate faster than that of men. Prison officials estimate that nearly 80% of those women are there for drug-related crimes and eight of every 10 have children.

—Schools, teachers and administrators are wrestling with the question of how to educate a huge population of babies exposed to drugs while in the womb, whose diminished abilities foretell an uncertain future. They may represent as many as 10% of all American children born annually, according to the National Assn. for Perinatal Addiction Research and Education. . . .

The Impact of Drugs

As students in an eighth-grade class in Laurel, Md., told their stories, Susan, 13, raised her hand. "I've seen it make people very violent and it tears families apart," she said.

How?

"Well, there was this family that lived near us when we lived in Newark, and the man used to do drugs," she said. "Most of the time the man was really violent. The wife would leave and take their children. You would be outside and he would throw things out of the window and be yelling and they would call the police."

When the bell rang, Susan lagged behind. Then, cautiously, she approached a reporter: "I want to talk to you," she said meekly. "You know that family I was talking about. That was my family."

Later, in a quiet corner of the library, Susan told her story:

"At first everything was all right. My mother was a nurse. She stayed at the same hospital for 10 years. We lived in a house. I had my own room. We had a back yard, a swing and everything. Now we live in an apartment and me and my sister share a room.

"Everything was all right until the drugs came in. My father used to do drugs . . . cocaine. He used to do it in the house and he and my mother used to fight all the time. The fighting was because of the drugs.

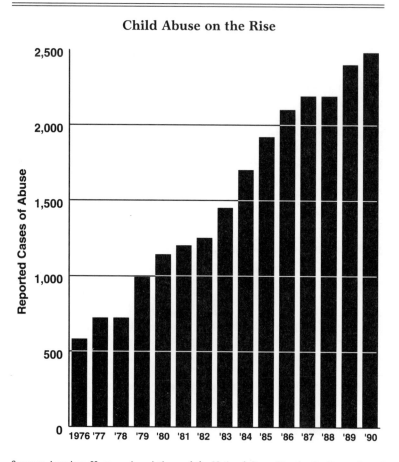

Child Abuse on the Rise

Sources: American Humane Association and the National Committee for the Prevention of Child Abuse.

"I can remember the first grade. They used to fight in the middle of the night and they would wake us up and take us to my grandmother's house. My mother had a 1980 Cadillac. My father broke her windows five times. . . .

"The fighting and stuff messed me up. In the fourth grade, I used to have temper tantrums. I was mad at everybody. . . . In the sixth grade, my sister was getting into trouble at school all the time. . . . I would stay up late at night worrying about my mother, go to school and worry about my mother. . . . I didn't want to come home. I always wanted to stay at my grandmother's house.

"Then one day my mother came down here [to Maryland] to find us a place to stay. At first we stayed with her friend. Then we got our own apartment. . . .

"I try to forget about it now. Those were hard times."

Drugs and Welfare

Susan and her sister, officials said, could have easily joined the thousands of cases that have flooded the offices of the nation's welfare system, a system "so overloaded by cocaine that it is about to short-circuit," says Rep. Thomas J. Downey (D-N.Y.).

According to a 1990 report by the House Ways and Means Committee, adult drug use has become the "dominant characteristic" in case loads of child protective service agencies in 22 states and the District of Columbia. It is the cause of dysfunctional families, child neglect and abuse in more than 70% of the cases in cities such as Los Angeles, New York and Washington.

"I would suspect that drugs or alcohol is at the bottom of probably eight of every 10 cases we get," said Brian Albiser, of Las Vegas, who oversees child protective services as administrative coordinator for the Clark County Juvenile Court.

The number of children placed in foster homes jumped 29% nationally in three years—from 280,000 in 1986 to 360,000 in 1989—according to a report by the human resources subcommittee of the Ways and Means Committee.

Jean Bridgeford, who is known to just about everybody as "Granny," has taken 235 foster children into her St. Paul home over the past 20 years. She needs only to look at the faces of the newest foster children scurrying around her six-bedroom house to know that adult drug use is driving children into foster homes. . . .

Twoana and James Shorter, who have been with Granny for two years, make up the last of her permanent charges. Their older sister, Deanna, used to live with them, but was taken to a detention center for running away from foster homes. A younger sister is in another foster home.

Their mother, a cocaine addict, lives in a halfway house in Minneapolis. A St. Paul judge stripped her of parental rights after she failed repeatedly to live up to the requirements of her rehabilitation program.

Twoana and her siblings came to the notice of local officials by chance when they were living with their mother in an aunt's home. For two weeks, the youngest child, less than a year old, had been sick, running a fever and vomiting periodically.

One morning, Deanna, then 11, decided something had to be done, so she bundled the infant up and carried her four blocks to the nearest hospital. When she arrived, curious hospital officials inquired about her mother.

"She's at home," Deanna lied. "She's asleep on the sofa."

In fact, her mother had not returned home from the night before. That day, child welfare officials discovered that the children had been surviving largely on their own, clothing and feeding themselves, preparing for school and doing their best to tend to each other's needs while their mother fed her addiction.

The children were taken to a foster home where they lived for two months, before moving to "Granny" Bridgeford's.

"Living with Granny is OK," Twoana said. "Granny really takes care of me real good. She takes care of my hair, she lets me get curls in my hair and everything. I have people who like me here . . . Granny's got rules. I like that . . . That means everybody will be treated fair."

Even so, Twoana said, "I want to go back and live with my mom. I never gave up hope that I wouldn't go back and live with my mom."

Child welfare officials estimate that thousands of children like Twoana, neglected, often abused while living with their addicted parents, never get help because they do not come to the attention of authorities.

"The dramatic increase in the rate of child abuse that we are now seeing can be reversed if the number of people living in poverty can be reversed."

Poverty Causes Child Abuse

Brian H. McNeill

Brian H. McNeill was a social worker in Hennepin County Child Protection in Minnesota from June 1988 to December 1990. In the following viewpoint, McNeill argues that the leading cause of child abuse in the United States is poverty. According to McNeill, increasing numbers of parents find themselves unable to cope with the stress of poverty. Their children, according to the author, often bear the brunt of parents' frustration through physical abuse and neglect.

As you read, consider the following questions:

1. Why is child abuse increasing, according to McNeill?
2. According to the author, what is the connection between capitalism and child abuse?
3. Why does McNeill argue against those who claim that child abuse is not an economic issue?

Bruce H. McNeill, "Dramatic Rise in Child Abuse from Growing Economic Stress," *New Unionist*, April 1990. Reprinted with permission.

The poorest group of people in the United States today are children. Thirteen million children, 20.6%, fall below the government's officially declared poverty line. The incidence of child poverty in 1990 is six percentage points higher than it was in 1969.

Most of these poor children live in households headed by single women. According to 1989 figures from the Bureau of the Census, 45.8% of white children, 68.3% of African-American children and an incredible 70.1% of Hispanic children living in households headed by a single female are poor.

Children in Poverty

In addition to getting poorer during the 1980s, while the rich among us were playing with their yachts, their $30,000 cars and their third and fourth vacation homes, large numbers of America's children not only did not have toys, they were also the victims of increasingly frequent abuse and neglect. According to the Denver-based American Association for the Protection of Children (AAPC), which compiled statistics on child abuse for the federal government from 1977 to 1989, between 1981 and 1988 the number of reports of child abuse received by government agencies increased 98%. Between 1976 and 1987, the number of reports of child abuse received by government agencies increased 225%.

It is currently being debated by those concerned with child abuse whether or not this dramatic increase in reports is the result of an actual increase in child abuse itself, or simply the result of a public more aware of the problem and willing to report it more often. While the academics and politicians are figuring that out, the AAPC estimates that there were 686,000 proven cases of child abuse in the United States in 1987, the last year that reliable statistics are available, constituting 37 to 40% of all reports.

Statistics No Longer Kept

In 1989, when the media was filled with stories about the increase and the horrors of child abuse, the government cut the funding of the AAPC, and currently no one in the United States is compiling national statistics on child abuse. It takes two years to come up with national figures. The 1987 figures came out in 1989. No one is working on the 1988 child-abuse numbers. There is talk of establishing a National Child Abuse Reporting Center, but it is years from being a reality.

The government that comes up with statistics on the economy as regular as clockwork, statistics serviceable to the financiers on Wall Street and to the bankers in your home town, has decided that it cannot afford to count how many of its children are being neglected, beaten, raped and killed.

Articles about child abuse in your local newspaper are usually based on statistics from state or county social-service agencies. These articles inevitably include a statement to the effect that child abuse hits all economic classes in society equally and is not confined to the poor and the working class. Such statements leave the impression that child abuse is primarily the result of the psychopathology of the parents. They imply that there is something wrong mentally with the parents and they need to see a therapist to stop abusing their children. These articles lead the reader to believe that child abuse is a criminal and mental-health rather than an economic issue.

Poorest of the Poor

The reality of the situation is completely different. Ask any social worker in a child-protection agency and they will tell you that the great majority of their clients, if not all their clients, are the poorest of the poor. In 1985, 48.3% of abused children lived in families receiving Aid to Families with Dependent Children (AFDC), popularly known as welfare. In 1978, the AAPC found that 90% of abusive families fell below the national median-income level. In an article entitled "Child Abuse and Neglect: The Myth of Classlessness," Leroy Pelton sums up the situation:

"The lower socioeconomic classes are disproportionately represented among all child abuse and neglect cases known to public agencies, to the extent that an overwhelming percentage—indeed, the vast majority—of the families in these cases live in poverty or near-poverty circumstances."

Economic Problems and Abuse

That the majority of chronically maltreating families fall within the lowest social echelons is no coincidence. Economic, sociocultural, and interpersonal factors act jointly in these families to create a situation of severe economic stress, hardship, and dependency that has been cited as the single greatest threat to adequate family functioning.

Joan I. Vondra, *Children at Risk*, 1990.

Perpetrators of child abuse are almost always parents or relatives who have easy access to the child. These relatives have almost always come from poor families where they themselves were abused as children. As a result, they do not have first-hand knowledge of how to cope with the stress of raising several small children with almost no money and little social support.

Given the obvious and direct link that exists between poverty and child abuse, given that poverty, according to studies, in fact in many cases can be said to cause child abuse, why do so many politicians and journalists insist that child abuse hits all economic classes equally?

The causal link between poverty and child abuse is denied by most because to admit it is to admit that the current economic system is responsible for what all people recognize as inhuman barbarity. To admit that poverty causes child abuse is to admit that capitalism causes child abuse, because capitalism always has and always will create and maintain a pool of poor and unemployed people in order to keep wages low.

Ruling Class Response

The ruling class responds to child abuse in three ways. First, they have their hired spokespersons, the politicians, pass laws on the state level requiring county social-service agencies to respond to reports of child abuse.

Second, the county social-service agencies hire social workers to investigate these reports and "work" with families that are identified as abusive. Sometimes this "work" involves removing children from the abusive parental home and placing them in a foster home, where they are at high risk for further abuse. At other times, the decision is made to allow the children to stay in their parent's home.

Third, the ruling class, through government and private funding, sets up a series of social programs whose purpose is to try to help abusive parents learn new parenting skills, or to stop taking drugs if that is part of the problem.

Learning How to Parent

This patchwork system has its own logic and sometimes actually works. That is, sometimes poor parents who enter the system once in a while actually do learn new parenting skills, sober up if they have been chemically dependent and are able to safely parent their children.

More often than not, the only thing that this system accomplishes is to keep a large number of social-service workers employed at low-paying jobs and to give the ruling class an alibi. They can say that they are doing everything possible to prevent child abuse because they are funding a large array of programs.

This system also gives the ruling class and their hired spokespersons, the politicians and the journalists, scapegoats to blame when the inevitable happens and children die. When that does happen, the media has a field day blaming everyone in sight. The television and newspaper reporters appear to take particular delight in focusing on those lazy county bureaucrats who are not doing their jobs.

The fact of the matter is that the social-service workers are the only ones in sight who really give a damn, but they cannot possibly undo the social damage that the capitalist economic system has inflicted on generations of poor families. Not only are the social-service workers asked to do more than is humanly possible in terms of case loads, they simply do not have the resources necessary to begin healing those who more often than not have turned into abusers after they themselves were abused as children.

Capitalist Exploitation

The social-service programs are a joke, mere window dressing. The programs have nowhere near the level of funding necessary to seriously address the economic, educational and psychological deficits created by capitalist exploitation of working people that results in child abuse.

The increase in child abuse that we are seeing in this country at this time is an indication that the stress of living under a capitalist economic system is increasing. Both parents must work to maintain the same standard of living that one parent could provide 30 years ago. As the capitalists increasingly organize their enterprises on an international scale, workers' standards of living in the developed nations increasingly come closer to the standards of living of workers in the developing nations of Africa, Asia and Latin America. The readjustment involves more than doing with a little less. To some of the children of parents who cannot cope with this economic wrenching, the "readjustment" means burns with hot irons, broken bones and even death.

Although no political or economic program can promise to eliminate child abuse, the dramatic increase in the rate of child abuse that we are now seeing can be reversed if the number of people living in poverty can be reversed. That goal can be accomplished by the workers taking control of their workplaces and creating a more humane economic and political system that is concerned with the welfare of all people, in place of the current system that is in reality designed for just one thing: the profits of the capitalists.

"Child maltreatment can . . . be explained in terms of attitudes that have taken root and been nourished for many, many generations."

A Violent Society Causes Child Abuse

Vincent J. Fontana and Valerie Moolman

In the following viewpoint, Vincent J. Fontana and Valerie Moolman argue that society's tolerance of violence—especially violence toward children—causes child abuse. Fontana, a doctor, has served as the head of the Mayor's Task Force on Child Abuse and Neglect in New York City. As the medical director and pediatrician in chief at the New York Foundling Hospital, he established the Foundling's Temporary Shelter for Abusing Parents and the Crisis Nursery for Parents and Children. Moolman is an author in Brooklyn, New York.

As you read, consider the following questions:

1. Who is the typical child abuser, according to the authors?
2. According to Fontana and Moolman, how have society's attitudes toward children changed and how have these changes affected the incidence of child abuse?
3. How does abuse affect the children that survive it, according to the authors?

Save the Family, Save the Child: What We Can Do to Help Children at Risk by Vincent J. Fontana and Valerie Moolman. New York: Penguin, 1991. Copyright 1991 by Vincent J. Fontana. Reprinted with permission.

People say: "Eliminate poverty, and you'll eliminate child abuse!"

I wish it were true. It would be wonderful if we could eliminate poverty, and God knows it would help to ease a great many of our national ills, including child abuse, but it would not be a cure. Most poor people do not abuse or neglect their children, or commit other crimes. Many well-off people do. Poverty, like other stresses, exacerbates the factors that drive people to mistreat their fellow beings, their children, and their pets, but it is not a primary cause. Is it something in the genes? Maybe, sometimes. Usually not.

Why, then, do people abuse their children?

I suspect that if we could trace our way back to the beginning of human life and the human psyche, and if we could point to the first individual to maltreat a child, we would still not be able to identify the origins or answer *why*. We have an inheritance that we carry around with us, but it is not—with some exceptions—genetic, and it has no single source. Perhaps child maltreatment can better be explained in terms of attitudes that have taken root and been nourished for many, many generations.

Violence

A key theme is violence, violence to both body and soul.

Though we are all born with a self-protective mechanism, we are not born violent or with a disrespect for human life. The will to violence is an acquired attitude; juvenile violence, leading to adult violence, is a learned behavior. We do not all learn it; and even some of us who do manage to, unlearn it.

Although violence begins with the individual and is not an inherited trait or ancestral throwback, there are contributing elements that reach well beyond the individual. We have to reckon with the psychological forces that interweave with the social environment of the times. In different periods of history, the pattern of violence changes, and the factors leading up to it change, too. With reference to the causes of disturbed behavior, Freud, in one of his last writings, observes that "we must not forget to include the influence of civilization." I believe it is not difficult to see what influence *our* civilization has on the developing individual.

My own personal experiences with parents and children over the last three decades have convinced me that much of the physical and emotional abuse that we inflict on our children is an extreme of the violent and self-serving child-rearing practices firmly established in Western culture. These practices are rooted in our cavalier attitude toward children as possessions —often balky ones that have no right to balk—and our own upbringing. We are sickened when a parent scalds a child to death or slams him against a wall with such force that the skull is fractured, but we are well accustomed to the spanking, slapping, yelling, scolding, yanking, ear-pulling, and name-calling practiced on even little kids by our own friends and neighbors—all done under the guise of caring for the child and disciplining him.

Within the definition of the maltreatment syndrome, I can say without question that child abuse in one form or another is taking place in the majority of our American homes today, and the alarming part about it is that it is not being recognized as child abuse. Most parents—yes, *most*—fail to draw the line between discipline and physical punishment. They may not recognize what they are doing, but they are maltreating their kids. If this should be called to their attention, they are astounded. They say, "The kid will only learn if I use the strap! A good paddling never hurt anybody! That's the way I was brought up! There's nothing wrong with me!"

I look at them, and I wonder.

Abuse Crosses Generations

What is really happening is that the parents are replaying an old scene; what they are doing to their children is a variation on what was done to them. In the name of discipline, they themselves were thrashed, manipulated, lied to, deceived, and threatened with the loss of parental love. Now they can do the same. Their children, in turn, are helpless and dependent, easy targets for the owner-adult who has grown up into a position of power. The stored-up hatred and anger of the cruelly treated child-become-parent spills out and engulfs the next generation. Parental cruelty, intentional or otherwise, can take innumerable forms. How satisfying it can be, sometimes, to mock, demean, humiliate, and physically punish even while proclaiming love! And how confusing for a child.

Psychoanalyst and author Alice Miller says: "Beatings, which are only one form of mistreatment, are *always* degrading, because the child not only is unable to defend him- or herself but is also supposed to show gratitude and respect to the parents in return. And along with corporal punishment there is a whole gamut of ingenious measures applied 'for the child's own good' which are difficult for a child to comprehend and which for that very reason often have devastating effects in later life."

One of the devastating effects may be a smoldering but unrecognized hatred that expresses itself in unbridled cruelty.

Never mind that practically every child development expert alive regards corporal punishment as an unacceptable and outdated form of discipline: the habit seems to be ingrained in the

American way of life. It is a legacy that travels down the generations, stopping—when? Only when it is consciously, deliberately stopped. I believe the tradition continues to be handed down because of our casual acceptance of violence in general, because of our belief that children are our possessions to do with as we please, and because we feel that parents have the right to raise their children in the manner of their choice. Parents, we believe, have the right to mind their own business. Sadly, what they are likely to achieve is a wary, defensive child with a tendency to lash out at others, maturing into a punitive adult.

Societal Violence

Some societal values may perpetuate child abuse and neglect. For example, the acceptance of violence as a way of life, the conviction that parents have the right to treat children as they please, and the desire to avoid outside involvement in family life may influence the occurrence of child abuse and neglect.

U.S. Department of Health and Human Services, *Child Abuse and Neglect: A Shared Community Concern*, March 1989.

Corporal punishment only teaches that it's okay to use violence in solving problems, that it's okay for a powerful person to hurt someone who is less powerful, that hitting is okay if practiced by certain people at certain times. Loving discipline, on the other hand, is an educational, civilizing experience that teaches the child about life and the rules required for getting along with others on terms of mutual respect. . . .

Domestic Violence

According to the combined figures of several recent studies, children are present in at least 50 percent of the homes visited by the police in connection with domestic violence calls. The majority of battered women never press charges, which increases the possibility that the abuse will escalate and include the child. Because the most severely abused women are usually the least likely to seek help, many children in violent homes *never* come to the attention of agencies that might provide protective services—a grim thought, since a nationwide study has found that over 50 percent of the children of known battering couples had been physically or sexually abused.

This is, of course, extreme. But an acceptance of less violent patterns of maltreatment is imbedded in the family code today. "There is a high level of sanctioned violence within the

American family that makes it difficult to define and prevent child abuse or spouse abuse," says Murray A. Straus. "Law and social custom condone an intrafamily 'right to hit,' which far exceeds what might be permitted on the street or on the job."

So much for the safety of the family bosom. Clearly, there is much risk here for the children.

A Typical Abusive Family

If we were to look for a likely family in which to find or expect child abuse, we would draw up a trial model of a family unit characterized by a pattern of isolation from the community and of violence within; social deviance or criminal behavior; a mother bearing her first child before the age of twenty; poor prenatal care, or none; marital conflict; and a record of previous child abuse and neglect, possibly culminating in the removal of a child by court order. We would not be surprised to find that one or both parents had been abused, neglected, or otherwise demeaned as a child, or had been raised in hatred masquerading as love. One is a substance abuser, the other an enabler. One may be mentally ill or retarded. One or both may be unemployed. There is likely to be a child in the family with medical or mental problems. If there is a grandmother in the household who might be expected to lend stability, she is likely to be a permanent adolescent herself—a teenage mother in her time, and a 28-year-old grandma.

Let me hasten to point out that this profile is a conglomeration based on known families of abuse: the highly visible ones in contact with social agencies. Obviously, in more affluent circles, the portrait of the household is bound to be different. The portrait of the abuser, however, is very much the same, no matter what the social class.

He or she tends to be a social isolate of minimal self-esteem, usually maltreated as a child, lacking a parental role model, looking to the children to provide the warmth and attention not forthcoming from his or her own parents; he does not have much in the way of coping strengths. There is a pervading sense of despair, of giving up. These sad people have no awareness that in hitting out at innocent, powerless little targets they are expressing repressed anger and hatred. They are so cut off from their feelings that they neither know nor care about the pain and misery they are inflicting. If the abuser is the male, the woman in the case is a passive collaborator who is either so addicted to or afraid of the man that she cannot intercede.

Some major studies of child deaths due to abuse and neglect have concluded that most of the homicides are committed by mothers, followed by the mothers' boyfriends and the biological fathers. This may be true, but the mothers also cover up for their men: if they do not confess to guilt themselves, they profess to have no idea what could have happened, or go out of their way to insist that the male partner could not possibly have been involved. My feeling, based on police investigations and years of personal observation, is that the "boyfriend" is most often the perpetrator. However, the dumping of newborns into the trash—an escalating phenomenon—is almost certainly the work of mothers "stuck" with babies they didn't want.

Predicting Abuse

Thus, within limits, it is possible to predict the kinds of situations in which abuse is likely to occur. We can look into our schools, too, and pinpoint predictive risk factors through what we see of the lives of children and parents. We have learned that such factors as low birth weight, having a teenage mother, untreated health problems, lack of language and coping skills at school entry, and failure to develop warm and trusting relationships early on in life correlate with troubles in elementary school. In turn, we find that poor school performance and truancy as early as third or fourth grade permit us to predict delinquency, dropping out, early pregnancy, and long-term damage in general. Knowing these things, we can attack the risk factors with intensive intervention programs providing preschool education and intensive family support. . . .

Rather than receding, violence is becoming more deeply entrenched in our society. If we cannot trace the practice of violence against children back to its historical roots, we know very well where it has nestled and been nurtured: in the bosom of the family. The civilization of the times plays its role, too. "Civilization" is the environment of the family of man, and a quick look around will show us a present-day environment that is poison for families and a new breed of family that is hell on the environment.

*"Cutting children off from the potential
friendship of strangers has the effect of further
burdening already overburdened parents, some
of whom will become more abusive."*

A Lack of
Community Ties
Causes Child Abuse

Richard Farson

In the late twentieth century families have become isolated
from the extended families of grandparents, aunts, uncles, and
cousins that had characterized society for generations. In the
following viewpoint, author Richard Farson argues that fear of
strangers leads parents to isolate themselves and their children
still further. This isolation, Farson contends, causes parents to
feel alone and unable to parent effectively, increasing the likelihood that these overburdened parents will abuse their children.
Farson, a psychologist in La Jolla, California, writes on issues related to women's and children's civil rights.

As you read, consider the following questions:

1. How, according to the author, does fear of child abuse lead to
   abuse?
2. What solution does Farson recommend to reduce child abuse?
3. Why does the author say that parent training leads to abuse?
   What alternative does he suggest?

Richard Farson, "Child Protection That Backfires." Reprinted, with permission, from the
Bulletin of the Park Ridge Center, vol. 6, no. 1 (Jan. 1991). Copyright 1991 by the Park Ridge
Center for the Study of Health, Faith, and Ethics, Chicago.

A friend who happens to run a toy store remarked to me the other day that he no longer talks to the children who play in the park across the street from his store. He has become afraid that he will be seen as a potential child abuser.

I am sure his story could be repeated by many thousands of others who have recently become unwilling to risk befriending children. They are afraid because of what we might call the milk carton alarm.

Frightened Parents and Frightened Children

Pictures of missing children on milk cartons and shopping bags, it has been reported, frighten children. Probably so. But a greater danger is that they frighten parents. This fear in turn frightens away people like my friend. As well intended as these efforts to protect children may be, by further separating them from the community at large they probably place children at even greater risk.

The reasons are not all that obvious. To understand them, we have to start with the fact that America is currently obsessed with the subject of child abuse. While children have been our number one subject of conversation for many years (no society is as concerned or anxious about children as ours), recently that conversation has turned into nothing less than a national preoccupation with child abuse and a pervasive fear of strangers.

Fear Can Lead to Abuse

One might applaud the long overdue recognition that this dark subject is finally receiving were it not for the fact that as we make parents more frightened of other people, particularly strangers, we actually increase the likelihood that their children will be abused. Not by strangers, but by the parents themselves.

Strangers can be dangerous to children, of course. But the risk is small when compared to the dangers that parents represent. Cutting children off from the potential friendship of strangers has the effect of further burdening already overburdened parents, some of whom will become more abusive as they become more isolated in their 24-hour child care responsibility. Isolation contributes to the frustration and anger that sometimes lead to frantic acts of violence.

We are the only society in the world, and the only in history, to define parenthood in this lonely way. In all other societies, the raising of children is more of a community responsibility, with many adults helping as their time, talents and roles permit.

But we are driving away this potential source of parental assistance. Newspaper and t.v. stories about molestation in child care centers, missing children, dangers of kidnaping, and so forth have diverted us from the more basic causes of child abuse, and worse, have led us to take the wrong kinds of protective measures.

America is among the leading nations in child abuse, a million or more cases per year. We don't even know how to count all the incidents. How, for example, do we regard the parent who allows a nagging and tugging child to fall, or who lets a squirming and resistant child slip in the bathtub? Do these instances count? Not in most statistics. But they stem from the same source as other abuses—frustrated and desperate parents, alone with increasing and unprecedented feelings of responsibility.

Isolation from Community Causes Abuse

Many studies of child abuse suggest that isolation is a major factor. When families have difficulties, perhaps from unemployment or some other social problem, they may respond to their problem in a number of ways. The families that respond by isolating themselves, by withdrawing from friends and neighbors, are the most likely to be abusive.

Other studies have shown that abusive families tend to be more isolated than other families. They tend to have fewer friends, less contact with neighbors, and less access to resources such as the welfare system or social service system; churches, synagogues, and other religious groups; and other community organizations. Isolation seems to be both a cause and an effect of abusive patterns.

Susan Mufson and Rachel Kranz, *Straight Talk About Child Abuse*, 1991.

Displaying missing children's pictures, legislating stronger surveillance of child care centers, warning children and adults of the potential dangers of strangers, do not strike at the core of the child abuse problem. The measures fail to recognize that parents are by far the main abusers of children, including the most horrifying acts. Moreover, they ignore the major causes of child abuse, which are the legitimization of violence against children, the increased burdens of modern parenthood, and the growing isolation of parents from the community that could help them.

If most courses of action are actually making matters worse, what then would be effective counterproposals for reducing child abuse?

1. End corporal punishment. Most Americans (70% of all educators) believe that it is acceptable (even desirable) to commit acts of violence against children, in the form of spankings (or worse), to bring about acquiescence to adult authority. Spanking

may not be the worst thing we do to children, but the line between spankings and beatings is just too difficult to draw, especially when the parent or teacher is alone and frantic.

Scandinavian countries have successfully enacted laws against such punishment in both school and home. That is the simplest and surest single act we as a society can take to bring about a new nonviolent attitude toward our children.

A U.S. Supreme Court decision to protect children from corporal punishment would help, but given its continuing decisions supporting corporal punishment, we are not likely to see a rapid change in the Court's attitude toward this practice. However, a Court decision to declare corporal punishment a violation of children's constitutional rights could make an important difference.

Parents Need Help

2. Connect overburdened parents with other people. When parents (increasingly single parents) are near the end of their rope almost anyone can help, if only the frantic parent could call upon someone.

Parents need to be able to rely more on the community and, yes, on strangers sometimes. That has been the practice in every society. We are the only one that asks parents to do the whole job themselves. Other people can be very good for our children. Children can be taught not to get into automobiles with strangers, but we have become afraid if we see a stranger tying our children's shoes, wiping their noses, or buttoning their jackets.

We are now even afraid of professional child care workers. Consequently child care centers, most of which have adopted stringent rules against touching children (how terrible that must be for them and the children!), are closing because they cannot afford the increased cost of liability insurance. This means that even more children will have to be cared for by potentially abusive parents.

Education for Compassion

3. Give parents education, not just training. Paradoxically, people who have parent training are more likely to treat their children harshly because the training makes them feel more responsible in situations where they, like all of us, are still largely helpless.

That combination of feelings—responsibility plus helplessness—predictably leads to abuse. That is why doctors who are unsuccessful in curing their patients or teachers who are unable to teach their students do not become compassionate but instead become abusive.

If parents were educated rather than trained, they would learn, for example, that parenthood, like childhood, is in itself an invention. It keeps being reinvented in every age, as the particular burdens carried by parents today are not "natural" but result largely from other developments in our society, our cultural anxiety about children, our belief that all problems have solutions, and our willingness to impose on parents new responsibilities for their children without regard for how these responsibilities may impossibly burden parenthood.

Recognize Children's Right to Resist

4. Teach (and allow) children to say no. This may not be so easy in a society that does not recognize children's rights, particularly their right to resist adult authority. But if we were to gain a new consciousness of children's full right to personhood, they would be able to resist improper actions against them by whomever is the perpetrator, including the parent, and all of us would regard them (as we do others who can legitimately resist us) as less likely targets for our hostility.

These steps are by no means all we need to do to make the world safer for children, but they do represent a beginning. Ultimately we may come to see the best way to protect children is to recognize their full status as persons under the law, to grant and protect their civil rights, which means, of course, protection against those of us who think we know what is good for them.

If, however, we proceed along the paths we are now taking, frightening ourselves and our children about strangers, reducing the ability of the community to help parents with the increasingly difficult responsibilities of parenthood, only those with perverse interests in our children will risk approaching them, and parents will be ever more burdened and abusive.

106

"Many child abusers were also survivors of child abuse themselves."

A Family History of Abuse Contributes to Child Abuse

Susan Mufson and Rachel Kranz

In the following viewpoint, Susan Mufson and Rachel Kranz maintain that parents who were themselves abused as children are more likely to abuse their own children. Such parents, the authors contend, come to believe that abuse is the proper method of child rearing. Mufson is a member of the New York City Task Force Against Sexual Assault and a consultant to the Crime Victims' Counseling Service. She conducts numerous workshops, presentations, and training seminars on all forms of abuse. Kranz is the author of numerous books for young adults on a variety of social issues.

As you read, consider the following questions:

1. How do parents abused as children justify their abuse of their own children, according to the authors?
2. According to Mufson and Kranz, what characteristics do abusive parents attribute to their children?
3. In families where only one parent is abusive, how does the other parent typically react, according to the authors?

If child abusers aren't monsters, then why do they act the way they do? If we believe that some of them, at least, love the children they abuse, how do we understand their actions?

There's no one answer to these questions, but there are some explanations that may help us understand. First, some abusers may simply not know any other way to act. This is particularly true of parents who physically abuse or neglect infants. Some parents, particularly young or teenage parents, don't have a realistic idea of how easily an infant can be hurt or of how much stronger they are than their babies. They don't realize how unsafe it is to leave infants or toddlers alone in the house or how damaging it is to tie them to a bed to "protect" them while the parent goes out. These parents need education and help to enable them to act differently.

Generations of Abuse

With other abusive parents, the problem goes deeper. Many child abusers were also survivors of child abuse themselves. If they were physically, emotionally, or sexually abused as children, or possibly if they grew up with someone who was abused, they may grow up to repeat the abuse as adults.

Some people in this category are simply unaware of any other way of acting. They may believe that it's normal to beat a child or to vent one's anger with harsh insults. They may believe that it's normal to engage in sexually abusive behavior, since that's what they grew up with.

For many parents who were abused as children, their reason for abusing their own children is that they need to prove that their parents were right. They do this by treating their children exactly as their parents treated them. You'll recall that many children find it easier to pretend that they are somehow responsible for the abuse, or that their parents are acting out of love, rather than to hold their parents responsible for acting badly. When those children grow up, they still don't want to admit that their parents acted badly. So they act just like their parents, because, they reason to themselves, their parents were acting out of love.

Deserving Abuse

Sometimes these parents decide that their children "deserve" to be abused, just like they "deserved" it when *they* were kids. Sometimes these parents identify with their own parents: "He got to beat me, so now I get to beat you—it's my turn now." Sometimes children remind parents of someone who abused them or someone whom they're angry at, such as a husband who left home. Parents may not be aware that they're taking out their feelings against this person on a child who in reality has done nothing wrong.

In addition, people who were abused as children would generally have felt very helpless as they grew up. After all, the adults that they depended on were not very dependable—instead, they were abusive. When these children become adults, they still have the feeling of being helpless and abused by a powerful, angry person. In this frame of mind, they often perceive children or growing teenagers as a "powerful" person.

In reality, of course, a parent is always much more powerful than a child. But in his or her own mind, the parent feels like a child, and the crying baby or the arguing teenager seems to have all the power of an angry father or mother. So the parent feels justified in doing anything to make this seemingly powerful person "behave."

The Effects of Maltreatment

Not only does the experience of maltreatment have potentially profound effects on the individual, but . . . the effects of such a history can manifest themselves in the next generation, insofar as that individual is at risk of mistreating his or her offspring.

Lise M. Youngblade and Jay Belsky in *Children at Risk*, 1990.

No matter how much they may love their parents, abused children probably also feel anger and resentment, along with the love. So when these children grow up, they may still feel angry and resentful that they weren't treated properly. They may still be waiting for someone to come along and treat them like a loving parent, instead of an abusive one. They may even expect that they will get this kind of love from their children. But children cannot act like loving parents since they are not old enough. So all of the parent's leftover anger against his or her own parents gets let out on the child, even though the child has done nothing to deserve it.

Parents who expected only love and caring from their children may be very frustrated when they discover that little babies have needs of their own. One young mother who abandoned her child later said, "I thought that finally someone would love me, but this baby is always crying—he doesn't love me, either." In reality the baby was crying because he was hungry or tired or wanted something. But the mother could only see her own need to be loved, and therefore misinterpreted her baby's actions, which led her to act abusively.

This pattern is also experienced by emotionally abusive parents. Even though these parents may not batter their children, they may make inappropriate demands on them. Because the parents felt unloved as children, they want their children to make up for it. But a child cannot make up for a parent's disappointments. So both parent and child continue to be frustrated and hurt. And the parent continues to take that frustration out on the child by making unfair demands or expressing unfair criticisms.

Sometimes emotionally abusive parents who themselves were deprived as children may unconsciously resent the idea that anyone will get something they themselves were denied. They may also simply not know how to give emotional support, since they themselves never got any. They may feel so deprived of love themselves that they cannot conceive of how to love their own children. Or they may love their children, but not be able to provide a sense of security, respect, or any other quality that was missing from their own childhood.

Sexual abusers were often sexually abused themselves as children. Again, they may be trying to make up for the experience, proving to themselves that the adults who abused them "weren't so bad" by imitating those adults.

Some sexually abusive adults and teenagers may feel that no one loves them or cares about them. They may feel that everyone their own age dislikes them or doesn't love them enough. It may scare them that they cannot control these other people, that they cannot make sure that the people they love will love them back the way they'd like. Such people may feel that in a sexual relationship with a child they have finally found someone to love them—someone whom they can also control. Because a child is so dependent on adults (and on teenage authorities like baby-sitters), and because a child or a teenager knows less and has less power than an adult, that younger person will be far more easy to control than someone of the abuser's own age. So the abuser feels safer with the younger person.

Such abusers may lie to themselves, telling themselves that the younger person wants the relationship as much as they do. In fact, the abusers are using their power to get the love that they fear they can't get in any other way.

The Nonabusive Parent

Frequently in families only one parent is abusive, and the other parent does not act abusively. What about these other parents? If they aren't abusers themselves, how can they allow abuse to go on?

Again, this is a complicated question and there's no one simple answer. In the case of physical abuse, the nonabusive parent may also be scared of or abused by the battering parent.

Especially in the case of battering men, wives and children may be equally at risk.

In this case, the mother may have many different reasons for going along with the abuse. She may believe that she deserves to be beaten, perhaps because she too was an abused child. She may believe that someday the man will stop, and that meanwhile, he really loves her—which may also be feelings that she had about a battering parent when she was a child. Since as a child she was powerless to stop the abuse of her parents, she may not realize that as an adult she has more power than before. She may not realize that even if she can't stop the abuse, she could leave the abuser—an option she didn't have as a child.

Or the mother may want to leave, but not know how she'll financially support the family without a man. She may also believe, perhaps correctly, that the battering man will hurt her and the children even more severely if she leaves.

A man whose wife is physically abusive is less likely to be physically frightened of her or economically dependent on her. But he may still feel powerless to affect her actions. Again, if he grew up with an abusive mother, he may still carry around those childlike feelings of being helpless and dependent. He may not realize that he could affect the actions of his wife in a way that he could not affect the actions of his mother. He may not realize that as an adult, he can leave the house and take his children with him—since he certainly couldn't act that way as a child.

Parents "Know Best"

A nonabusive parent of either sex may also believe that the abusing parent is acting "correctly." Again, this may well go back to their own experiences as children. If as children they believed that their parents knew best and that they themselves knew nothing, it may be easy to continue those feelings as adults and decide that another parent "knows best."

Sometimes a nonabusive parent is aware of the children's pain, but still feels more loyal to the other adult. If that parent is not willing to lose the relationship with the abuser, he or she will not be willing to challenge the abuser or insist that the abuse stop.

Such a parent may try to "make things better" by comforting children after the abuse, or by trying to help them learn how to avoid "making Daddy or [Mommy] angry." Unfortunately, this behavior usually doesn't prevent abuse—because the child's behavior was never really the cause of the abuse. However, the child may get the message from the nonabusive parent that somehow he or she *is* causing the trouble. The child may believe that if only he or she could be "good" enough, the abuse

111

would stop. Even though the nonabusive parent isn't hitting the child, he or she is reinforcing a negative message.

The nonabusive parent may also try to make the child feel sorry for the abusing parent. The child may be told that "Daddy can't help it" or "You know that Mommy loves you even if she hits you."

Effects of Abuse on Children

Unfortunately, this also carries a negative message. Children are being told that they are loved by a person who has just finished battering or abusing them. They may get the message that anyone who loves them will also beat or abuse them. Or they may get the message that they should feel sorry for the abusing parents, rather than angry with them. Instead of learning to defend themselves against bad treatment, these children are being taught to take the side of the abuser and to look at things from his or her point of view. This may make it difficult for them later, when they meet abusive people who are *not* their parents.

Intergenerational Abuse

Recent . . . investigations provide support for the link between a history of maltreatment and subsequent maltreatment of one's own children. For example, in an investigation of 282 economically at-risk parents of newborns admitted to an intensive care nursery, 49 parents reported a history of abuse and/or neglect at the initial interview. One year later, 10 of these babies were confirmed as being abused or neglected; nine of the abusing parents had a history of childhood maltreatment.

Lise M. Youngblade and Jay Belsky in *Children at Risk*, 1990.

These patterns also apply to emotional and sexual abuse to some extent. If a mother lets loose a stream of unfair criticism, a child's natural reaction would probably be to get mad and tell her to stop. But if the father is saying "Don't get mad—you know she doesn't mean it," then the child becomes confused. It sounded like she meant it. It hurt as much as if she meant it. What is the child supposed to do with the hurt and angry feelings?

Thus, even if the other parent is not directly abusing the child, he or she may be contributing to the feeling that the child is somehow responsible for the abuse. Children need their parents for protection, and for an accurate view of reality. One of the bad effects of abuse is that it teaches children that their parents will not protect them, and that their parents will not tell them the truth about reality. Instead, both their parents, whether abusive or not, ask the child to believe that the child's own feelings don't count and that the child's perceptions of reality aren't accurate.

The pattern may be the same with sexual abuse if the other parent is aware of the abuse. However, because of the secrecy that frequently surrounds sexual abuse, a parent may not be aware that a child has been abused. The child may also be unsure whether the parent is aware or not.

Being Blamed for Abuse

If a child or teenager has been sexually abused by someone who is not living in the home, it's quite possible that the parents are not aware. Even in that case, the child's decision whether to tell them will be influenced by the messages that these parents have given. If the parents have encouraged their child to trust his or her own perceptions and to stand up for his or her rights, the child may feel more secure in telling about what happened and asking the parents for support. (Children who have been threatened with physical harm to themselves or to others may also be unwilling to tell their parents, regardless of how good the relationship is.) If these parents have encouraged the child to believe that anything bad that happens is somehow the child's fault, the child will be a lot less likely to turn to the parents for help. Rightly or wrongly, such a child may fear that he or she will be blamed for having been abused.

If you or someone you know is in such a situation, we encourage you to find an adult that you do trust. This person will almost certainly tell your parents, but at least you will have the support of another adult and you will have taken an important step toward stopping the abuse.

"Child abuse is always supposed to happen 'somewhere else.' But in reality it can happen anywhere."

Many Factors Contribute to Child Abuse

Elaine Landau

In the following viewpoint, Elaine Landau discusses many of the factors that have been identified as causing child abuse. Landau maintains that problems such as the long-held attitude that children are parents' property, intergenerational abuse, social isolation, and substance abuse can all result in parents' abusing their children. Landau is the former director of the Sparta Public Library in Sparta, New Jersey, and a free-lance author.

As you read, consider the following questions:

1. Before the late nineteenth century, child abuse was not considered a problem, according to Landau. Why?
2. According to the author, what kind of opposition is there to removing children from abusive situations?
3. What role can physicians play in ending abuse, according to the author?

How can child abuse in America continue after so many cases of violence against young people have been documented? Any examination of child abuse requires questioning a basic assumption of our society: "The parent owns the child."

Perhaps this premise was first challenged in 1874, when the earliest child-abuse case in America was brought to court. It all started when one day Henry Bergh, founder of the ASPCA [American Society for the Prevention of Cruelty to Animals], was combing the streets of New York City in search of wounded and abused animals. As Bergh walked past an apartment building, he heard a child's screams from inside.

The First Child Abuse Case

Bergh ran into the apartment to find a ten-year-old girl named Mary Ellen being repeatedly stabbed with a pair of scissors by her parents. Mary Ellen's mother and father thought that their young daughter was a witch.

Henry Bergh wanted to take the child away from her parents, but at the time there weren't any child-abuse laws in existence. He argued in court for Mary Ellen's safety on the ground that children should be entitled to protection from abuse just as dogs and cats were.

Formerly it was assumed that children didn't need protection from their own parents. Mothers and fathers supposedly acted only in the best interests of their children. Discipline and supervision were left solely in the parents' hands. It was as if children belonged to their parents and in many ways were considered their property.

Unfortunately, remnants of this assumption still exist. Parental discipline is supposedly administered for the child's own good, but in many instances child abuse has been committed in the name of discipline. Children are generally not thought to need protection because they have parents to look out for them, although many times children do need protection—from their own parents.

As Donald Bross, a lawyer, medical sociologist, and advocate for abused children stated, "We still think of children as their parents' private property—and that is the heart of the problem. Yes, family privacy is a good thing, but not in the case of the battered wife or the abused child."

At times it is difficult to know when outside intervention is appropriate. In at least one community, people were so outraged by the removal of children from an abusive, neglectful home that bomb threats were made against the social services building.

Some citizens strongly feel that government shouldn't meddle in people's lives or that judges, attorneys, and social workers have no right to tell people how to bring up their own children.

It is not uncommon for social workers to hear of well-intentioned people who suspected trouble at a neighbor's house, but were reluctant to become involved because they felt it didn't concern them. Until those priorities are changed, more and more children will die.

Parents do not own their children. They merely care for them in trust for the rest of society. To maximize healthy growth and development, all children should grow up surrounded by social relationships that are close, personal, and enduring.

Forms of Abuse

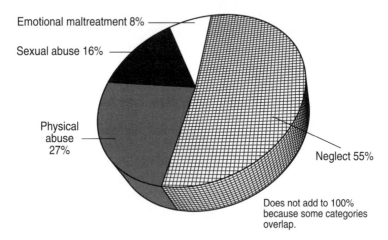

Emotional maltreatment 8%

Sexual abuse 16%

Physical abuse 27%

Neglect 55%

Does not add to 100% because some categories overlap.

Source: American Humane Association and the National Committee for the Prevention of Child Abuse.

When a newborn infant leaves the hospital with his parents, the child's progress may not come to the attention of any social institution until he enters school at the age of four or five. If his parents are responsible, mature individuals who are capable of adequately meeting his needs for nurture and protection, all will go well for him. However, abuse may arise when parental power is misused.

Parental authority and power are misused when they are employed to damage the child either physically or emotionally, or administered in any manner that reduces or limits the child's opportunity for normal growth and development. The absolute authority of the parent is rarely questioned in our society when it is exercised judiciously with no visible harmful effects. The

116

important ethical question of whether the child has a right to his own integrity as a separate individual is generally left unexamined.

What common factors are present in homes with abusive parent-child relationships? Social isolation seems to be a major component. Ours is a highly mobile society. Job changes and educational needs frequently take people to new parts of the country. Often they live far from their relatives and don't develop strong new ties to a church or synagogue. In many instances, it's hard to initiate new friendships with busy neighbors who have tight schedules.

A Stressful Situation

This may leave the parent at home with a baby or small child in a stressful predicament. Being cut off from support systems that might enable the parent to deal more effectively with the frustrations inherent in caring for a small child can lead to abuse.

Kate, an attractive redhead in her early thirties, left her job at a bank when her son was born. She planned to devote all of her time to the baby. But unfortunately, it wasn't long before she began to regret her decision. Her husband, a successful administrator, was away at work for about ten hours a day, while Kate was left by herself with the baby in their eastern Massachusetts home.

Their son was a colicky infant who had trouble sleeping and seemed to cry most of the time. Kate found herself unprepared for the loneliness and exhaustion she experienced as a new parent. She missed her old friends from work. Her family was hundreds of miles away, and she didn't know any mothers with very young children.

Kate became depressed. She began to hold her infant son responsible for her unhappiness. Kate felt that she hated the baby for what her life had become.

Before long Kate found herself hitting her son at the slightest provocation. The infant had merely to drop his bottle to feel the sting of her hand. To hide any bruises, Kate made certain that her blows landed only on the baby's back. She took care never to hit his face.

Kate knew that what she was doing was wrong, but she couldn't seem to stop herself. Afterward, she always felt remorseful. She said, "Every time I hit him, I would cry and apologize and promise him that Mommy would never do it again."

At that point Kate thought that she had to be the world's worst mother. She felt she was probably the only person in suburbia who hit her own baby.

But she was wrong. Child abuse in America has reached epidemic proportions. Over 2.2 million cases of child abuse and neglect are reported every year.

Abusive Situations

Disciplinary situations are more likely to turn into child abuse in families that are socially isolated or cut off from support networks that could intervene and provide help. A parent in a stressful situation is far less likely to be abusive to his child if he can turn to another person or a social agency for assistance. Often just being able to ask a relative or friend to take the child out for a few hours or for a weekend can make a difference.

Support can also be provided by play groups, such as those sponsored by a church or social agency. While the children are there, the parents can relax and have a chance to let off some steam or gather their thoughts. They may simply need a break from an exasperating situation.

Support systems generally arise through a sense of connectedness with the community. A parent or family in trouble needs a variety of resources to call upon in times of personal crisis or excessive stress. Such resource people might include the extended family, other parents, clergy, educators, social workers, mental health practitioners, and others.

Unfortunately, abusive parents may tend to distrust and retreat from society. Parents who habitually abuse their children generally prefer not to seek help in resolving crises. In addition, abusive parents often attempt to prevent their children from forming normal healthy relationships outside the home.

Deborah Daro, research director of the National Committee for the Prevention of Child Abuse, said of the Steinberg case, "Though Lisa Steinberg was an exception to the rule in many ways, in other ways her family was typical of the child-abuse home. The family was isolated from other families and friends. . . ."

Of course, everyone needs some privacy, and lack of social contact does not *cause* abuse or neglect. No one factor produces the same reaction in all people. Depending on their individual circumstances, some children may find themselves more vulnerable than others. Still, isolation has been identified as a known factor that places the parent-child relationship in special jeopardy. In America, privacy and an individual's right to it have become a treasured ideal. However, each year hundreds of thousands of children pay for their parents' privacy with their tears.

Substance abuse is also a factor that may intensify stressful parent-child relationships. At least forty percent of all abuse cases involve the parent's use of alcohol or drugs. Alcohol has long been a catalyst in domestic violence, but the growing use of crack in recent years has served to worsen matters. Loretta Kowal of the Massachusetts Society for the Prevention of Cruelty to Children stated, "Crack can turn a loving mother into a monster in ten minutes."

In the beating death of Lisa Steinberg, the comatose girl was left to lie naked for hours on a bathroom floor, while her "adoptive" parents free-based cocaine. Darwin Carlisle's mother was on cocaine when she left her nine-year-old daughter locked alone in an apartment for nearly a week in January. The Gary, Indiana, child suffered a severe case of frostbite. Both her legs had to be amputated at the knee. Darwin's twenty-five-year-old mother pleaded guilty to felony child neglect and was sentenced to fourteen years in prison.

The National Committee for the Prevention of Child Abuse estimates that in as many as forty percent of the deaths due to child abuse, the abusive parent had a drug or alcohol problem. Substance abuse impairs thinking and judgment, lessens inhibitions, and often acts as a barrier in preventing parents from coming to grips with problems.

A third common component in child abuse is its connection with wife beating. In thirty to forty percent of child-abuse cases, the wife was also a victim of physical abuse. Since four to six million women are abused each year by their husbands and boyfriends, the number of children in jeopardy is overwhelming. Lisa Steinberg's "adoptive" mother, Hedda Nussbaum, had been abused by Joel Steinberg for over a decade at the time of Lisa's death. A fourth element that may contribute to child abuse is the fact that many child-abuse victims grow up to become abusers themselves. Often adults who mistreat their children are found to have little or poor preparation for their role as parents. They have no history of good experiences as children. They lack appropriate role models on which to pattern their behavior as parents. Someone who was never given a sense of dignity and self-esteem as a young person may find it difficult to provide his own child with either a sense of well-being and worthiness or appropriate discipline.

Abuse Crosses Generations

Parents who were abused children are six times more likely to abuse their own children than are parents from "normal" homes. Dr. Vincent Fontana, who in 1962 first identified the "maltreatment syndrome in children" and designed a specialized program to aid abusive parents and their children at New York Foundling Hospital, explained, "These parents never had parental love and care themselves. They don't know what being a loving parent is. Many of these people have been programmed for violence, and some of them expect their little children to 'parent' them. When the child does not provide this mothering or fathering—when the child cries or has a temper tantrum—they think this means 'I hate you,' and they strike out at the child."

Parents who were themselves emotionally impoverished often experience a great deal of trouble learning the role of parent. Many lack insight and knowledge in dealing with infants and children, and they often express unrealistic expectations about their offspring.

Although significant research exists to support the theory that abusive behavior repeats itself in successive generations, studies conducted by researchers Joan Kaufman and Edward Ziegler indicate that this need not always be the case. In certain situations, mitigating factors have altered the effects of the environment on the child.

Their studies show that abused children who as adults have a loving, supportive relationship with a spouse or lover, as well as those who are aware of having a history of abuse and are consciously resolved not to repeat it, are more likely to break the cycle. As Kaufman and Ziegler found, "Being maltreated as a child puts one at risk for becoming abusive, but the path between these two points is far from direct or inevitable."

Bad Parents

A final factor in the incidence of child abuse often proves to be a general lack of parenting skills. When a person becomes a parent he must undergo a definite series of changes. He has to reorganize his values and priorities to include a baby. He must set aside the immediate gratification of his own needs, as the helpless child must now come first. Abusive parents have often been described as individuals who experience difficulty in balancing their own needs against the needs of their child.

A person who has not learned to function as a competent parent may find a nearly intolerable situation even further aggravated by outside factors. An unwanted or unplanned pregnancy, seemingly relentless demands from older children in the family, overwork or job-related problems, financial difficulties, and countless other sources of stress may eventually help to create an abusive family situation.

Anne, a former elementary school teacher, experienced problems in parenting her two-year-old daughter. Every time Anne was about to leave the house, her daughter would have a tantrum.

Anne didn't know how to discipline her child effectively. She'd ask her to behave in a pleasant manner, but the little girl refused to listen. Meanwhile, Anne began to feel inadequate and angry. Finally, she'd reach her boiling point. Then Anne would roughly shake and push the child.

The most upsetting incident took place when Anne told her daughter to take a nap and the child refused. Anne sat on the child to hold her down while she placed a pillow over her daughter's head. The child cried and screamed, but her mother persisted.

Finally, Anne realized that her child was gasping for air. That made Anne stop, but she knew now that if she didn't get help soon, she might one day kill her daughter in anger. Both the mother and child were frightened.

A Pattern of Maltreatment

Emerging understanding of both the necessary and sufficient causes of maltreatment points to broad and interacting sets of factors that contribute to individual instances of abusive behavior or, more commonly, a pattern of chronic emotional maltreatment and neglect of the physical and/or psychological needs of the developing infant, child, or adolescent. These factors arise from within and outside the family and, more often than not, converge to create a family situation characterized by both extreme need and an inability to develop or maintain the external supports that could help bolster this very fragile system. Indeed, if research has accomplished little else, it has demonstrated again and again that recurrent maltreatment is *not* the outcome of any single factor—whether parental psychopathology or the experience of maltreatment in childhood, child temperamental or behavioral deviance, marital conflict or violence, economic hardship and job stress, inadequate and ineffective social supports, or sociocultural mores that encourage punitive, authoritarian parenting.

Joan I. Vondra, *Children at Risk*, 1990.

Anne was fortunate that she was able to secure effective help immediately. She contacted a local chapter of the National Exchange Club, an organization that offers counseling in such situations. Anne began to learn new parenting skills that helped her to deal with her daughter in a more positive way.

Anne realized that she'd been trying to be a perfect mother, and that such unrealistic expectations only added to the frustrations of child rearing. She learned that it's better to "blow off steam" occasionally than to let the pressure build up inside to a dangerous boiling point. Now when tensions arise between Anne and her daughter, she sends the little girl to her room until they've both had an opportunity to regain their composure.

Although many people believe that poverty increases the likelihood of child abuse, no one knows for certain. The National

121

Committee for the Prevention of Child Abuse has reported numerous instances of abuse by people from well-to-do, well-educated families. In addition, Dr. Eli Newburger, director of the Family Development Study at Children's Hospital in Boston, has stressed that violence in middle- and upper-class homes is far more common than is generally known. Middle-class professional parents may know how to look for help discreetly. These parents may also have a more sophisticated understanding of how to shift suspicion from themselves when talking to teachers, doctors, and police.

Stereotyping the Abuser

According to a nationwide survey of hospitals conducted by Newburger, it was race and social status of the family, not the severity of the child's injuries, that determined whether doctors reported suspected abuse cases to the authorities as they are required to do by law. Newburger believes that too often physicians have a stereotyped view of a child abuser and tend not to suspect a parent who doesn't conform to that negative image.

Another dangerous tendency cited by Dr. Newburger is that physicians may deliberately look the other way when faced with child abuse involving their more affluent patients. Many middle-class families use a physician whom they've known and trusted for years. These doctors may feel hesitant to report their patients to the authorities and betray their confidence. They also may be reluctant to lose steady clients. At times physicians' desire to maintain a good doctor-patient relationship with their clients has been placed above the overall welfare of a child. . . .

The Parents Anonymous Hotline, which confidentially helps parents who have been, or fear becoming, violent with their children, reports that many of its calls come from middle-class people. But child-abuse cases among the middle class still tend to shock the public. It is always difficult to believe that things could go so wrong for people like Joel Steinberg and Hedda Nussbaum, who seemingly have so much. Middle-class child abuse defies the American dream and tarnishes the myth of the "ideal family." Child abuse is always supposed to happen "somewhere else." But in reality it can happen anywhere.

Periodical Bibliography

The following articles have been selected to supplement the diverse views presented in this chapter.

Malcolm Bush
"Hard Times for Children," *Bulletin of the Park Ridge Center*, January 1991. Available from 211 E. Ontario, Suite 800, Chicago, IL 60611-3215.

Christianity Today
"Making Porn Pay," April 27, 1992.

Don Feder
"Child Pornography: Enough Is Enough!" *Conservative Chronicle*, December 16, 1992. Available from PO Box 11297, Des Moines, IA 50340-1297.

Thomas Fleming
"Uncommon Properties," *Chronicles*, January 1993. Available from the Rockford Institute, 934 N. Main St., Rockford, IL 61103-7061.

Daniel Goleman
"Sad Legacy of Abuse: The Search for Remedies," *The New York Times*, January 24, 1989.

Linda Gordon
"The Politics of Child Sex Abuse," *Against the Current*, March/April 1989.

Haven Bradford Gow
"Drugs, Homosexuality, and Child Abuse," *Conservative Review*, April 1992. Available from 6861 Elm St., Suite 4H, McLean, VA 22101.

Loring Jones
"Unemployment and Child Abuse," *Families in Society*, December 1990. Available from Family Service America, 11700 W. Lake Park Dr., Milwaukee, WI 53224.

Barbara Kantrowitz and Karen Springen
"Parental Indiscretion," *Newsweek*, April 22, 1991.

Beverly Merz
"Wheel of Misfortune," *American Medical News*, January 6, 1992. Available from American Medical Association, 515 N. State St., Chicago, IL 60610.

Joel S. Milner and Chinni Chilamkurti
"Physical Child Abuse Perpetrator Characteristics," *Journal of Interpersonal Violence*, September 1991. Available from Sage Publications, 2455 Teller Road, Newbury Park, CA 91320.

Hollida Wakefield, Martha Rogers, and Ralph Underwager
"Female Sexual Abusers: A Theory of Loss," *Issues in Child Abuse Accusations*, Fall 1990. Available from the Institute for Psychological Therapies, 13200 Cannon City Blvd., Northfield, MN 55057-4405.

How Widespread Is Child Sexual Abuse?

Chapter Preface

More than 60 percent of sexually abused children are abused by family members. Most of the remaining victims are abused by trusted caretakers—day-care workers, teachers, scout leaders, and clergy. Such caretakers have recently been the focus of lurid and sometimes fantastic accusations of sexual abuse. Widely reported stories of satanic abuse and child pornography rings in day-care centers, camp counselors who assault children during overnight campouts, and pedophile priests with multiple victims make it seem that the nation is a hotbed of child sexual abuse.

This perception may be no more accurate than the belief many people once had that child sexual abuse was exceedingly rare. While "nobody knows for sure whether child-abuse numbers are inflated with spurious allegations, or vastly underrepresent a crime that is often kept secret," according to *Newsweek* senior writer Laura Shapiro, the truth is probably somewhere in between. It may be merely the awareness of and willingness to acknowledge child sexual abuse that have changed, and not its incidence. For example, studies of the number of girls aged fourteen or younger who were sexually abused by a male at least five years older "have shown a fairly consistent rate of 10 to 12 percent since the 1940s," Shapiro reports.

Because child sexual abuse is a crime victims are often unwilling to report, but also a crime subject to exaggeration by the media and the public, it is difficult to determine how widespread it is. The authors in the following chapter present diverse views concerning the extent of child sexual abuse.

"The volunteer organizations are just perfect for
pedophiles. "

Scouting Often Exposes
Boys to Sexual Abuse

Patrick Boyle

Boy Scouts is an organization that is supposed to help boys become strong, healthy, competent men. However, according to
Patrick Boyle, more than a thousand Scouts reported being sexually molested by their leaders between 1971 and 1989. Adding
to the problem, the author maintains in the following viewpoint,
has been a concerted effort to keep the abuse secret, which has
allowed molesters to escape punishment and, in some cases, to
continue abusing children. Patrick Boyle is a reporter on the
metro desk at the *Washington Times*, a daily newspaper.

As you read, consider the following questions:

1. What factors, according to Boyle, help Scoutmasters molest
   boys?
2. Why did Scout executives often suppress reporting of sexual
   abuse charges?
3. Give two reasons for and two reasons against keeping
   molestation charges a secret.

From Patrick Boyle, "The Scouts' Badge of Dishonor," *Insight on the News*, June 17, 1991.
Reprinted with permission.

For parents, the local Boy Scout troop is a safe place to send the kids. For child molesters, it's an ideal place to meet them.

The result: More than once a week for the past two decades, on average, a Cub Scout, Boy Scout or Explorer has reported being sexually abused by a Scout leader.

"They've got a real problem on their hands," says Atlanta psychiatrist Gene Abel, who has extensively studied child molesters. "The Scout leader is not the only position that a sex offender can take, but it is an ideal one for a pedophile."

At least 1,151 Scouts have reported being abused by their leaders over the past 19 years, making sex abuse more common in Scouting than accidental deaths and serious injuries. In that time, at least 416 men have been arrested or banned from Scouting for molesting the boys in their care. Those are among the findings of an investigation that turned up abuse by Scout leaders in all 50 states and the District of Columbia.

Boy Scouts Not a Sanctuary

"I was naive to think the Boy Scouts was such a safe place," says the mother of a Maryland boy abused by his Scoutmaster. "I thought the Boy Scouts was a sanctuary."

In fact, an examination of sex abuse in Scouting reveals a longstanding paradox for the nation's most revered youth group: for 80 years the Boy Scouts of America has given boys some of the best experiences of their lives, but throughout that time men have used the organization to have sexual relations with boys.

Among the findings of the investigation:

• Each year from 1971 through 1989, an average of at least 21 male Scout leaders and camp workers were banned from Scouting or arrested for sexual misconduct with Cub Scouts, Boy Scouts and Explorers. The acts ranged from proposing sex and fondling boys in their sleep to performing oral sex and intercourse with them.

• During that time an average of at least 60 Scouts were reported abused each year, with some of them abused dozens of times before they told anyone.

• Scout officials tried to hide the sex abuse problem from the public and press, and sometimes from parents and police. National Scout officials have given the news media incorrect information about the extent of abuse in Scouting, and in a few cases, local Scout officials may have violated child abuse reporting laws by not reporting suspected abuse to authorities. "The attitude was more one of sweeping it under the rug and hoping it goes away," says Edward Allinson, a Scout leader in Prince George's County, Md.

• Camping trips—in many people's eyes the essence of Scouting—are the most popular places for Scout leaders to have sexual relations with boys.

- Over the past five years, the Boy Scouts of America and local Scout councils have agreed to pay at least $15 million to settle lawsuits brought by families of abused Scouts.
- The molesters often joined troops and molested boys even after being caught. At least 21 of the men had prior criminal records—mostly for sex offenses with children. Others had left troops or youth groups under suspicion but were not charged.

An Ideal Situation for Molesters

In many ways, the problem of child sex abuse in Scouting reflects the problem of sex abuse in America, especially in volunteer groups that serve children. "All volunteer organizations are troubled . . . by this same issue," says Abel. "The volunteer organizations are just perfect for pedophiles, in the sense that they are just the ideal situation if they can get to a large number of kids, to kind of check out which ones might be the easiest victims."

The molesters in Scouting come from all walks of life: they're priests and policemen, teachers and truck drivers, laborers and lawyers. Far from being the dangerous strangers that parents warn their children about, they are usually upstanding members of their communities and well-liked by children and parents—common for pedophiles, who have a knack for establishing sympathetic relations with boys.

"I felt I could pull myself down to their level to talk to them," says John Fitzgerald, a former Scout leader now in a New Jersey prison, serving time for molesting Scouts. "I could almost understand what they would feel, what they would think."

The Scouts say sex abuse has not been a statistically significant problem in their organization, considering they have more than 1 million adult volunteers and more than 4 million Scouts. However, more than half the volunteers play administrative roles, such as working on the committees and councils that oversee troops.

The vast majority of abuse in Scouting is committed by a narrow group of volunteers: male Scoutmasters and assistant Scoutmasters, who number about 147,000. The victims also are usually from one group: Boy Scouts who range in age from 11 to 17 and numbered 959,000 at the end of 1990.

The Thomas Hacker Story

As Danny remembers it, the first thing Thomas Hacker did when he walked into the tent that night was turn around and zip it shut.

"He just, you know, zipped the outside door so you can't see inside the tent at all," says Danny. "It was at night and we were supposed to be going to bed, you know, for the night, and he came in and he was talking to us and I was laying on my stomach on my sleeping bag."

It was the summer of 1985, and Danny's troop was spending a weekend at Camp Falcon in Illinois. Hacker, the Scoutmaster who arranged the trip, was 48. Danny was 11.

This is how Danny—whose name was changed for this story—told his tale four years later from the witness stand: "He sat down next to me and started to give me a back rub and he was talking to me about Scouts. He was saying that I was, like, good material for Scouts. I could learn a lot of things. As he was rubbing my back, he started to bring his hand down slowly and he started to massage my butt."

Hacker seduced boys in this fashion for 25 years. He later told a psychiatrist that he lost count of the boys he had sexual relations with, but it was "well above a hundred."

Was Baden-Powell a Pedophile?

If the founder of the Boy Scouts ran a troop today, he could get kicked out as a potential child molester. His diaries and letters say he enjoyed photos of nude boys and admired their bodies at swimming holes.

There's no evidence that Lord Robert Baden-Powell, the British war hero who started the Scout movement in 1908, had sexual relations with children. But some people believe the man who founded the world's most popular youth movement was a pedophile who kept his sexual desires in check. . . .

In fact, Baden-Powell cautioned men against letting their feelings for boys evolve into physical relationships. Writing in 1923 about a Scoutmaster who went to jail for sexual activity with boys, he said, "Had the law allowed it one would have been glad to see a flogging inflicted."

Patrick Boyle, *Insight*, June 17, 1991.

By anyone's standards, including the Boy Scouts', Hacker should not have been at Camp Falcon. Two states had convicted him of sex offenses with children. He had been forced to resign from at least three schools after being caught fondling students. One Scout troop had already kicked him out for molesting boys.

Yet for several years Hacker repeatedly molested Danny and more than 30 other boys in Troop 1600, based in the Chicago suburb of Oak Lawn and sponsored by St. Louis de Montfort Catholic Church.

The boys kept quiet about it because of their loyalty to Hacker, the thrill of the sexual intrigue and their fear of getting in trouble if anyone knew what they did. After his arrest in February 1988, Hacker said he loved the boys and was doing God's work by teaching them about sex. In 1989 he was convicted of sexual assault and sentenced to 100 years in prison.

People Thought He Just Liked Kids

"He expressed to me that he had been very interested and always obsessed . . . with young boys," psychologist Larry Heinrich testified at Hacker's trial. "He developed his life pretty much around . . . putting himself in situations where he would have contact with youth."

Other people thought Hacker just liked kids. "He goofed around with us like he was one of the guys," testified a Scout abused by Hacker.

Hacker's talent for goofing around with boys surfaced soon after he began teaching junior high school in 1960. In his unpublished autobiography, written 28 years later as a therapeutic exercise while he was in a psychiatric hospital, Hacker remembered his students "sitting on my lap, rubbing my back, and generally providing me with needed affection. I didn't see anything socially unacceptable." He lost his first teaching job when a mother discovered he was pulling boys' pants down. No charges were filed against him.

A Pattern of Abuse

That set the pattern for Hacker's life. He would move someplace and become a pillar of the community—president of the Holy Name Society, vice president of the Little League, an award-winning teacher and Scout leader. Then someone would catch him fondling boys. Shocked adults would offer a deal: resign or they'd tell the police. He'd quit and move.

"He was so charming nobody put him in jail," testified Marvin Schwarz, a psychiatrist. Hacker knew, however, that if he didn't stop, he could go to jail. He hoped marriage would save him.

"He told me he thought if he got married, that would probably hopefully take away all of these urges," Heinrich testified. Hacker also told the doctor that to have intercourse with his wife, he fantasized she was a boy. They had three children.

Hacker's Boy Scout career supposedly ended in 1970, when he pleaded guilty in Indiana to sexually assaulting a 14-year-old boy. His troop dismissed him. Local Scout leaders said they sent his name to national headquarters so it could be placed in the "confidential files," a list of adults banned from Scouting.

Hacker moved to Illinois, but in 1971 he was again arrested on sex charges; he pleaded guilty to taking indecent liberties with a boy. He did not get a prison sentence for either conviction.

Nevertheless, he was able to join a troop in Illinois. The troop leaders never checked his references. His registration papers were sent to national headquarters, but somehow his name didn't show up in the confidential files [the Ineligible Volunteer File, created around 1920 to keep a list of volunteers who had been banned from the Boy Scouts because they were deemed unfit as role models]. Joseph Anglim, national director of administration for the Boy Scouts, isn't sure why.

"My question would be the same as yours," Anglim says. "Why didn't we catch this?"

Perhaps it's because the organization's controls have never been especially tight. Even now, on a new application for volunteers, the organization merely asks: "Have you ever been convicted of a criminal offense? Have you ever been charged with child neglect or abuse?"

"I don't know anyone who's going to say yes to that," says Bennett Wolff, a Louisiana attorney for a boy molested at a Scout camp.

A Better Way

Soon, however, there may be a better way. A Senate committee is considering the creation of a national database of every person convicted of child molestation, so that youth groups could check up on people who apply to work with children. Right now, most youth groups cannot run such criminal background checks since federal law doesn't let them use the FBI's files.

Having slipped through the cracks, Hacker was free to act with impunity. With the boys of the new troop, he wrote, "I fell back into a pattern of taking their pants off. This went on for a year or two."

He was caught and arrested. The youths' parents agreed to drop the charges if he got psychiatric help. Troop leaders didn't report Hacker's behavior to national headquarters.

He moved again and landed in the Chicago suburb of Burbank around 1980, where he eventually became director of a municipal agency that ran public parks. He also became assistant Scoutmaster of Troop 1600.

Hacker loved campouts, and made sure there was one a month. He talked about movies and games the boys liked. He let them do things their parents wouldn't. He let them steer his car. He bought them *Playboy*. He also told them that God loved them and they should go to church. Sometimes, the boys testified, he said this during back rubs.

Parents liked Hacker because he had so much time for their children. One mother would drive her son to Hacker's house for tutoring. The boy testified that he and Hacker engaged in sex acts every time. For a while, the boy said, they slept naked together on every campout.

Hacker photographed many of the boys nude, and some of them performed sex acts on him. He wouldn't force himself on a Scout who said no, although children testified that he once had intercourse with a boy while the boy cried.

News Alerts for Damage Control

National Scout headquarters in Irving, Texas, advises local leaders on what to tell the media in sex abuse cases. Among the usual responses:

• The Boy Scouts have more than 1 million volunteers and get only a few sex abuse reports each year.

• Scout leaders are chosen by parents and other local people who run the troop, not by the Boy Scouts of America.

• The Scout leader has been dismissed or is being dismissed, and action was taken as soon as the accusations arose.

• The Boy Scouts try to screen volunteers, but there is no foolproof system for detecting child molesters.

• The incident did not occur during a Scout activity or the victims were not Scouts.

Patrick Boyle, *Insight*, June 17, 1991.

All this went on despite the fact that parents were usually on the campouts, sleeping in other tents.

Hacker didn't pursue all the boys, only those who were between 10 and 15. He lost interest when they developed pubic hair. That's why a Boy Scout troop was perfect for Hacker. A steady supply of 10- and 11-year-old Cub Scouts graduated into his troop.

Ironically, it all ended for Hacker because of a petty theft. In 1987 local police investigated the theft of $575 from a safe in his park office and decided to check the criminal records of key employees. Hacker panicked. He said he didn't take the money, but he paid back $600 to halt the probe. He told police he didn't want his conviction record exposed.

Police went ahead with the investigation, Hacker quit his job, and a local paper, the *Daily Southtown Economist*, wrote about his criminal record. Parents asked their sons if Hacker had done anything to them. Dozens were stunned by the answers; Scouts told tales of sex acts with Hacker dating to 1981.

Hacker's attorney argued for treatment, not jail. He got both. He is now at the Menard Psychiatric Center, an Illinois corrections facility.

So Far, No Bad Publicity

In the spring of 1982, a disturbing letter made its way to Irving, Texas, where it landed on the desk of Paul Ernst, director of registration for the Boy Scouts of America.

The letter said a South Carolina Scout leader had been arrested for taking pictures of naked children.

But there was good news: "So far, we have received no bad publicity from this," wrote Chubby Earnest, the local Scout executive who oversaw the troop. "We'll keep our fingers crossed."

"I hope the media maintains its silence relating to his involvement with Scouting," Ernst wrote back. "This will certainly help us, not only in your area but across the country."

In 1983 the leaders of a troop in Coconut Grove, Fla., put a Scoutmaster on probation after learning he took Scouts to his bedroom and fondled them. The conditions of probation: no private meetings with boys and "no touching of any area of the body, genital, anal and/or chest that is generally accepted as private," according to a memo from the pastor of the Episcopal church that sponsored the troop. Parents weren't told about the probation.

The next year Scout officials got more evidence of sex abuse and forced the man to resign. Parents were not told why. Troop officials didn't tell police, either. (Two of the Scouts eventually did, and the man was convicted of sex abuse.)

That's how sex abuse in the Boy Scouts has remained such a secret.

"Like anybody, we were not interested in broadcasting it," says Anglim, the director of administration for the Boy Scouts. "For years and years it was one of America's greatest secrets." . . .

Local Scout officials often made deals with molesters: They wouldn't call the police if the accused man would resign, and maybe move away. Scout files show this was often done with cooperation of parents, who wanted to spare their children and families the embarrassment of a trial.

"I think they were aware they'd be in the public limelight and their kid would be embarrassed," says George Traquair, a retired Scout executive who oversaw troops in Massachusetts. Traquair says he handled about six abuse cases during his several decades in Scouting, and the men usually left the troops quietly with no charges filed. . . .

"Most people, when they're presented with the option, they decide not to press charges," Traquair says. "I preferred not to have that kind of publicity."

Scout officials now admit this practice was a mistake because it let molesters move on to other troops and other children. Many states require child care workers to report suspected child abuse to police or social service agencies. In one case in Pennsylvania in 1984, police charged a local Scout official with violating state law by not reporting suspected abuse by a Scout leader.

At times, however, police cooperated in the secrecy, quietly dropping charges or helping keep abuse reports out of the press. When a Scout leader was arrested for molesting boys in a Pennsylvania troop in 1981, the local Scout executive visited the police chief, then wrote to Ernst: "He told me that he would do everything he could to keep this account out of the newspaper to protect the name of the Boy Scouts.". . .

In 1984—the last year for which all the files on sex abuse in the Boy Scouts are available—the organization banned 36 men for sexual misconduct. In some years, about one of every four men banned from Scouting are banned for that reason.

Paul Ernst, the Scout's director of registration, says the number of cases didn't seem high, since the Scouts had more than 1 million adult volunteers. So the cases were not reported to the Scouts' health and safety committee, which got reports about injuries and safety hazards in troops and helped create programs to protect boys. Through the 1970s and 1980s, the committee created programs to promote water safety and seat belt use. It even studied the safety of the gunpowder that troops used in muskets for America's Bicentennial celebration.

In a 1987 deposition, health and safety committee chairman Walter Menniger said Scout officials never gave the committee any reports about sex abuse, although they routinely provided tallies for other injuries.

"There is a greater threat to Scouts of drowning and loss of life from accidents than there is from sexual abuse by a Scoutmaster," he said.

Scout statistics show the opposite. While an average of 60 Scouts have reported being sexually abused each year for the past 19 years, in the same span an average of 13 Scouts died each year during Scout activities. The Scouts report that each year about 30 Scouts suffer "serious injuries"—life-threatening or requiring a 24-hour hospital stay.

Something else contributed to the silence over abuse: The men running the Boy Scouts had trouble believing some men join troops to have sex with boys.

"Here we are, an organization chartered by Congress for the best program of Americanism and country and God," says retired professional Scouter Mickey McAllister. "We did not feel originally that this could infiltrate our organization."

134

"These are protective strategies designed to give youth the power to help protect themselves."

Scouting Teaches Boys to Avoid Sexual Abuse

Boy Scout Handbook

Boy Scouting has always focused on teaching boys how to handle themselves in any situation. Today, this includes teaching Scouts how to avoid sexual abuse and what to do if they are abused. The Scouts' sex abuse education program includes a video, discussions, a new section in the *Boy Scout Handbook* on child abuse, and a special tearout section in the handbook for parents. Participating in the discussion exercises in the parents' guide is now a requirement for becoming a Boy Scout. In the following viewpoint, excerpts from the parents' guide explain the Boy Scouts' new policy on child sexual abuse.

As you read, consider the following questions:

1. In the scouting program, who is responsible for stopping or avoiding abuse?
2. What are the three R's of youth protection, according to the handbook?
3. How does Scouting reconcile the desire to be helpful and obedient with the need to avoid abusive situations?

From the *Boy Scout Handbook*, tenth edition. Reprinted with permission of Boy Scouts of America.

The Boy Scouts of America is deeply concerned about the general welfare of our nation's children. There are many challenges that confront today's youth and child abuse is one of these. Child abuse is a fact in our society and a matter of great concern for all parents. Fortunately, child abuse is preventable, but parental action is important to protect children. The first responsibility that parents have is to be sure their children are safe from abuse in the home. Unfortunately, studies show that more children are abused in the home than anywhere else, often because of inappropriate or excessive punishment. . . .

Parents also need to discuss the possibility of abuse outside the home with their children and provide reassurance that any time a child feels threatened, the parents will be there to discuss the problem and support the child.

One form of abuse that parents find especially difficult to discuss with their children is sexual abuse. By overcoming the discomfort that they experience when children bring up sensitive subjects such as sexual abuse, parents may greatly reduce their children's chances of being abused.

The Three R's of Youth Protection

The three R's of youth protection are the key to an effective youth protection strategy:

Recognize. The child needs to be able to recognize the situations in which he may be at risk of abuse. Traditionally, children have been told of the risks associated with strangers. As we have come to learn, in most cases, child abuse is committed by a person known to the child, often one in a position of authority over him. Therefore, if we only teach them to be wary of strangers, we are not protecting our children as completely as we must. . . .

Resist. The child needs to be able to assert his rights to resist the abuser. Interviews with child molesters document that when a child resists advances made by a molester, the molester will usually abandon further attempts with that child. Only a very small percentage of child molestation involves the use of physical force. Children need to be trained to "run, scream, or make a scene" when inappropriately approached by *anyone—* friend, relative, or stranger.

Report. The child needs to be able to tell an adult when he has encountered abuse, with the expectation that the adult will take action to prevent further abuse. Children need to be taught to tell their parents, teachers, or other adults whenever they encounter questionable situations or attempted abuse. Since adults do not always listen when children talk to them, the children need to be told to keep on telling until someone listens.

Sometimes, a child may not be able to talk about what has

136

happened, but will communicate in other ways. For example, he may go out of his way to avoid being alone with a particular person. This is a kind of communication to which parents need to be sensitive, as it may be an indicator of abuse.

When a Child Discloses Abuse

If your child becomes a victim of abuse, your initial reaction can be very important in helping him through the ordeal. The following guidelines may help you.

• DON'T panic or overreact to the information disclosed by the child.

• DON'T criticize the child or claim that the child misunderstood what happened.

• DO respect the child's privacy and take the child to a place where you and he can talk without outside interruption and distractions.

• DO reassure your child that he is not to blame for what happened. Tell him that you appreciate his telling you about it and that you will help make sure that it will not happen again.

• DO encourage your child to tell the proper authorities what happened, but try to avoid repeated interviews. This can be very stressful for the child.

• DO consult your pediatrician or other child abuse authority on the need for counseling to help your child.

Help Yourself, Help a Friend

Most relationships with others can be warm and open. That is because they are built on trust. A pat on the back, a hug of encouragement, or a firm handshake are ways we can show someone we care about them.

However, it is a sad fact that some adults use their size and power over children to abuse them. You need to know about child abuse so that you will understand what to do if you are ever threatened. You may also be able to help stop the abuse of a friend.

Boy Scout Handbook, 1990.

Finally, if abuse happens to your child, do not blame yourself. Individuals who victimize children are not readily identifiable; they come from all walks of life and all socioeconomic levels. Often they present a nice image—they go to church and are active in the community. The molester is skilled at manipulating children, often by giving excessive attention, gifts, and money.

Most abuse occurs in situations in which the child knows and trusts the adult.

If you would like to learn more about child abuse and protecting your child, the Boy Scouts of America provides a ninety-minute training program, Youth Protection Guidelines: Training for Volunteer Leaders and Parents. Contact your local council for scheduling and availability.

Teaching Your Child to Be Assertive

It is important that your child understands the right to react assertively when faced with a situation he or she perceives as dangerous. When teaching your child self-protection skills, make it clear that although some basic strategies involved seem to contradict the sort of behavior you might normally expect of your child, these strategies apply to a situation that is *not* normal. When feeling threatened, your child must feel free to exercise the right to:

- trust his or her instincts and feelings
- expect privacy
- say no to unwanted touching or affection
- say no to adult demands and requests
- withhold information that could jeopardize his or her safety
- refuse gifts
- be rude or unhelpful if the situation warrants
- run, scream, and make a scene
- physically fight off unwanted advances
- ask others for help

It's important to remember these are protective strategies designed to give youth the power to help protect themselves. . . .

Child Abuse and Being a Good Scout

When a boy joins the Scouting program, he assumes an obligation to be faithful to the principles of Scouting as embodied in the Cub Scout Promise, Law of the Pack, Cub Scout motto, Scout Oath, Scout Law, Scout motto, and Scout slogan.

The principles of Scouting do not require that a Scout place himself in potentially perilous situations—quite the contrary, we want Scouts to "be prepared" and "do their best" to avoid these situations.

We hope that you will discuss these with your Scout and be sure that he understands the limitations to the requirements in consideration of the rules of safety.

Cub Scouts. The Cub Scout Promise includes the phrase, "to help other people." This means that a Cub Scout should be willing to do things for others that would please them, but *only* when his parents have given permission, and know where he is and who he is with.

The Law of the Pack includes the statement, "The Cub Scout follows Akela." Akela is a good leader and should never ask the Cub Scout to do something that the Cub Scout feels bad about. If Akela, who may be a teacher, coach, or other youth leader, ever asks the Cub Scout to do something the Cub Scout thinks is bad, the Scout has the right to say NO! and will tell his parents.

Recognize, Resist, and Report

Some adults or older youths may try to use your normal curiosity about sex as an opportunity to attempt sexual abuse. Sex is a normal bodily function that you need to understand. If anyone makes it seem dirty or secretive, you should be very cautious.

People who sexually abuse young people are called child molesters. . . . The molester may be a member of the family, a schoolteacher, religious leader, or youth group leader. . . .

Molesters look for victims who do not know enough to resist the abuse. You have the right to control your body. Anytime a person does something to your body that makes you feel bad or you know is wrong, you have the right to stop them even if you must be rude. You should be ready to run, scream, or make a scene in public in order to protect yourself. When faced with resistance, most molesters will stop.

Anytime you feel that a person has tried to molest you or someone you know, you must report it.

Boy Scout Handbook, 1990.

Boy Scouts. The Scout Oath includes the phrase, "to help other people at all times." The Scout Law says that a Scout is helpful, and the Scout motto is "Do a Good Turn daily." There are many people who need help and a Boy Scout should be willing to lend a hand when needed. Sometimes, people who really do not need it will ask for help to create an opportunity for abuse. Boy Scouts should be very familiar with the rules of safety so that they can recognize situations to be wary of. For example:
 • It is one thing to stand on the sidewalk away from the car to give directions and something else to get in the car and go with the person to show them where to go. A Scout should never get into a car without his parent's permission.
 • It may be okay for a Scout to help carry groceries to a person's house, but he should never go into the house unless he has permission from his parents.
The Scout Law also states that a Scout is obedient—but a Scout does not have to mind an adult when that person tells

him to do something that the Scout feels is wrong or that makes the Scout feel uncomfortable. In these situations, the Scout should talk with his parents about his concerns. . . .

Family Meeting

The one most important step that parents can take to protect their children from abuse is to establish an atmosphere of open communication in the home. Children must feel comfortable bringing sensitive problems to their parents or relating experiences in which someone approached them in an inappropriate manner or in a way that made them feel uncomfortable. Studies have documented that over half the abuse of children is never reported because the victims are too afraid or too confused to report their experiences.

It is important that your children be allowed to talk freely about their likes and dislikes, their friends, and their true feelings. One way to create open communication is through family meetings at which safety issues can be addressed by the entire family. The "what if" exercises could be done as part of a family meeting, as could the development of safety rules for the safety notebook.

Basic Rules of Safety for Children

As we address the basic rules for child safety, it is important to stress that traditional cautions about strangers are not sufficient to protect our children. Because the child abuser is usually known to the child, a more appropriate protection strategy is based upon teaching children to recognize situations or actions to be wary of. Children should be taught:

• If you are in a public place and get separated from your parent (or authorized guardian) do not wander around looking for him or her. Quickly go to a police officer, checkout counter, the security office, or the lost and found department and tell them that you have been separated from your parent and need help.

• You should not get into a car or go anywhere with any person unless you have your parent's permission.

• If someone follows you on foot or in a car, stay away from him or her. You do not need to go near the car to talk to the people inside.

• Adults and older youths who are not in your family and who need help (such as finding an address or locating a lost pet) should not ask children for help; they should ask other adults.

• You should use the "buddy system" and never go anywhere alone.

• Always ask your parent's permission to go somewhere, especially into someone else's home.

• Never hitchhike.

- Never ride with anyone unless you have your parent's permission.
- No one should ask you to keep a special secret. If this happens, tell your parents or teacher.
- If someone wants to take your picture, tell your parents or teacher.
- No one should touch you in the parts of your body that are covered when you wear a bathing suit (unless it is your doctor while treating you or during a physical examination), nor should you touch anyone else in those areas. Your body is special and private.
- You have the right to say "NO!" to someone who tries to take you somewhere, touches you, or makes you feel uncomfortable in any way.

These are some simple safety rules that can be approached in the same non-frightening manner in which you tell your child not to play with fire. They emphasize situations common to many child molestation cases.

"Satanism is creeping into the underworld of child pornography, drugs, and sexual abuse as an ideology that goes well with crime."

Satanic Ritual Abuse of Children Is Widespread

Carl A. Raschke

Stories of child abuse practices as part of satanic cult ritual have emerged numerous times in recent years. Carl A. Raschke, author of the following viewpoint, verifies these stories, arguing that secret cults practice, as criminal black arts, ritual child sexual abuse, mutilation, and murder. In the following viewpoint, the author argues that satanism provides a fertile field for the sowing of such underworld activities as child pornography, drug dealing, and sexual abuse. The lurid details reported by victims, Raschke urges, must not discount the reality of the abuse they have suffered. Raschke is director of the Institute for Humanities and professor of religious studies at the University of Denver.

As you read, consider the following questions:

1. According to Kurt Jackson, what makes children easy victims of satanic ritual abuse?
2. How is satanist "theater" used by criminals, according to Raschke?
3. According to the author, what is likely to be the source of the improbable fantasies of victims of ritual abuse?

Item: An Indiana state trooper told reporters he had been investigating satanic cult operations in his locale since he arrested a child abuse suspect in March 1988, according to published accounts. Another individual associated with the case had already been sentenced to the state penitentiary for statutory rape and related crimes. The mother of the abused children had been apprehended in January for terroristic threats and endangerment of the welfare of her two sons, ages eight and fourteen. The boys testified they had been taken to satanic rituals entailing animal sacrifice. The boys said groups of twenty to thirty people, including children, participated in the rituals.

Item: Al Sarno, a psychiatrist in the Kansas City area, has said he has thirty-five clients who have been involved in satanic cults, either as victims or abusers. His clients have reportedly described rituals involving very brutal sexual abuse of children and the slashing of flesh, as well as urinating and defecating on victims. "Our minds are not prepared to deal with this kind of trauma," said Darrell Miller, a clinical social worker at a local mental health center. Miller added that three of his patients had reported witnessing human sacrifice.

Item: Kurt Jackson of the Beaumont, Texas, police department talked about satanic ritual abuse of children to a gathering of California psychologists. He said that crimes committed against children by "black satanic cults" are reaching epidemic proportions and that they encompass sexual abuse, child pornography, animal killings, human sacrifice, and forcing children to ingest drugs, blood, urine, feces, and human flesh. The same criminal activities involve donning robes in dark, candle-lit rooms, according to Jackson. Children become victims because "they make the worst possible witnesses in court, are easy to force into silence about the abuse, are trusting and easy to handle," he said.

The McMartin Case

On Tuesday, July 13, 1987, following three and one half years of legal skirmishes and pretrial hearings, the infamous McMartin case commenced in the superior court of Los Angeles. This was the child molestation case involving alleged sexual and satanic abuse at the McMartin preschool in Manhattan Beach, California. The seven defendants were the former owners and operators of the preschool—Virginia McMartin, 78; Peggy Buckey, 58, the school's director who is also Virginia's daughter; granddaughter Peggy Ann Buckey, 29; grandson Raymond Buckey; and three instructors by the names of Babette Spitler, Mary Ann Jackson, and Betty Raidor. Later charges were dropped against five of the seven. Raymond and Peggy Buckey were left to stand trial. [They were acquitted in 1990.]

The "McMartin Seven" were initially charged with twenty counts of felony child molestation. A count of conspiracy had been laid against the son. The defendants had pled not guilty to the charges. Their attorneys contended that the prosecution was guilty of what the satanists said their detractors always suffer from—paranoia and community hysteria. The primary evidence to be admitted in the first part of the trial was the testimony of thirteen young children, who were allegedly victimized at the school. The children told social workers and police investigators that they not only suffered from perverted sexual handling, they witnessed satanic practices, including people chanting in black robes and ritual sacrifice of babies.

NOW I UNDERSTAND WHY YOU MADE HELL, LORD...

Newspaper
Child Sexually Assaulted and Murdered

The subject was lurid, and the credibility of many of the children appeared in doubt because the stories had changed slightly. The cry of witchhunt had been heard many times by those sympathetic to the defense. The children could be "confabulating," said some psychiatrists, meaning that certain events or incidents may have been fantastically embroidered by what they saw on television or suggestions may have been planted in their heads by well-meaning but irresponsible mental health professionals. Early interviews by the Children's Institute International (CII) may have been flawed, according to the district attorney's office in charge of the case.

"Naked Movie Star"

At the nub of the McMartin case was testimony by the children themselves that they played a game called "Naked Movie Star" in which they were routinely photographed without clothes. The children's parents, as well as the prosecuting team, had suggested that child pornography was involved. *McMartin* was well on its way to becoming the national codeword for virulent and orchestrated child abuse. But what made the case even more chilling and sensational, though at the same time exceedingly tangled, was the contention that behind the systematic abuse were satanic practices and rituals. The allegations of satanic influences were abundant:

• A four-year-old at the preschool told his mother one day without any prompting, "I am the son of the devil." The child had been stretched out on the couch at times during the preceding days with glazed eyes and was constantly making two horns with his fingers.

• Several children said former teachers buried the bones of rabbits after mutilating them in front of the children. Another child claimed a pony had been hacked to death before their eyes.

• One boy said he had been forced to drink animal blood.

• A fourth-grade boy claimed he had been taken to the St. Cross Episcopal Church in Hermosa Beach where adults wearing dark robes and moaning with strange sounds sacrificed an animal on the altar. He also insisted that, he along with other children, were sexually abused in the storage room of Harry's Meat Market in Manhattan Beach.

• The children told prosecutors about an unidentified "devil house" where adults dressed in a Satan suit and a tiger costume.

• McMartin pupils identified as one of their tormentors a thirty-five-year-old handyman named Robert Winkler, arrested on separate child molestation charges. During a raid at the home of the man's girlfriend in Lomita, California, sheriff's deputies confiscated a black robe, a dark candle, and rabbit ears such as had been allegedly chopped off during a ritual at the preschool. Torrance, California, police officers had supposedly found "cult books" in Winkler's motel room, which at first they thought were not relevant to the crimes for which he was accused.

• A six-year-old girl said she had witnessed the killing of three babies. She also related that she had been tied up and compelled to watch the killing by gun of animals, kept in cages.

145

The insinuations of satanic practice at the preschool went hand in hand with declarations by the children that vile sexual acts had been perpetrated upon them. An eleven-year-old girl, whom the prosecution regarded as the lead witness because approximately a third of the child molestation counts involved her and her brother, told the court she had been forced into having intercourse, sodomy, and oral sex with one of the defendants. The child had spent many afternoons at the preschool and thus could have been expected to have longer exposure to the defendants. Her testimony was disturbingly explicit. She finished her recollections by saying the defendant held up a knife and a gun and threatened to kill her parents if she tattled.

The Defense: Therapist-Induced Fantasies

From the start, the defense made a pitch that would become the trademark of child abuse perpetrators around the country. The children were "fantasizing," and the child therapists used the power of suggestion to influence the children. . . .

The assault on the credibility of the plaintiffs and the witnesses was one of the most massive campaigns ever staged in legal proceedings. The out-of-court sideshow, particularly with regard to the media, was also astounding. The most dramatic effort was to discredit, not only the mother [Judy Johnson] who first complained and was subsequently found dead of an apparent suicide, but also McMartin's chief prosecutor, Lael Rubin. . . .

Parents, however, consistently refuted the charge that their children were coached by therapists at CII to dream up fantasies of satanism and abuse. "What's in it for us?" one of the parents asked. "Nothing, except to keep people off the street who would do these things."

One father said he and his wife had discussed with their daughter on at least six occasions the goings-on at the McMartin school. The daughter could not "remember" anything happening. But after one of the other children, a friend of his daughter, let the little girl know he had been able to "tell secrets" to the therapists, the daughter was also able to "recall" things that had happened.

Using anatomically correct dolls, the daughter showed how Raymond Buckey had molested her. The parent said he tried to comfort his daughter later with regard to having to talk about the alleged abuse incidents. He said that during her stay at the school the girl had awoken with fits of shaking during the night, that she had redness in the region of her vagina, and that she was dead set against taking a nap at the school. He said she grew "more defiant" toward her parents "and less warm and affectionate" toward her father and other male members of the family. The counseling at CII, however, had created a more "positive" relationship between the child and the family.

Dr. Roland Summit, assistant clinical professor of psychiatry and head physician at the UCLA Medical Center where Judy Johnson's child was first diagnosed, has been outraged at the propensity of the media and public officials to dismiss child abuse. He is also upset at the way in which abusers and their defenders routinely appeal to Americans' native fear of moral vigilantes, allowing an entire industry of abuse and exploitation aimed at America's young to flourish.

Summit has been a consultant to federal law enforcement agencies, customs, postal inspectors, and child protective services. He gave written testimony for the U.S. attorney general's commission on pornography in 1985. "I believe that as a people, as a nation and as a collection of child caring institutions we have maintained, like the three monkeys, a self-protective posture of see no evil, hear no evil, and speak no evil," Summit wrote. " Our need to deny is bolstered by the relentless irrelevance of protective institutions and the paralyzing, calculated confusion imposed by an unknown number of influential citizens whose private lives are devoted to the sexual subjugation of children."

Ritual Abuse Exists

The truth is that *ritual abuse exists*. It is hideous and devastating. . . .

If we want to stop ritual abuse, the first step must be to believe that these brutal crimes occur. Society's denial makes recovery much more difficult for survivors. Those who have suffered from ritual abuse need the same respect and support that would be given to survivors of any tragedy.

Elizabeth S. Rose, *Ms.*, January/February 1993.

According to Summit, it is more comfortable to believe in a happy childhood and a just society than to confront the tragic truth of child abuse. The fact of widespread child abuse, particularly in day-care centers, challenges the proud myth of the sixties generation, which said that institutionalizing the care of children was not only harmless, but productive to the goals of society. . . .

As Summit has stressed, there are powerful interests—the criminal interests—who want the public to remain confused [about the relationship between satanism and sexual abuse]. Whether babies are actually sacrificed by day-care providers in front of the eyes of kids is not nearly as relevant as the fact that drug-use or child pornography are strongly implicated. . . .

Satanism Goes Well with Crime

The fact of the matter is that satanism is creeping into the underworld of child pornography, drugs, and sexual abuse as an ideology that goes well with crime in the first place. Satanist "theater" may also be used by criminals, first to frighten and intimidate the children, then to devise stories that make the little witnesses lose their credibility—allowing the criminals to go free and to undermine the plausibility of the attack on child sexual abuse in the first place. The common cord that binds most of the controversy is that parents, who generally know their children, believe what they are being told or at least believe that some kind of serious trauma has happened and should not be dismissed by officials.

Some of the more far-out fantasies of young children that are the victims of ritual abuse, trotted into court by the defense to underscore how ridiculous the prosecution's case is, may simply be the result of slipping the kids LSD or similar hallucinogens, which can then be manipulated by the power of suggestion. Satanic cults are known by police all over the country to avail themselves of LSD in their ceremonies. A local television station in Denver filmed a sandstone cave west of the city next to a popular rock concert amphitheater. The cave was employed as a satanic ritual site for adolescents following concerts, where they would be given LSD and introduced into the experiential mysteries of the dark.

And as for the beheaded babies, it all may be a matter of aesthetic terrorism in a very clever sense of the word. Alice Cooper would ritually decapitate dolls onstage. And police in California raided a warehouse where cultists had reportedly been active. They found a whole cache of aborted fetuses.

"The problem is bad enough; it is not necessary to exaggerate it."

Satanic Ritual Abuse of Children Is Not Widespread

Kenneth V. Lanning

Accusations of large numbers of well-organized satanic cults that practice ritual child sexual assault, among other horrific crimes and degenerate practices, are exaggerations or complete fabrications, according to Kenneth V. Lanning, author of the following viewpoint. Lanning argues that accusations of satanism stand in the way of law enforcement efforts to investigate and curb child abuse. While some child molesters may use the trappings of satanism to frighten their young victims, Lanning asserts that large-scale conspiracies and multiple human sacrifices are just as unlikely as the tales of victims cut apart and put back together. Lanning, supervisory special agent for the FBI Academy's Behaviorial Science Unit in Quantico, Virginia, specializes in studying the sexual victimization of children.

As you read, consider the following questions:

1. What are the four common dynamics of cases in which ritual abuse is alleged, according to Lanning?
2. Why, according to the author, is the use of the term "ritual child abuse" misleading?
3. What dangers does Lanning foresee in concentrating on the "ritual" elements in child abuse cases?

Society's attitude about child sexual abuse and exploitation can be summed up in one word: *denial*. Most people do not want to hear about it and would prefer to pretend that child sexual victimization just does not occur. Today, however, it is difficult to pretend that it does not happen. Stories and reports about child sexual victimization are daily occurrences.

It is important for professionals dealing with child sexual abuse to recognize and learn to manage this denial of a serious problem. Professionals must overcome the denial and encourage society to deal with, report, and prevent sexual victimization of children.

Some professionals, however, in their zeal to make American society more aware of this victimization, tend to exaggerate the problem. Presentations and literature with poorly documented or misleading claims about one in three children being sexually molested, the $5 billion child pornography industry, child slavery rings, and 50,000 stranger-abducted children are not uncommon. The problem is bad enough; it is not necessary to exaggerate it. . . .

"Stranger Danger"

During the 1950s and 1960s, the primary focus in the literature and discussions on sexual abuse of children was on "stranger danger"—the dirty old man in the wrinkled raincoat. . . .

In today's version of "stranger danger," it is the satanic devil worshipers who are trafficking in child pornography and snatching and victimizing the children. Many who warned us in the early 1980s about pedophiles snatching 50,000 kids a year now contend they were wrong only about who was doing the kidnapping, not about the number abducted. . . .

Sometime in early 1983 the author was first contacted by a law enforcement agency for guidance in what was then thought to be an unusual case. The exact date of the contact is unknown because its significance was not recognized at the time. In the months and years that followed, the author received more and more inquiries about "these kinds of cases.". . .

These cases involved and continue to involve unsubstantiated allegations of bizarre activity that are difficult either to prove or disprove. Many of the unsubstantiated allegations, however, do not *seem* to have occurred or even be possible. These cases seem to call into question the credibility of victims of child sexual abuse and exploitation. These are the most polarizing, frustrating, and baffling cases the author has encountered in more than eighteen years of studying the criminal aspects of deviant sexual behavior. . . .

What are "these kinds of cases"? They were and continue to

be difficult to define. They all involve allegations of what sounds like child sexual abuse, but with a combination of some atypical dynamics. These cases seem to have the following four dynamics in common: 1) multiple young victims, 2) multiple offenders, 3) fear as the controlling tactic, and 4) bizarre or ritualistic activity.

Multiple young victims. In almost all the cases, the sexual abuse was alleged to have taken place or at least begun when the victims were between the ages of birth and 6. This very young age may be an important key to understanding these cases. In addition, the victims all described multiple children being abused. The numbers ranged from three or four to as many as several hundred victims.

The Panic of the 1990s

A study by the Committee for the Scientific Examination of Religion, an international group of scientists, found that of more than 1 million recent violent crimes in the United States, only about 60 could be tied in any way to satanic belief.

"Satanism is one of many panics that have swept this country," explains Shawn Carlson, a physicist at the Lawrence Berkeley Laboratory who helped conduct the study. "In the 1950s it was the communists, the Great Red Scare. In the early 1980s it was people being abducted by UFOs. Now it's satanism."

Guy-Alban de Rougemont, *Mother Jones*, January/February 1993.

Multiple offenders. In almost all the cases the victims reported numerous offenders. The numbers ranged from two or three all the way up to dozens of offenders. In one case, the victim alleged 400-500 offenders were involved. Interestingly, many of the offenders (perhaps as many as 40-50 percent) were reported to be females. The multiple offenders were often family members and were described as being part of a cult, occult, or satanic group.

Fear as controlling tactic. . . . In almost all of the cases studied by the author, the victims described being frightened and reported threats against themselves, their families, their friends, and even their pets. They reported witnessing acts of violence perpetrated to reinforce this fear. It is the author's belief that this fear and the traumatic memory of the events may be another key to understanding many of these cases.

Bizarre or ritualistic activity. This is the most difficult dynamic of these cases to describe. *Bizarre* is a relative term. Is the use of urine or feces in sexual activity bizarre, or is it a well-documented aspect of sexual deviancy, or is it part of established satanic rituals? . . . The ritualistic aspect is even more difficult to define. How do you distinguish acts performed in a precise manner to enhance or allow sexual arousal from those acts that fulfill spiritual needs or comply with "religious" ceremonies? Victims in these cases report ceremonies, chanting, robes and costumes, drugs, use of urine and feces, animal sacrifice, torture, abduction, mutilation, murder, and even cannibalism and vampirism. All things considered, the word bizarre is probably preferable to the word ritual to describe this activity. . . .

What Is "Ritual" Child Abuse?

The author cannot define *ritual child abuse* precisely and prefers not to use the term, but is, however, frequently forced to use it (as throughout this discussion) so that people will have some idea of what is being discussed. Use of the term is confusing, misleading, and counterproductive. The newer term, satanic ritual abuse (SRA), is even worse. Certain observations, however, are important for investigative understanding.

Most people today use the term to refer to abuse of children that is part of some evil spiritual belief system, which almost by definition must be satanic.

Dr. Lawrence Pazder, coauthor of *Michelle Remembers*, defined ritualized abuse of children, in a presentation in Richmond, Virginia, on May 7, 1987, as "repeated physical, emotional, mental, and spiritual assaults combined with a systematic use of symbols and secret ceremonies designed to turn a child against itself, family, society, and God." He also states that "the sexual assault has ritualistic meaning and is not for sexual gratification."

This definition may have value for academics, sociologists, and therapists, but it creates potential problems for law enforcement. Certain acts engaged in with children (*i.e.*, kissing, touching, appearing naked, etc.) may be criminal if performed for sexual gratification. If the ritualistic acts were in fact performed for spiritual indoctrination, potential prosecution can be jeopardized, particularly if the acts can be defended as constitutionally protected religious expression. The mutilation of a baby's genitals for sadistic sexual pleasure is a crime. The circumcision of a baby's genitals for religious reasons is most likely NOT a crime. The intent of the act is important for criminal prosecution. . . .

Almost all parents with religious beliefs indoctrinate their children into that belief system. Is male circumcision for religious reasons child abuse? Is the religious circumcision of females child abuse? Does having a child kneel on a hard floor reciting the rosary constitute child abuse? Does having a child chant a satanic prayer or attend a black mass constitute child abuse? Does a religious belief in corporal punishment constitute child abuse? Does group care of children in a commune or cult constitute child abuse? Does the fact that any acts in question were performed with parental permission affect the nature of the crime? Many ritualistic acts, whether satanic or not, are simply not crimes. To open the Pandora's box of labeling child abuse as "ritualistic" simply because it involves a spiritual belief system, means to apply the definition to all acts by all spiritual belief systems. The day may come when many in the forefront of concern about ritual abuse will regret they opened the box. . . .

Where Is the Evidence?

Some of what the victims in these cases allege is physically impossible (victim cut up and put back together, offender took the building apart and then rebuilt it); some is possible but improbable (human sacrifice, cannibalism, vampirism); some is possible and probable (child pornography, clever manipulation of victims); and some is corroborated (medical evidence of vaginal or anal trauma, offender confessions).

The most significant crimes being alleged that do not *seem* to be true are the human sacrifice and cannibalism by organized satanic cults. In none of the multidimensional child sex ring cases of which the author is aware have bodies of the murder victims been found—in spite of major excavations where the abuse victims claim the bodies were located. The alleged explanations for this include: the offenders moved the bodies after the children left, the bodies were burned in portable high-temperature ovens, the bodies were put in double-decker graves under legitimately buried bodies, a mortician member of the cult disposed of the bodies in a crematorium, the offenders ate the bodies, the offenders used corpses and aborted fetuses, or the power of Satan caused the bodies to disappear.

Not only are no bodies found, but also, more importantly, there is no physical evidence that a murder took place. Many of those not in law enforcement do not understand that, while it is possible to get rid of a body, it is even more difficult to get rid of the physical evidence that a murder took place, especially a human sacrifice involving sex, blood, and mutilation. Such activity would leave behind trace evidence that could be found using modern crime scene processing techniques in spite of extraordinary efforts to clean it up.

The victims of these human sacrifices and murders are alleged to be abducted missing children, runaway and thrownaway children, derelicts, and the babies of breeder women. It is interesting to note that many of those espousing these theories are using the long-since-discredited numbers and rhetoric of the missing children hysteria in the early 1980s. Yet, a January 1989 *Juvenile Justice Bulletin*, published by the Office of Juvenile Justice and Delinquency Prevention of the U.S. Department of Justice, entitled "Stranger-Abduction Homicides of Children" reports that researchers now estimate that the number of children *kidnapped and murdered* by nonfamily members is between 52 and 158 a year and that adolescents 14 to 17 years old account for nearly *two thirds* of these victims. These figures are also consistent with the Justice Department's 1990 *National Incidence Studies on Missing, Abducted, Runaway, and Thrownaway Children in America.*

We live in a very violent society, and yet we have "only" about 23,000 murders a year. Those who accept these stories of mass human sacrifice would have us believe that the satanists and other occult practitioners are murdering more than twice as many people every year in this country as all the other murders combined.

Human Nature Disproves Conspiracy Theory

In addition, in none of the cases of which the author is aware has any evidence of a well-organized satanic cult been found. Many of those who accept the stories of organized ritual abuse of children and human sacrifice will tell you that the best evidence they now have is the consistency of stories from all over America. It sounds like a powerful argument. It is interesting to note that, without having met each other, the hundreds of people who claim to have been abducted by aliens from outer space also tell stories and give descriptions of the aliens that are similar to each other. This is not to imply that allegations of child abuse are in the same category as allegations of abduction by aliens from outer space. It is intended only to illustrate that individuals who never met each other can sometimes describe similar events without necessarily having experienced them.

The large number of people telling the same story is, in fact, the biggest reason to doubt these stories. It is simply too difficult for that many people to commit so many horrendous crimes as part of an organized conspiracy. Two or three people murder a couple of children in a few communities as part of a ritual, and nobody finds out? Possible. Thousands of people do the same things to tens of thousands of victims over many years? Not likely. Hundreds of communities all over America are run by mayors, police departments, and community leaders who are practicing satanists and who regularly murder and eat people? Not likely. In addition, these community leaders and high-ranking officials also supposedly commit these complex crimes leaving no evidence, and at the same time function as leaders and managers while heavily involved in using illegal drugs. . . .

Many people do not understand how difficult it is to commit a conspiracy crime involving numerous co-conspirators. One clever and cunning individual has a good chance of getting away with a well-planned interpersonal crime. Bring one partner into the crime and the odds of getting away with it drop considerably. The more people involved in the crime, the harder it is to get away with it. Why? Human nature is the answer. People get angry and jealous. They come to resent the fact that another conspirator is getting "more" than they. They get in trouble and want to make a deal for themselves by informing on others.

Unresolved Issues Cause Ritual Abuse Panic

Several years and scores of cases since allegations of ritual child sexual abuse first surfaced throughout the United States, authorities still have no more evidence of such crimes than they did when McMartin parents and children began talking. . . . The ritual abuse scare is a deeply rooted expression of anxieties this culture harbors about unresolved family and sexual issues. Without thoughtful, public discussion of such problems, the moral panic about diabolic, conspiratorial child molesters will no doubt continue to victimize adult defendants—and children—at least for the foreseeable future.

Debbie Nathan, *The Satanism Scare*, 1991.

If a group of individuals degenerate to the point of engaging in human sacrifice, murder, and cannibalism, that would most likely be the beginning of the end for such a group. The odds are that someone in the group would have a problem with such acts and be unable to maintain the secret. . . .

The conspiracy theory is a popular one. We find it difficult to believe that one bizarre individual could commit a crime we find so offensive. Conspiracy theories about soldiers missing in action (MIAs), abductions by UFOs, Elvis Presley sightings, and the assassination of prominent public figures are the focus of much attention in this country. These conspiracy theories and allegations of ritual abuse have the following in common: 1) self-proclaimed experts, 2) tabloid media interest, 3) belief the government is involved in a cover-up, and 4) emotionally involved direct and indirect victim/witnesses. . . .

Why are victims alleging things that do not *seem* to be true? . . .

The author has identified a series of possible alternatives to this question. The alternative answers also do not preclude the possibility that clever offenders are sometimes involved. The author will not attempt to explain completely these alternative answers because he cannot. They are presented simply as areas for consideration and evaluation. . . .

Possible Answers

The first possible answer to why adult victims are alleging things that do not *seem* to be true is *pathological distortion*. The allegations in question may be errors in processing reality influenced by underlying mental disorders such as dissociative disorders, borderline or histrionic personality disorders, or psychosis. . . .

Although not always pathological, many "victims" may develop pseudomemories of their victimization and eventually come to believe the events actually occurred. . . .

The second possible answer is *traumatic memory*. Fear and severe trauma can cause victims to store memory of those events in a fragmented way which can distort reality and confuse events. This is a well-documented fact in cases involving individuals taken hostage or in life-and-death situations.

The author does not believe it is a coincidence nor the result of deliberate planning by satanists that in almost all the cases of ritual abuse that have come to his attention, the abuse is alleged to have begun prior to the age of 7 and was perpetrated by multiple offenders. It may well be that such abuse, at a young age by multiple offenders, is the most difficult to accurately recall with the specific and precise detail needed by the criminal justice system and the most likely to be distorted and exaggerated when it is recalled. . . .

The third possible answer may be *normal childhood fears and fantasy*. Most young children are afraid of ghosts and monsters. . . . While young children may rarely invent stories about sexual activity, they might describe their victimization in terms of evil as they understand it. . . .

Misperception, confusion, and trickery may be a fourth answer. Expecting young children to give accurate accounts of sexual activity for which they have little frame of reference is unreasonable. The Broadway play *M. Butterfly* is the true story of a man who had a fifteen-year affair, including the "birth" of a baby, with a "woman" who turns out to have been a man all along. If a grown man does not know when he has had vaginal intercourse with a woman, how can we expect young children not to be confused? Furthermore, some clever offenders may deliberately introduce elements of satanism and the occult into the sexual exploitation simply to confuse or intimidate the victims.

Simple magic and other techniques may be used to trick the children. Drugs may also be deliberately used to confuse the victims and distort their perceptions. Such acts would then be MO [modus operandi] not ritual. . . .

Overzealous intervenors, causing intervenor contagion, may be a fifth answer. These intervenors can include parents, family members, foster parents, doctors, therapists, social workers, law enforcement officers, prosecutors, and any combination thereof. . . .

Allegations of and knowledge about ritualistic satanic abuse may also be spread through *urban legends*. . . . Some urban legends about child kidnappings and other threats to citizens have even been disseminated unknowingly by law enforcement agencies. Such legends have always existed, but today the mass media aggressively participate in their rapid and more efficient dissemination.

Combination. Most multidimensional child sex ring cases probably involve a *combination* of the answers previously set forth, as well as other possible explanations unknown to the author at this time. . . . All the possibilities must be explored if for no other reason than the fact that the defense attorneys for any accused subjects will almost certainly do so.

Most people would agree that just because a victim tells you one detail that turns out to be true, this does not mean that every detail is true. But many people seem to believe that if you can disprove one part of a victim's story, then the entire story is false. . . . One of the author's main concerns in these cases is that people are getting away with sexually abusing children or committing other crimes because we cannot prove that they are members of organized cults who murder and eat people.

The author has discovered that the subject of multidimensional child sex rings is a very emotional and polarizing issue. Everyone seems to demand that one choose a side. On one side of the issue are those who say that nothing really happened and it is all a big witch hunt led by overzealous fanatics and incompetent "experts." The other side says, in essence, that everything happened; victims never lie about child sexual abuse, and so it must be true.

There is a middle ground. It is the job of the professional investigator to listen to all the victims and conduct appropriate investigation in an effort to find out what happened, considering *all* possibilities. Not all childhood trauma is abuse. Not all child abuse is a crime. The great frustration of these cases is the fact that you are often convinced that something traumatic happened to the victim, but do not know with any degree of certainty exactly what happened, when it happened, or who did it.

"When there's a problem priest, the bishop or archbishop has been able to sweep it under the rug, move them about, and carry on."

Child Sexual Abuse in the Catholic Church Is Widespread

Jeffrey Anderson, interviewed by Vicki Quade

In the past decade, hundreds of clergy from many denominations have been publicly accused of sexually abusing children. Several Catholic priests in particular have been accused of pedophilia. In the following viewpoint, Jeffrey Anderson, a lawyer who has been involved in many such cases across the country, states that church officials have ignored or denied priest pedophilia, or responded by moving offending priests from place to place, allowing them access to new victims. These actions by the church have made it difficult to prosecute, or even to force acknowledgment of, the abuse, Anderson concludes. Anderson was interviewed by Vicki Quade, editor of the American Bar Association's *Human Rights* magazine.

As you read, consider the following questions:

1. According to Anderson, how is the problem of clergy abuse different in the Catholic church than in other denominations?
2. Why does the author believe that clergy abuse has only recently been revealed?
3. What effect does Anderson believe making these cases public will have?

Editor's note: *In December of 1990, a jury in Anoka, a small town near St. Paul, awarded about $3.5 million to a man who as a minor was molested for eight years by Father Thomas Adamson. Testimony revealed that over a 23-year period, the Diocese of Winona in Minnesota knew of Adamson's sexual problems yet continued to assign him to parish work, transferring him within the diocese. By 1980, the Archdiocese of St. Paul and Minneapolis also knew of his problem, yet continued to assign him to parish work where he had access to children.*

Jeffrey Anderson, the lawyer for the victim, had previously settled several cases involving other victims of Adamson. This was his biggest success to date.

Anderson was a young lawyer when he agreed to take on his first case involving sexual abuse and the clergy. One of the first lawyers in the U.S. to chart this new field of civil torts, Anderson is one of the few specializing in this legal field.

Since the verdict in Anoka came down, the trial court let stand $855,000 in compensatory damages, but reduced the punitive damages of $2.7 million. Damages of $2 million against the archdiocese were reduced to $50,000, while damages of $700,000 against the Diocese of Winona were reduced to about $135,000. . . .

Anderson is now handling more than 125 cases in 22 states, and has settled successfully in dozens of others. . . .

*P*ayouts from the Catholic Church could total $1 billon within the next five years related to charges of child abuse against its priests. How is the church confronting this problem?

Historically they have failed to deal seriously with lawsuits, litigation, and what we call civil responsibility.

They ignored the issue, hoping it would go away. Now they're starting to respond to what is a crisis in their midst.

Sometimes they deny responsibility and attempt to blame the victims and/or their families. Or find fault with the lawyers who bring the claims.

On occasion they've acknowledged responsibility and tried to amend some of the harm that has been done. . . .

A Crisis in the Church

Is this the biggest crisis within the church right now?

That's a tough question.

Time magazine described it as the most significant moral crisis facing the Catholic Church in North America.

I would say the church has a failure to deal openly and honestly with issues around sexuality and sexism. And that manifests itself in a lot of their religious practices, such as the tenet of celibacy.

What is the church's response to this issue?

They are clearly beginning to acknowledge that they have a serious problem.

We are seeing them establish policies and procedures in various dioceses, but it's not comprehensive and that's one of the problems.

How big a problem is this?

Nobody knows. It's estimated that as many as 20 to 40 percent of Catholic clergy are sexually active. But sexual activity by clergy does not evidence child abuse.

It's also estimated that as many as five percent of the sexually active clergy are sexually interested in children. If that translates to the number of priests in the country, it's a phenomenally dangerous number.

Are other religious denominations affected by this problem?

It's a problem in all religious denominations, but more so in the Catholic Church.

Is that because it's been publicized within the Catholic Church?

No. It's an institutional problem.

When the church discovers sexual abuse by one of its own, that person is simply moved to another parish.

Other denominations have not been as institutionally inclined to conceal it.

The Catholic Church operates uniquely in some ways. It wields a tremendous amount of influence, but doesn't answer to a constituency of voters. It has the ability to deal with problems internally without public scrutiny or accountability.

As a result of that type of power, when there's a problem priest, the bishop or archbishop has been able to sweep it under the rug, move them about, and carry on.

And as a result of that kind of institutional response, the church is facing the liability crisis.

I have a number of cases against other denominations across this country, but the scope and depth of the problem is pale compared to that in the Catholic Church.

Everyone Kept the Secret

If that's true, why hasn't it been revealed until now?

People who have been abused and family members who learn of it have not felt comfortable about coming forward and speaking their truth.

The victim says, "Who would believe me?" And there's an overwhelming fear of doing anything against the church. Also, you're dealing with individuals who have a tremendous loyalty to their religion.

Lawsuits against the Catholic clergy and the church arising from sexual abuse are a recent phenomenon. The conduct underlying it is not recent, but the lawsuits are. You won't see any lawsuits publicly recorded before 1986.

How successful are those lawsuits?

I'm not aware of any cases civilly prosecuted and properly handled that haven't resulted in a settlement.

And to that extent, I think they're successful.

They're more successful in that they're exposing an underbelly that has never been exposed before.

How Many Chances Should a Molester Get?

Bishops have historically sent repeat offenders to new parishes, with parishioners unaware, while treating victims as pariahs. . . .

How many youths must a man molest before he is considered unfit to be a priest?

Jason Berry, *Commonweal*, January 15, 1993.

Are these mostly civil or criminal cases?

There are some criminal cases, but most are civil.

More often than not the same influences that have kept people from reporting the abuse have kept priests from being prosecuted by authorities.

There's been a reluctance by law enforcement or prosecuting authorities to actually prosecute priests.

There are occasional prosecutions of priests. Some are in jail right now. . . .

How difficult is it to fight a behemoth the size of the Catholic Church?

It poses special problems. And special challenges.

But it's not unlike any behemoth. To the same extent it's difficult to sue and do battle with General Motors, it's difficult to sue and do battle with the Catholic Church.

Except there's one additional dimension: the amount of influence and sometimes blind loyalty the Catholic Church enjoys in our culture.

There can be a certain illogicality to faith.

Faithful people believe in their church. They perceive anybody who disagrees vis-à-vis lawsuit or otherwise as a demon, an Antichrist, a devil, or worse.

It is a special challenge in jury selection, in evaluating how people are going to perceive the case, client, and claim.

But this is also a behemoth that is somewhat inexperienced in litigation in the sense that none of these people have ever been subjected to the process of law. To that extent, they're naive. While they're strong and powerful, they are also vulnerable.

You won't find a General Motors or other corporate giant power-ful, yet naive.

It's not to say that the church doesn't hire the best lawyers and biggest law firms. They always have the best legal talent available. They never hire fumblers and bumblers because they have the resources to do just what General Motors does—fend off an onslaught. . . .

What have you learned?

We've learned that if it's a Catholic Church case involving a cover-up, certain Catholics profile as very favorable jurors because they understand the special trust, power, and position a Catholic priest occupies in their lives and our society.

When that is betrayed, they understand the damage, and they are the ones who, as jurors, are the most outraged and angered.

There are certain types of jurors who would not find in your favor, no matter what, because of faith. Those are the ones you have to screen out.

Part of the reason I handle these cases is not for compensation for the victims, but for social, cultural, institutional change.

It's no accident that a large number of these cases are made public. That's not because I'm interested in having my name in the newspaper. It's because change is going to be effectuated through public attention. Pressure is going to be brought to bear on every protective institution.

A General Failure to Prosecute

Has there been a general failure to prosecute these offenders?

The first impression by law enforcement authorities, judges, prosecutors is to disbelieve the charges.

If you don't believe it, you don't take action.

Many prosecutors, judges—people in position of power, trust, and authority—are very loyal to the church. They feel they're serving the interest of the church as well as the priest by not taking action.

When child abuse happens by a clergyman, it's a child—often frail, vulnerable, maybe troubled—who's reporting this.

And the crime happens in secrecy, silence, and shame. It doesn't happen in the presence of others. So it's the child's word against the priest.

Is there an unwillingness among lawyers to embarrass the church?

Many lawyers are reluctant to prosecute any cases against the Catholic Church. And in particular these kinds of cases.

But what about representing the victim?

The first case I handled came as a referral from a friend who had worked for me and was now in private practice.

The child's parents had just learned that their son, who now is an adult, had been abused by a priest. As all Catholics typically do, they went to someone in the church—in this case to a bishop—and reported what happened.

The bishop did not act surprised.

Shortly after that, the family received a check from the church for about $1,600.

The parents didn't know what to do so they went to see my friend. He told them he just couldn't handle a case like this, especially against the Catholic Church.

But he said he knew somebody who wouldn't be afraid and he gave them my name.

I hadn't had any dealings with the Catholic Church, at least not professionally. I have two children who were raised Catholic.

So, I met with the parents and got the information. I remember telling them, "I don't know what's involved here, but something doesn't smell or look right. And let me look into it. In the meantime, cash the check, take the money, and I'll look into the matter."

I did some preliminary investigation and began to uncover what we learned to be a conspiracy and a cover-up.

Wasn't that your first case against Father Thomas Adamson? Were criminal charges filed?

It was my first case. And no, criminal charges were never filed.

Adamson had been sexually abusing children for a period spanning 23 years. Thirty-eight young boys. He had not been prosecuted even though it had been brought to the attention of church authorities on at least eight different occasions.

The passage of time prevented criminal prosecution. While that priest has admitted abusing dozens of youths, he has never spent one day in jail. . . .

The Church's Legal Tactics

What legal tactics are used by attorneys for the church?

They claim it's a falsehood and threaten to sue in defamation.

They will make a counterclaim for negligence, that the victim, even if he is 12 years old, was negligent. And they will claim the parents should not have entrusted their son to the priest.

There is a cruelty to that. They did that in the first and most recent case we tried.

The church and its attorneys are reluctant to discuss these cases. Is that because they fear others will come forward with their own charges?

They've been successful; these things have been kept beneath the surface. Maybe they feel by talking about it more, it invites more people to come forward and speak their truth.

The simple reality is that when I confront a priest through a lawsuit, that causes other victims to come forward.

Isn't that what happens in tort actions?

In most tort actions, the wrongdoer is operating in an isolated incident. For example, an automobile accident is an isolated incident.

The cases I handle are more similar to defective product cases. I'm not trying to equate a person who is a priest to a product, but there is a similarity in that they've injured a number of other people.

In defective product cases, often class actions are brought. Has there ever been a class action against the church?

No, there has not, although they have said they fear that might happen.

These cases and the individual damages in each are so unique that they don't lend themselves to class action suits.

Does the growing shortage of priests have anything to do with the church's reluctance to prosecute these cases?

No question about it. Because there is such a shortage, when a report is made there is an apparent reluctance to just remove the priest. Some archdioceses can't afford to lose any priests, they're so short-staffed.

Isn't there something called the doctrine of charitable immunity which bars lawsuits against charitable institutions?

Some states have charitable or religious immunities. . . .

These doctrines are archaic, antiquated, outrageous. But they represent the vestiges of the influence that religious organizations have exercised in lawmaking in our culture.

Priest Molests Children for Decades

James Porter, a former Roman Catholic priest, has admitted to molesting between 50 and 100 children over the last 30 years. He allegedly assaulted children in parishes from Fall River, Mass., to Las Vegas, Nev. He left the priesthood and later married. In 1992 he was convicted in Minnesota of molesting his own children's babysitter in 1987.

David A. Kaplan, *Newsweek*, January 18, 1993.

Are there other state laws that work against bringing charges against charitable or religious institutions?

I don't think so. The immunity doctrine applies to the churches themselves. There's nothing that prevents a priest from being prosecuted criminally or from being sued individually.

Does the National Conference of Catholic Bishops have any policy guidelines on this issue?

No. And that's where they have been remiss.

In 1985 they had an opportunity based on a report submitted to them that suggested that they take immediate action and adopt certain policies and certain procedures.

They didn't respond to that in any affirmative or significant way. They left it essentially to the bishops and the archbishops who preside in their various dioceses to develop policies.

As a result, policies do exist on a haphazard basis.

"Something Very Large, Very Dark"

When you first became involved in these cases, what was your initial reaction? Did you think this was too big to handle or that you didn't have the expertise needed?

I never felt it was too big to handle, in part because I didn't understand the scope of it.

But when I started to uncover and learn about the issue, I felt like all of a sudden I had stumbled upon something very large, very dark. And very much in need of change and attention.

So more than being intimidated or scared, it motivated me. I felt a sense of urgency about dealing with it.

I didn't feel like they're too big and I'm too small, and they can bury me.

There are times when you can get outspent, but I've felt I could always muster whatever resources necessary to do battle with them. . . .

You seem to have a perfect background for these kinds of abuse cases—working in products liability, class action, some criminal practice.

I had always represented little guys getting stomped on by the big guys, the behemoths.

Maybe that accounts for why my practice flourishes.

I never envisioned that I would be in this area. I don't think anybody ever envisions this area as a specialized practice of law. It's tragic that it is.

It's a shame that people are sexually abused and that we have so many clients. I'd much rather that this specialty didn't have to exist. . . .

Where are most of your cases brought? Do you concentrate mostly in the Minneapolis area?

The cases are all across the country.

I'm handling 125 cases right now in 22 states.

I'm in Albuquerque one week, Pennsylvania the next. I'm in Chicago the week after, then onto Seattle. I'm handling a case in Hawaii right now. I've been invited to represent families in Canada, although I've declined those cases for now.

Geographically, these cases are coast to coast.

Do you feel you're on a mission?

Not in a religious sense, but it's significantly more than a simple practice.

I have always felt like there were goals. Not economic. I've always felt driven to accomplish certain things in law. A lot of what I'm doing has social overtones to it; something more than just work.

Do you take on any of these cases pro bono?

A large number of the cases are pro bono.

I've never translated the cases into dollars, and I never thought the cases that I had handled would translate into the kinds of dollars they have.

When I first started taking them, many of those around me described it as a folly because the statutes of limitations had expired, there were barriers to recovery that had never been broken before.

Those barriers have now been broken, in part through my efforts.

So what is your desire in these cases?

I'd like to see it stop happening, although I don't think it's ever going to stop.

I'd like to see the church and church authorities deal with the crisis openly and candidly and change the way they do business around it. To that extent, there will be less child abuse and less harm done.

"The panic over . . . 'priestly pedophilia' . . . is a
classic example of the artificial generation of a
social panic for partisan ends."

Accusations of Abuse Are Anti-Catholic Propaganda

Philip Jenkins

In a manufactured panic over priest pedophilia, liberals and feminists have found the perfect vehicle for attacking the Catholic church, Philip Jenkins asserts in the following viewpoint. He contends that the problem of a few individuals with serious moral failings has been inflated to serve as a battering ram against such basic Catholic tenets as celibacy, confession, and the male priesthood. The question of child sexual abuse by priests is indeed a crisis for the church, he agrees, but the danger comes from activists attempting to harm the church, not from the rare few clergymen who molest. Jenkins is a professor in the Administration of Justice Department at Pennsylvania State University.

As you read, consider the following questions:

1. What financial "vested interests" are served by creating a panic about molesting priests, according to Jenkins?
2. On what grounds does the author object to the use of such terms as *pedophilia, molestation,* and *abuse* when referring to most of the reported cases of priest sexual misconduct?
3. How has the church dealt with the problem of priests who abuse children sexually in the past, according to the author?

From Philip Jenkins, "Priests and Pedophiles: The Attack on the Catholic Church," *Chronicles: A Magazine of American Culture,* vol. 16, no. 12 (December 1992). Reprinted with permission.

"Catholic priests claim to be celibate, but we know what they're really up to. Most of them seduce women, the rest like little boys. Priests trap them in the confessional, and when the priests are found out, the bishops let them off with a slap on the wrist. Celibacy, hierarchy, secrecy, the confessional—those are the things that make the Catholic Church the sink of iniquity it is." Put in various ways, sentiments like these have been the common currency of anticlerical and anti-Catholic rhetoric for almost as long as there has been a Catholic Church. We might think that these ideas would by now have gone the way of the other myths and stereotypes that once adhered to (say) Jews or blacks; but in fact, the attack on Roman Catholic clergy as sexual monsters is at this very moment reaching a crescendo in North America.

The panic over "clergy sex abuse," or "priestly pedophilia," has reached far beyond the trashy television talk shows and now threatens to become a devastatingly effective vehicle for anti-Catholic activism and legislation. This manufactured and manipulated crisis is being used as a justification for the wholesale evisceration of Catholic tradition, with liberal and feminist groups the chief beneficiaries. This is a classic example of the artificial generation of a social panic for partisan ends; and as yet, few of those under attack seem to understand what is happening, still fewer are able to organize a defense. . . .

Reviving an Ancient Stereotype

For all the media attacks, the Church has remained remarkably resilient and has even won political successes, for example through its leadership of the pro-life movement. Its opponents had therefore to be even more resourceful in seeking effective weapons for sabotage. . . . The ideal solution would have been identify the Church with racism; but that was wholly implausible in view of the consistent liberal activism of clergy in this area. That left the two other modern shibboleths, namely sexuality and children, here combined in the late 20th-century nightmare of the sexual abuse of children. Might it be possible to revive the ancient stereotype of the priest as sexual predator?

The solution to the anti-Catholic dilemma emerged in the mid-1980's, with the first of several cases involving the repeated sexual abuse of children by priests and members of religious orders. One of the most celebrated was that of Father Gilbert Gauthe in Louisiana, who was first identified as a molester in the early 1970's but was moved to several other parishes before his crimes came to public awareness. In other words, the local hierarchy seemed to connive with his horrific crimes by failing to intervene at a sufficiently early stage and in fact by placing at risk the children to whose parishes he was subsequently sent.

168

This tragic case involved (at best) serious misjudgments and organizational failings on the part of the Church, and there was a widespread scandal when the affair came to court in 1985.

Over the next three years, there were dozens of notorious cases following broadly similar lines, sometimes involving the manufacture and distribution of child pornography. In response, there emerged literature suggesting that there was more to the problem than the existence of a few individuals with serious moral failings. Clergy sex abuse was a social epidemic on a vast scale, and it was permitted, even encouraged, by the structure and institutions of the Church. The lack of full investigation and disclosure permitted "pedophile priests" to carry on their sinister careers for years. Another recurrent theme concerned the reluctance of secular law enforcement authorities to arrest and prosecute these legions of delinquent clergy. This appears to revive the archaic charge of "dual loyalty," the suggestion that Catholics holding secular office obey the demands of their Church before their public duties.

A Feminism-Based Panic

By the late 1980's, the materials for a panic were in place, in terms of cohorts of self-styled "experts" like Jason Berry and Marie Fortune and of a literature applying to clerical problems the wisdom of secular child abuse experts. This literature broadly accepted an essentially feminist analysis, that child abuse was a manifestation of patriarchal tyranny, an all but ubiquitous atrocity that had appalling and lifelong effects on its millions of victims. As Father Andrew Greeley has written, abusers are far worse than alcoholics or drunk drivers: "alcoholics are dangerous only to themselves, their families, and the people they smash with their cars, but each pedophile is a threat to the future lives of hundreds of children."

These beliefs supported the view that clerical abuse was both pervasive and destructive, which came as music to the ears of a growing profession of lawyers who now won huge liability lawsuits against Catholic dioceses. It is estimated that by the mid-1990's, the cumulative total of damages from this type of case will exceed a billion dollars. The ensuing scandals have had a snowball effect, encouraging past victims, real or imaginary, to come forward and register their complaints—all of which gives real social momentum to the panic. Lawyers have been among the greatest beneficiaries, but also significant were the profits to be made in organizing and teaching the countless seminars, workshops, training programs, and "encounter groups" on abuse-related issues that now litter the advertisement pages of every religious newspaper and journal. Of course, Catholic clergy were not the only targets of the panic, and we found lawsuits against most of the major Christian denominations, as well as Jewish groups; but the image of the celibate priest naturally attracted particular suspicion and hostility.

Catholic Clergy an Inviting Target

Certainly there is an element of sensationalism in the recent media coverage involving Catholic priests and the sexual molestation of children. Prurient interest, a staple of popular culture, accounts for some of this fascination. The very idea of celibacy as well as Catholic attitudes and beliefs about the sacramental character of sexuality, so at odds with the utilitarian ethos of secular culture, also make Catholic clergy an inviting target. Exposing the sexual hypocrisy or worse of Catholic priests is an old story and an old controversy. So Catholics have reason to think that the front-page stories reflect as much the culture war over sexual issues as they do genuine alarm over priests and pedophilia.

Commonweal, November 20, 1992.

There were sizable vested interests at stake (both financial and ideological) in generating a "clerical abuse" problem, and these efforts reached fruition in the early years of the 1990's. Following new Catholic-focused scandals, especially in the diocese of Chicago and in the Canadian province of Newfoundland, reports of "priestly pedophiles" became an almost daily occurrence in the media—though in some cases, investigations were reaching back to alleged misdeeds committed many years before. There has been great scandal about a case of this sort where a priest in North Attleboro, Massachusetts, was said to have been involved in hundreds of incidents as long ago as the 1960's. The literature on the topic mushroomed, with major investigative reports in most leading newspapers, as well as in *Time, Newsweek*, and journals like *Ms.* and *Vanity Fair.*

In this atmosphere, both secular and ecclesiastical authorities struggled to respond, with proposed solutions potentially draconian. The diocese of Chicago has now suggested a lay-dominated board that would hear and investigate charges against priests, even when such accusations were received over an anonymous hotline. Accused clergy would be suspended at an early stage of the process.

For no one was permitted to doubt that this was a crisis. The language employed by the media repeatedly suggested both the vast scale of the problem and the role played by official cover-ups and wrongdoing in high places. This was the "S&L disaster of the Catholic Church," an "ecclesiastical Watergate," a "meltdown." Andrew Greeley drew comparisons with the Clarence Thomas/Anita Hill farrago, which in contemporary liberal martyrology represents the ultimate manifestation of a patriarchal cover-up of male wrongdoing. According to Catholic writer Thomas Doyle, pedophilia represents "the most serious problem that we in the Church have faced in centuries": quite a claim when the issue is considered alongside the Enlightenment, Darwinism, wholesale secularization, Communism, and Nazism. When the problem was quantified, it appeared to be immense. Several accounts indicated that five or six percent of American priests might be "pedophiles" or molesters, suggesting a total of nearly three thousand troubled and dangerous individuals.

In a full-scale panic, it is often difficult to pause and ask whether the concern is entirely justified or whether there is any substance whatever to the issue; but this "crisis," more than most, presents a number of quite significant difficulties. For example, it cannot be denied that some priests, being human, commit serious crimes, while large institutions tend sometimes to favor self-interest and self-protection over the public good. But we knew this already. What is more contentious, and indeed wildly speculative, is the estimate of the scale of the problem. Who has the slightest idea whether the number of priests who molest children is twenty percent of the total or whether it is a fraction of one percent? And contrary to the impression derived from "experts," we do *not* know much about the impact of noncoercive molestation on children or adolescents: in the late 1970's, most therapists thought the effects were relatively trivial; in the early 1990's, we think they are devastating. Who is to know?

Most Cases Are Not Pedophilia

Problems are defined by language. . . . In the Catholic Church, we hear much about "pedophilia," an attractive term because of the alliterative quality of "priestly pedophilia." Like "molestation" or "abuse," this word suggests involvement with children, ranging in age from toddlers to pubescent youngsters, and further suggests forced acts that partake to some extent of the nature of rape. These acts have certainly occurred, indeed in some of the more notorious cases. However, by no means did all of the scandals involve "molestation," and many did not include victims we can accurately characterize as "children." When considered in detail, perhaps eighty or ninety percent of the cases involved sexual liaisons between priests and boys or young men in their teens or early 20's.

This behavior may be reprehensible in terms of ecclesiastical and moral codes of sexual conduct, specifically in violating vows of celibacy; and it might well be that the power relationship between priest and young parishioner renders it difficult to speak of it as fully consensual. However, the nature of the act would seem to be better characterized as "homosexuality" than "pedophilia" or molestation. In the words of a Nova Scotia bishop, following the scandal at the Mount Cashel home in Newfoundland, "we are not dealing with classic pedophilia. I do not want to argue that homosexual activity between a priest and an adolescent is therefore moral. Rather it does not have the horrific character of pedophilia."

This is neither to defend nor to justify the conduct, but it is necessary to stress that conventional language may exaggerate both the degree of force used on and the nature of harm done to the supposed victim. Failure to discriminate between homosexuality and pedophilia was long a feature of antihomosexual polemic; it is surprising to find such a confusion of terminology in contemporary liberal circles.

Humane Treatment Outrages Liberals and Feminists

But there are many oddities in this controversy, many areas in which our normal expectations about partisan attitudes are confounded. For instance, the Catholic Church has for years recognized the problem of abusers in its ranks and has attempted to deal with the problem in a humane and therapeutic way, refusing to invoke the criminal justice system. Offending clerics have been treated both as sinners capable of reform and as sick individuals deserving treatment rather than punishment. This would seem to be a model example of penological liberalism, yet it is this very humanity that has earned the wrath of liberals and feminists who demand that offenders be subject to the rigorous penalties of law for their sexual misdeeds.

Can this be correct? Liberals denouncing homosexuality? Liberals calling for the police and courts to enforce moral laws? This would all be very surprising if we did not recognize the deeper anti-Catholic agenda at work here. Priestly pedophilia has become a superb weapon to be used against the Church, because it presents a stereotype that appears gravely threatening to the most loyal Catholic parishioners themselves. Pedophilia also seems so unquestionably evil that it becomes impossible to challenge the critics: to question the panic is to attack the pathetic victims or—still worse—to exhibit the grave pathology known as "denial." It is simply not acceptable to believe or to state that some, even a handful, of the alleged victims might be less than impeccable in their stories. In child abuse, as in Catholic doctrine, there is a firm but selective belief in infallibility.

Moreover, if in fact the problem is as bad as has been described, then desperate measures are required to deal with it; and by a remarkable coincidence, the best solutions appear to be found in the traditional liberal and anti-Catholic agenda—

measures that strike at the heart of Catholic belief, teaching, and practice. If this statement seems hyperbolic, consider several specific practices that have long been attacked by liberal critics of the Church—celibacy, confession, the male priesthood. All have been denounced in the aftermath of the sex scandals, and the Church has had to struggle to defend its traditions— needless to say, with the critics receiving the wholehearted support of the media. As a rhetorical device, the association is brilliant: to oppose the "reform" of celibacy or women's ordination is to defend child abuse and even to attract suspicion to oneself as a friend and accomplice of abusers. . . .

Leave Titillation to the *National Enquirer*

Using the most recent statistics available, there are 53,086 Catholic priests in the United States, 6896 religious brothers, and 101,911 sisters. But let one of these be found guilty of child molesting and bells ring and lights flash in newsrooms across the nation. The crime involved need not be a recent one: there is no statute of limitations on reporting such stories. Armed robbery, even murders of which there are dozens in major cities every week, fade quickly from the news columns; but stories of illicit sexual encounters by priests, ministers, or other religious people continue to rebound again and again in prime time and prime space. . . .

Titillation, I know, sells papers and improves ratings; but is it too much to ask that we leave that device to the *National Enquirer* and other supermarket scandal sheets?

Robert E. Burns, *U.S. Catholic*, January 1992.

Abuse—whatever this means—has provided an excuse for a frontal assault on celibacy. The last few years have witnessed a spate of books on the unpopularity of clerical celibacy, and it has been alleged that priests and religious respond to their inner conflicts in one of two ways: either they ignore the discipline by forming relationships with women or they become pedophiles. Recent books—quoted with glowing approval in the major newspapers—have suggested that anywhere up to half of all priests effectively ignore celibacy regulations. Such studies cannot fail to have an impact, and opinion polls suggest that the number of Catholics favoring married priests rose from 58 percent in 1983 to 70 percent in 1992. Those supporting the ordination of women priests grew in the same period from 40 percent to nearly 70 percent. These changes cannot be entirely attributed to the panic over child abuse, but the coincidence in timing is striking.

The question of child abuse has done much to subvert a series of fundamental Catholic institutions that had remained largely unchallenged since the Reformation. It is quite possible to imagine a Catholic Church with married clergy, with women priests, and without auricular confession, though many would question how far such a body could claim an authentic link to Catholic tradition. But such changes appear mild when compared with the intellectual and cultural revolution that is now threatened in the name of feminist theology, in which the theme of child abuse plays a fundamental role. Christian feminists have often been criticized for their ambition to create new systems oriented toward the worship of a nurturing goddess rather than a traditional Judeo-Christian deity. In the process, they have shown a disturbing willingness to synthesize practices and beliefs from other female-oriented religions (including New Age groups and "Wicca" witches). Creeping neopaganism has often used the issue of abuse as a means of self-justification, leading many activists to challenge virtually all of the basic concepts not merely of Catholicism, but of Christianity as such.

Feminists Denounce Key Christian Beliefs

Christian churches have differed over many aspects of their faith, but the great majority have held fast to certain key notions: human sinfulness, the atonement, the sacrificial death of Christ, redemptive suffering, and the forgiveness of sins as the highest virtue. All of these ideas have been denounced by leading feminists like Mary Daly, Alice Miller, Matthew Fox, and Joanne Carlson Brown, precisely because these mainstream Christian notions represent what they term a "theology of abuse." In this view, guilt and a sense of sin represent the psychic scars of the primal rape and abuse suffered by the believer, while God becomes the ultimate abuser. *Episcopal Life* quoted a theorist who challenged the theology of the crucifixion: "To me, it is an abusive act of a father toward a child. The theology of sin in the church is all about human worthlessness." Absurd as it may seem, the Trinity becomes the celestial archetype of the dysfunctional family.

The essays in one of feminism's major texts—*Christianity, Patriarchy and Abuse*—repeatedly challenge Christian beliefs in this same vein. For example, "We do not need to be saved by Jesus' death from some original sin. We need to be liberated from the oppression of racism, classism and sexism, that is, from patriarchy. . . . Peace was not made by the Cross, . . . suffering is never redemptive, and suffering cannot be redeemed." Furthermore, "As an aspect of trinitarian thought, Christology is often based on implicit elements of child abuse." Even forgiveness is prohibited in some instances, because the offense of

174

child abuse is so immeasurably severe and because forgiving gets in the way of the "healing" of the alleged victim. Perhaps, after all these centuries, we have finally identified the mysterious "sin against the Holy Spirit," which cannot be forgiven? The Christian and specifically Catholic condemnation of sexual immorality is dismissed in these same pages as "theological pornography.". . .

In the brief time since a "child abuse problem" was defined in this country, the problem—and the ideology based upon it—has gained such support that it has revolutionized our justice system and undermined our churches. The panic is in a sense a perfect weapon, because so few are prepared to question this orthodoxy and hence to challenge its practical consequences. Realizing this, liberals and feminists have used the abuse ideology as a Trojan Horse to enter and to subvert many traditional institutions. In religion, the panic threatens to overthrow not merely the Catholic Church but much of the essence of Christianity itself. Child abuse might indeed be the greatest threat the Church has faced in centuries, but the danger comes less from the handful of pedophile clergy than from the cynical activists who are exploiting their misdeeds.

Periodical Bibliography

The following articles have been selected to supplement the diverse views presented in this chapter.

David Alexander	"Giving the Devil More Than His Due," *The Humanist*, March/April 1990.
David Alexander	"Still Giving the Devil More Than His Due," *The Humanist*, September/October 1991.
Jason Berry, editors of *Commonweal*, and anonymous	"'Priests & Sex': Other Views" (letters to the editor and responses), *Commonweal*, January 15, 1993.
Robert E. Burns	"Let the Publicity Fit the Crime," *U.S. Catholic*, January 1992.
Alexander Cockburn	"Out of the Mouths of Babes: Child Abuse and the Abuse of Adults," *Nation*, February 12, 1990.
Canice Connors	"Priests and Pedophilia: A Silence that Needs Breaking?" *America*, May 9, 1992.
Eric Felten	"Ritual Child Sex Abuse: Much Ado About Nothing," *Insight*, October 7, 1991. Available from 3600 New York Ave. NE, Washington, DC 20002.
Susan J. Kelley, Renee Brant, and Jill Waterman	"Sexual Abuse of Children in Day Care Centers," *Child Abuse & Neglect*, vol. 17 (1993). Available from Susan J. Kelley, Boston College School of Nursing, Chestnut Hill, MA 02167.
John Allan Loftus	"A Question of Disillusionment: Sexual Abuse Among the Clergy," *America*, December 1, 1990.
Dorothy Rabinowitz	"From the Mouths of Babes to a Jail Cell: Child Abuse and the Abuse of Justice: A Case Study," *Harper's*, May 1990.
Elizabeth S. Rose	"Surviving the Unbelievable," *Ms.*, January/February 1993.
Hollida Wakefield and Ralph Underwager	"Assessing Credibility of Children's Testimony in Ritual Sexual Abuse Allegations," *Issues in Child Abuse Accusations*, Winter 1992.
David Whitman	"Beyond Thrift and Loyalty: An Identity Crisis Looms for the Boy Scouts," *U.S. News & World Report*, January 14, 1991.
Kenneth L. Woodward	"The Sins of the Father," *Newsweek*, June 1, 1992 .

How Should the Legal System Respond to Child Abuse?

Chapter Preface

Until recently, children were judged not competent to testify in court. Since many cases of child abuse—especially sexual abuse—have no witnesses other than the child and the abuser and leave no clear physical evidence, the child's memories are often the only evidence available to prosecutors. This once meant that many child abusers went free. Since the passage of the Victims of Child Abuse Act in 1990, though, children have been presumed to be competent witnesses under federal law. Because children can now testify, the suggestibility of their memory has become a question with grave legal consequences.

Scientists do not yet understand exactly how memory works, but they have learned that it can be tampered with. For example, memory researchers have found that leading or suggestive questions may help people remember events, and make the memories stronger and more easily recalled later. However, as Anastasia Toufexis warns in *Time*, "Suggestion is a potent disrupter of truth." Researchers have found that under suggestive questioning, some children can infer what adults want to hear and incorporate this information into their answers. Some think the children may even come to believe these answers: "Kids can be fed ideas they quickly come to believe are true," asserts professor of psychology Lenore Terr.

Other researchers find that while children may adopt such false information on minor points, on major points—such as whether they were sexually assaulted—their memories are at least as reliable as those of adults. With proper questioning techniques, they contend, children can be excellent witnesses, and when they say they were abused, they should be believed. As researcher Debra Whitcomb writes in *When the Victim Is a Child*, children's errors of memory are more likely to be omission than commission—forgetting, rather than adding false information. "Even after a one-year delay," she notes, "children do not make false reports of sexual abuse, although they may mistakenly report certain facts about the incident in question."

Judging the reliability of adult witnesses has traditionally been within the purview of the jury. Now jurors must also judge for themselves the competency and reliability of child witnesses. The stakes are high: Innocent adults could be sent to prison, or children may be returned to molesters to be assaulted again. The challenge for the legal system is to protect children and punish abusers while still ensuring that innocent adults are not unfairly convicted of child abuse. The authors of the following viewpoints examine how the legal system can meet this challenge and adequately respond to charges of child abuse.

"The veracity of sexually abused children has been analyzed by researchers, all of whom report that false accusations are extremely rare."

Child Testimony Must Be Believed

Billie Wright Dziech and Charles B. Schudson

Prosecutors' misunderstanding of children and jurors' predisposition to doubt children's testimony make it difficult for young victims of abuse to win justice in the legal system, according to Billie Wright Dziech and Charles B. Schudson. In the following viewpoint, the authors examine children's testimony in light of information on child development and find that, when properly examined, children can and do give reliable testimony. Dziech, assistant to the dean and professor of language arts at the University of Cincinnati, has written and lectured on sexual harassment and women's issues. Schudson, a Wisconsin court of appeals judge, is a member of the faculties of the National Council of Juvenile and Family Court Judges and the National Judicial College.

As you read, consider the following questions:

1. According to Dziech and Schudson, what are the major motivations for preschoolers to lie?
2. In what cases might children be less susceptible than adults to manipulation of testimony, according to the authors?
3. Why do the authors believe that children's fantasizing does not affect their ability to give reliable testimony about abuse they have suffered?

The history of childhood is a record of neglect and violence by adults who learned too little too slowly about children's differences. Even at the end of the twentieth century, child libertarian Richard Farson can observe: "Our world is not a good place for children. Every institution in our society severely discriminates against them. We all come to feel that it is either natural or necessary to cooperate in that discrimination. Unconsciously, we carry out the will of a society which holds a limited and demeaned view of children and which refuses to recognize their right to full humanity." Nowhere is discrimination against children more apparent than in the legal system's treatment of victims of sexual abuse. Because we do indeed hold "a limited and demeaned view of children," we cooperate in the discrimination they suffer in the system. . . .

Prosecutors' reluctance to pursue cases relying on children's testimonies is often reluctance born of misunderstanding—a misunderstanding of children corresponding to assumptions about children held by jurors. Significant numbers of child molesters are never brought to trial because prosecutors know that even when child witnesses do survive the rigors of the adversarial system in order to testify, juries are predisposed to doubt their testimonies. . . .

A Context for Evaluating Children's Testimony

If trials are genuine searches for truth, that truth must be sought in light of society's modern understanding of children rather than in subservience to age-old biases and ignorance. Adults who assume that their own perceptions, motivations, and fears are universal cannot empathize with children caught between the horrors of sexual abuse and the criminal justice system. Adults who doubt children because of false assumptions about their perception, memory, suggestibility, and truthfulness cannot fairly evaluate their testimony in the courtroom.

Yet there is a reliable body of information that could be used to establish a context for the evaluation of child testimony. While some of our knowledge of children is as yet inconclusive, we can differentiate with some precision the certainties from the areas of disagreement or lack of information. Although there are individual differences in children and although professionals have defined and described the various stages of child development in sometimes esoteric ways, it is possible to capture for the prosecutor, the judge, and the jurors the essential features of a child at a given stage of life. Many adult concerns about the child witness can then be addressed. . . .

Below is a series of questions that a typical adult might ask about a child witness in a sexual abuse case. The discussion following each question . . . explains why a child might respond to abuse in a particular fashion. . . . The question and answer segments here are based upon children at . . . the preschool stage. . . .

Do Children Lie?

[After alleging abuse], several times this child denied that an assault occurred. Isn't that proof there was no sexual abuse?

Any recantation demands attention, but denial is predictable in child sexual abuse cases and does not mean that assault did not occur. Once a child has disclosed an account of abuse, denials almost inevitably follow. . . .

Children's denial is a tempting way for adults to make the problem appear to go away, but they can never trust it as proof that nothing happened. Once a child risks an account of sexual abuse, the inevitable recantation must be judged in the total context of the child's statements and actions. Adults charged with protecting and providing justice for children must anticipate recantation and be prepared to ask why it occurred and what it means to the search for truth. Unfortunately, this seldom occurs. In case after case, recantations capture headlines and adversely affect jurors' decisions.

Don't children lie? Aren't false accusations about sexual abuse common?

Children do not commonly make false claims of being sexually abused. Underreporting and denial are far more common. In their article "The Testimony of the Child Victim of Sexual Assault," Lucy Berliner and Mary Kay Barbieri establish that

> while adults are often skeptical when children report sexual abuse . . . there is little or no evidence indicating that children's reports are unreliable, and none at all to support the fear that children often make false accusations of sexual assault or misunderstand innocent behavior by adults. The general veracity of children's reports is supported by relatively high rates of admission by the offenders. . . . Not a single study has ever found false accusations of sexual assault a plausible interpretation of a substantial portion of cases.

The veracity of sexually abused children has been analyzed by researchers, all of whom report that false accusations are extremely rare. A study by Jonathan Horowitz, professor of clinical psychiatry at Boston University Medical School, found a 5 percent invalidity rate among reports by Boston children. In Denver, David Jones, a psychiatrist at the Kempe Center, reported the fabrication rate to be 2 percent or less. In another survey of Child Protection Services social workers in North Carolina, M.D. Everson and B.W. Boat differentiated children according to age groups and found among children under the age of three a 1.6 percent false allegation rate; among three- to six-year-olds 1.7 percent, among six- to twelve-year-olds, 4.3

percent; and among adolescents, 8 percent. . . .

The adult notion that children lie about sexual abuse is illogical to those who have studied them closely. Few three-year-olds have the will or capacity to process a lie, and the ability of children of four or five to formulate an untruth is offset by their inability to sustain the falsehood. . . .

Courtroom trauma

David Seavey, © 1989 *USA Today*. Reprinted with permission.

Preschoolers' characteristic motivations for lying are simple to discern. They may lie to express very intense desires. A child desperately wishing to travel to Disney World might tell a friend, "This morning my mom and I went to Disney World, and then we came home and ate lunch." Children may also lie to avoid punishment. Confronted with his parent's discovery of a broken vase, a four-year-old boy may argue that his sister was the culprit; when that story is unsuccessful, he may persist:

"Well, she made me do it." But the motivation to avoid punishment usually leads to silence, not false allegations. The fear of punishment allows an abuser to convince a child that punishment will follow if the truth is told.

The third major motivation for preschoolers to lie is to please their parents. This is the most frequent cause of false allegations. In a study by David Jones and Mary McQuiston, for example, only 45 of 309 allegations were found to be fictitious, and 36 of these were adult-initiated. While the significance and potential danger of false allegations must be acknowledged, it is clear that educated professionals can develop awareness of these motives. . . .

Are Children's Memories Easy to Manipulate?

But even if this child believes the account she or he gave, how do I know an adult didn't create the story? Aren't children very open to suggestion by others?

How likely is the possibility that an adult will be able to deceive a child into believing that he or she was sexually abused? While much more needs to be known before we achieve full understanding of children's suggestibility, certain points are clear. Adults are not, as many assume, immune to suggestive influences; and children are not as easily or as often manipulated as some suppose. . . .

The bulk of current research suggests that children may be more open to external influence if an event is less personally interesting, significant, or memorable or if it did not actually occur. On the other hand, there may be instances in which they are less susceptible to suggestion than adults. Because of their greater experience, adults may draw inaccurate inferences when processing information, while children will be less likely to do so and will thus be less likely to respond to suggestive influence by others. For example, precisely because of their more limited knowledge of sexuality, preschoolers might be far more difficult to manipulate into giving repeated and complex false descriptions of a sexual act than an adolescent or adult. . . .

This may be a case where the child believes his or her own fantasy. After all, don't children tend to confuse fact and fantasy?

The assumption that children cannot distinguish their fantasies from reality derives from everyday experience. Children tell of imaginary playmates and impossible personal feats and are often convinced they can alter reality with their own wishes. . . .

Perhaps the salient issue is not whether or not children fantasize. Of course they do. The crucial question is whether their normal fantasizing process has an impact on their perceptions and descriptions of sexual abuse. While the research is limited, one conclusion is certain: children sometimes do not distinguish between what they actually have done and what they have fantasized doing; but they do readily differentiate what they've done and fantasized doing from what they have perceived. Marcia Johnson and Mary Ann Foley explain:

> The belief is pervasive that children have more difficulty than adults in discriminating what they perceive from what they imagine, but it has little direct experimental support. Children in our studies did not appear to be more likely to confuse what they had imagined or done with what they had perceived. On the other hand, young children did have particular difficulty discriminating what they had done from what they had only thought of doing.

Thus a young child might be expected to say, "I want to be a teacher" and "I am a teacher" with equal belief. However, this child would not confuse either assertion with "The teacher touched me between my legs." To say that children fantasize is to acknowledge the obvious, but fantasizing is part of a normal developmental stage with relatively clear boundaries. Fantasizing does not deprive children of the ability to perceive and tell about conduct outside their realm of reality or fantasy. . . .

Children Resist Misleading Suggestions

Children as young as age 4 are much less suggestible than previously thought. They are particularly resistant to misleading suggestions about "abuse."

Eugene Arthur Moore, Pamela S. Howitt, and Thomas Grier, *Juvenile & Family Court Journal*, 1991.

To some it may appear too frustrating, perhaps even impossible, for the courts to respond adequately to the rapidly growing body of knowledge about children. It took centuries for civilization to acknowledge their humanity, and it has been only in the last hundred or so years that adults have attempted to probe their separate realities and to understand the mystery of who children are and what they can and cannot do. America's courts have been slow in learning and applying even the most certain advances in child development knowledge. Because some of that information is inconclusive or obscure, the courts have not had to consider sweeping changes in the ways in which child witnesses are treated. There is, as Arlene Skolnick observes, "a tension between the tentativeness with which scientific findings should be regarded and the needs of policy-makers for clear-cut principles upon which to make decisions." What this means for the thousands of American children who are victims of sexual abuse is that recourse in the courts remains an uncertain prospect.

Child psychology will probably never yield "clear-cut principles"; but without the insight it can offer, intelligent and fair decisions are very difficult to achieve. However imperfect, developmental psychology has provided us a wealth of information about children. When that information is juxtaposed against the demands made on child witnesses, the injustice is clear. If the courts are to provide justice for children as well as defendants, they must seek greater understanding and accommodation of the realities of childhood.

"*Children can be led by a persistent interrogator to change their descriptions of what they have seen or what has been done.*"

Child Testimony Must Sometimes Be Doubted

Gail S. Goodman and Alison Clarke-Stewart

In experiments studying whether nonabused children might be led to make false reports of abuse, researchers Gail S. Goodman and Alison Clarke-Stewart tested young children to see if they would always tell the truth about events they had witnessed or experienced. As they report in the following viewpoint, the authors discovered that children may fail to disclose information unless they are asked specific, leading questions. On the other hand, suggestive leading questions can manipulate almost all young children into accepting the interviewer's interpretation of ambiguous events. The authors conclude that children may be led to make false accusations of abuse. Goodman is a professor of psychology at the University of California, Davis. Clarke-Stewart is a professor of social ecology at the University of California, Irvine.

As you read, consider the following questions:

1. What are some of the difficulties Goodman and Clarke-Stewart list in studying children's suggestibility in sexual abuse cases?
2. What dangers do the authors see in the use of leading questions in interrogating victims of child sexual abuse?

When an adult is suspected of sexually abusing a child, in most states a report is made to county child abuse registries and then referred to a social worker and police for investigation. A key part of these investigations is an interview with the child who is the alleged victim. The belief that children are susceptible to suggestions made by adult interrogators has raised apprehension about the accuracy of information obtained from children during such interviews. Similar concerns have been voiced about the credibility of children who testify in court after extensive "preparation" by authorities. Some fear that the use of leading questioning by legal and mental health professionals is resulting in false allegations of abuse and consequently prosecution and conviction of innocent adults. Others claim that children do not report abuse readily and that leading questioning may be necessary to facilitate children's disclosures. . . .

The studies described here represent two independent efforts to explore issues of children's suggestibility in relation to sexual abuse cases. To design research that approaches the issues of sexual abuse and suggestibility in an ecologically valid and ethical manner is a challenge. We could not, for the sake of our research, actively abuse or threaten children. We could not observe actual sexual abuse occurring naturalistically and then document children's recounting of their experiences. We could not pose as social workers or police about to remove children from their homes. In considering the experiments we describe, we acknowledge that sexual abuse of young children and subsequent social service and police investigations are unique events; they have no perfect analogies in the lab. The results of our studies, therefore, are inevitably limited in their applicability.

It should also be kept in mind, however, that our studies are not so much concerned with simulating abusive events as they are with testing the claim that nonabused children can be led by adult interviewers to make false reports of abuse when nothing sexual or traumatic happened. Our strategy was to expose children to nonabusive events and then to interview the children in ways that mimic important features of child abuse investigations. . . .

Study: Children's Reports of Genital Contact

Karen Saywitz, Gail S. Goodman, Elisa Nicholas, and Susan Moan examined children's suggestibility about an event in which the children were undressed, their naked bodies touched, and for half of the children their genital and anal areas examined. The event was a medical checkup conducted by a pediatrician at a hospital, a checkup that typically includes a genital and anal component. Seventy-two healthy 5- and 7-year-old girls participated. All of the children experienced a standard medical checkup, but for half this included an external genital/anal examination, and for the other half it included a test for scoliosis instead. Either one week or one month later, the children were asked to recall what happened, to reenact the checkup with anatomically detailed dolls, and to answer specific and misleading questions.

Children Are Suggestible

[In a study conducted by Stephen Ceci, a psychologist at Cornell University,] for several days, preschool children in a classroom were given information about a man named either Dirty Harry or Sam Stone. They were told he was not a nice man, that he broke toys or stole things. Then a man identified as Sam Stone briefly visited their classroom, wandered around for a few minutes, but did nothing wrong.

For two minutes a week for the next three months, children were subjected to suggestive interviews about the visit. The questions were modeled after actual child-abuse interviews. "The interviewer might say, 'Remember that day Naughty Harry visited and broke the toy stove? Did he do it on purpose, or was it an accident?'" Ceci said.

Then a forensic interviewer was brought in to ask children about what Sam Stone had done. With children under 5, nearly 100 percent said Stone spilled chocolate, ripped a book or did other things that were suggested in the questioning but had not happened. If pressed further, 50 percent said they saw the events, while the rest said somebody told them about it.

Jim Okerblom, *The San Diego Union-Tribune*, February 2, 1993.

The majority of the children who experienced genital and anal touching failed to report it in open-ended interviews. They disclosed the experience only when asked specific questions— questions that would be considered leading in an actual investigation. Out of 36 girls in the genital/anal condition, 28 failed to mention genital touching in free recall, and 30 failed to demonstrate it with anatomically detailed dolls. However, when asked a yes or no question about whether they were touched in the genitals (i.e., the interviewer pointed to the vaginal area of an anatomically detailed doll and asked, "Did the doctor touch you here?"), all but five finally disclosed the experience. (The same trend held for the children's reports of anal touching.) For the 36 girls in the scoliosis condition, only three children produced a commission error in response to the specific question about genital/anal touching, and none produced errors of this sort in free recall or doll demonstration. Two of the three children who erred could not provide any detail when probed further, whereas the third child falsely claimed that the doctor had placed a stick in her rectum.

These results highlight the dilemma faced by professionals who interview children in sexual abuse cases. The findings suggest that children may not disclose genital contact unless specifically asked, but that asking may increase the chance of obtaining a false report. However, in the present study, when all of the chances to reveal genital/anal contact were considered, children failed to disclose it 64% of the time, whereas the chance of obtaining a false report of genital/anal touching was only 1%, even when leading questions were asked.

Study: How Children Interpret Actions

In an on-going series of studies conducted by Alison Clarke-Stewart, William C. Thompson, Stephen S. Lepore, and associates, the focus was not on children's accuracy in recalling whether or not certain actions occurred, but on their interpretation of actions. The basis for this research strategy was the belief that part of what transpires in sexual abuse cases depends on the interpretations that children and investigators make of incidents as being either sexually abusive or innocent.

In a research room at the university, children saw and interacted with a confederate, who followed one of two scripts. Posing as a janitor, the confederate cleaned up the research room, and then he either cleaned and arranged some toys, including a doll of the same sex as the child, or he played with the toys in a somewhat rough and suggestive manner. In both scenarios, he invited the child to join in his activities ("Would you hold the doll while I straighten its legs?"). The two scenarios were balanced with respect to the confederate's specific actions, but those actions had different meanings depending on whether the confederate was cleaning or playing.

When he was cleaning, the confederate said such things as: "This doll is dirty. I'd better clean it" as he sprayed and wiped the doll's face. "I'd better see if it's dirty here, too," as he looked under its clothes. When he was playing, the confederate, performing roughly the same actions, said: "I like to play with dolls. I like to spray them in the face with water. I like to look under their clothes." In some cases, after the confederate had played with the toys, he also asked the child not to tell what he had done.

An hour or so later, an interviewer (the janitor's "boss") came into the playroom and interrogated the child in one of three ways. She was neutral and nonsuggestive, asking open-ended questions. Or she was "incriminating," accusing the janitor of

189

playing with the toys instead of doing his job. At first, she made a gentle suggestion: "Did you see the cleaning man when he was in here? I need to know what he has been doing. You know his job is to clean the room and the toys. But he sometimes stops working and plays with the toys. He's not supposed to do that. Would you tell me what the janitor did with the toys when he was in here?" Then, her suggestions became stronger and more accusatory: "This doll didn't need to be cleaned. Did you see any dirt on it? Why would the janitor clean a doll that wasn't dirty? Do you suppose he might just have wanted to play with it? Maybe he pretended to clean it but really he was playing?" And finally, if the child continued to insist that the janitor was just cleaning: "I happened to know that the janitor is not a good worker. I don't believe he was just cleaning the toys. So come on and tell me the truth. The janitor was playing, right?" The third style of interrogation was "exculpating," as the interviewer made the claim in progressively stronger suggestions, which paralleled the incriminating arguments, that the janitor was only cleaning the toys and not playing with them.

Open-Ended Questions

At the end of the interrogation, the interviewer asked the child an open-ended, free-report question: "Now just to be sure I have the story straight because I have to make a report, why don't you tell me again what the janitor did to these toys?" Then she asked 17 standard, factual questions (e.g., "Did the janitor wipe the doll's face? Did he kiss the doll?") and finally, she asked the child six fixed-choice, interpretive questions (e.g., "So what do you really think, was the janitor cleaning the toys or playing with them? Was he doing his job or was he being bad?").

After this first interrogation, a second interviewer followed up with another interrogation, which was either in line with the first or opposite it, and then, finally, at the end of the entire session, the child's parent asked the child about what the janitor had done. A week after the session, a follow-up questionnaire was mailed to the parent to investigate more long-term effects of the manipulation.

One hundred 5- and 6-year-old children were randomly assigned to the conditions in this ongoing study. Of particular interest are the children whose interrogations were inconsistent with what they had actually seen, the children who saw the confederate clean and then heard an incriminating interrogation, and the children who saw the confederate play and then heard an exculpating interrogation. Children who heard interrogations consistent with what they had witnessed, or who heard the neutral interrogation, provided necessary baselines for assessing children's testimony in this situation. . . .

Consistent with other research, when the children in this study were given no leading suggestions or no persuasive interrogation, or when the interrogation they received was consistent with what they had observed, their answers to the interviewer's questions were limited, but accurate. On the 17 standard factual questions, on the average, the children answered 14 questions correctly, and on the final, interpretive questions, they answered at least 5 of the 6 questions correctly. They continued to answer the questions accurately a week later on the follow-up questionnaire.

Results of Leading Interrogations

When children heard an interrogation that was inconsistent with what they had observed, however, it was a different story. Even after the first gentle suggestion, one-quarter of the children answered the interviewer's questions about what the janitor had done inaccurately, following the interrogator's suggestion. By the end of the interrogator's strong suggestions, only one-quarter of the children were still reporting accurately what the janitor had done; two-thirds had switched from what they had seen to what the interrogator had said; the other few children were maintaining that the janitor had both cleaned and played. On the six final interpretive questions at the end of this interrogation, 90% of the children who heard an interrogation that was inconsistent with the scenario they had witnessed answered at least four of the questions in line with the interrogation rather than the scenario; only one child answered all six questions accurately.

When the second interrogation was of the same type as the first, moreover, the suggestion planted in the first interrogation carried over to the second. When the second interviewer first asked what the janitor had done, only one-sixth of the children gave accurate responses, and, by the end of the second interrogation, only one child who heard an interrogation that was inconsistent with the confederate scenario gave fewer than 6 out of 6 responses to the interpretive questions in line with the interrogation. Nor did the children change their stories when questioned by their parents at the end of the session: All the children answered the questions posed by their parents consistently in line with the interrogators' interpretation of the confederate's activities, and one week later, on the follow-up questionnaire, the children generally retained these interpretations.

When the second interrogation was contradictory to the first, most children tended to change their interpretations in line with the second interrogation, but their reports were not as uniform as those of children who heard the same biased interrogation twice. A week later, their version of what had happened was a combination of cleaning and playing.

Although the biased interrogations strongly affected children's responses to the *interpretive* questions about what the confederate had done, their effect on children's recollection of the "facts" of the confederate's behavior was more subtle. Overall, the children who heard a biased interpretation inconsistent with what they had observed answered as many of the 17 standard factual questions correctly as the children who heard a neutral or a consistent interpretation. A handful of children (about one-fifth of the sample), however, consistently made errors that were in the direction suggested by the biased interpretation. Although no suggestions had been given regarding these particular details of the confederate's behavior, these children, who had seen the janitor playing with the toys and then heard interrogations suggesting that he cleaned the toys, answered affirmatively (and inaccurately) that the janitor had wiped the doll's face, said the doll's clothes were dirty, cleaned the doll's shoes, straightened the doll's cap, tied the doll's bow, and dusted under the table. . . .

Misleading Questions

Misleading questions by adults can cause children not just to lie but also to believe their falsehoods. Legal scholar Douglas Besharov of Washington's American Enterprise Institute cites the case of a three-year-old who told a social worker a story about a piece of candy being dropped into her underpants. After interviews by various child-protection workers, the story evolved into a tale that a candle had been inserted into the child's vagina. It took months of further interviews to discover that the original story had been correct.

Jerome Cramer, *Time*, March 4, 1991.

When the confederate asked the child to keep his play activities a "secret," only 7 out of 18 children admitted that he played; 3 were noncommittal, and 8 said he cleaned. These children kept up their defense of the confederate throughout the open-ended questions and, if they received a neutral interrogation, they maintained the confederate's innocence even in the final questions posed by the interrogators and by their parents. (If they received a biased interrogation, all the children went along with the interrogators' suggestions, even if the janitor had asked them to keep his secret.). . .

In sum, the children's interpretation of a somewhat ambiguous event was easily manipulated by an opinionated adult interviewer. In considering the implications of this research to sexual abuse investigations, however, the most important caveat to keep in mind is that the study did not involve allegations of sexual abuse but rather whether a janitor cleaned or played. Children may be more resistant to manipulation when the suggestions are about abusive acts, especially against the child himself or herself.

Benefits and Dangers of Suggestive Questioning

These studies suggest that obtaining accurate testimony about sexual abuse from young children is a complex task. Part of the complexity rests in the fact that there are dangers as well as benefits in the use of leading questioning with children. The benefits appear in the finding in the studies by Goodman and associates that leading questions were often necessary to elicit information from children about actual events they had experienced (genital touching). Benefits might also be inferred from the finding in the studies by Clarke-Stewart and associates that children were more likely to disclose the janitor's "secret" when the interviewer made strong and persistent suggestions.

The dangers of suggestive questioning lie in children's adding erroneous information to their accounts of what has occurred. The children in the study by Goodman and associates were generally accurate in reporting specific and personal things that had happened to them. If these results can be generalized to investigations of abuse, they suggest that normal children are unlikely to make up details of sexual acts when nothing abusive happened. They suggest that children will not easily yield to an interviewer's suggestion that something sexual occurred when in fact it did not, especially if nonintimidating interviewers ask questions children can comprehend. However, leading questions also resulted in a small number of children making errors that could be misinterpreted as suggesting that abuse had occurred.

A small number of children also made errors in reporting the details of what they had seen in the studies by Clarke-Stewart and associates. These errors were in line with suggestive questioning by a biased interviewer. In addition, in the Clarke-Stewart studies, even those children who reported the facts accurately were swayed in their overall interpretation of events. If these findings can be generalized to abuse investigations, they suggest that young children might be led to mislabel or misinterpret acts when something nonabusive occurred that could be confused with abuse. Children do not make up facts often, both studies agree, but Clarke-Stewart's findings indicate that children can be led by a persistent interrogator to change their descriptions of what they have seen or what has been done if the event is somewhat ambiguous to start. . . .

Our studies also do not directly answer the question, "Do children lie about sexual abuse?", and we believe there is no simple answer to this question. Even pinning down an acceptable definition of what constitutes a lie is problematic (e.g., is intentional deceit required or simply a misstatement of facts?). Children in our studies had motivation to lie, but the motivation derived mainly from social influence (e.g., social pressure to conform to suggestion) rather than other possible sources (e.g., the desire to protect or punish a parent). However, in many cases of sexual abuse—for example, when the alleged victims are young and the defendant a nonparent, as in most preschool cases—suggestibility and not intentional lying is the central issue. Thus our studies address what has historically been and what continues to be a crucial issue in forensic investigations of the sexual assault of children.

"Criminal prosecutions for [child abuse] . . . must balance the constitutional rights guaranteed the accused with the . . . well-being of the child victim/witness."

Abused Children Should Be Spared Having to Confront Abusers in Court

Katherine A. Francis

Increasing child abuse prosecutions have forced legislatures and courts to address special problems that arise in balancing victims' and defendants' rights when the victim is a child. In its 1990 decision in *Maryland v. Craig*, the U.S. Supreme Court decided that in some instances, protecting child witnesses from trauma outweighs the right of the defendant to confront his or her accuser. In the following viewpoint, Katherine A. Francis agrees with the reasoning of the Court, contending that defendant Craig's constitutional rights were not violated when the child victim's testimony was heard via one-way closed-circuit television. Francis received her law degree from the University of Cincinnati College of Law.

As you read, consider the following questions:

1. What did the U.S. Supreme Court state were the main goals of the Confrontation Clause of the U.S. Constitution?
2. In the *Craig* case, what was the compelling state interest that justified denying the defendant's right to physical confrontation of her accusers?

From Katherine A. Francis, "To Hide in Plain Sight: Child Abuse, Closed Circuit Television, and the Confrontation Clause," *University of Cincinnati Law Review* 60 (3): 827-56, © 1992 by The University of Cincinnati. Reprinted with permission.

In October, 1986, Sandra Ann Craig was charged with child abuse, first and second degree sexual offenses, perverted sexual practice, and battery. Brooke Etze, the six-year-old victim, had attended for two years a prekindergarten and kindergarten center owned and operated by Craig. Prior to trial, the State of Maryland moved to invoke a Maryland statutory procedure that allowed the judge to receive, via one-way closed circuit television, Brooke's testimony and the testimony of several other child witnesses alleged to be victims of Craig's abuse. Pursuant to this procedure, the trial judge made a preliminary finding that, if forced to testify in the courtroom, Brooke and the other child witnesses would suffer severe emotional distress and would be unable to communicate. Once the procedure was invoked, Brooke, the prosecutor, lead defense counsel, and a video technician went into the trial judge's chambers while the judge, jury, Craig, Craig's other defense attorney, and another prosecutor stayed in the courtroom. During direct and cross-examination in the separate room, Brooke's testimony was transmitted and displayed in the courtroom for the judge, jury, and Craig. Craig was at all times in electronic communication with defense counsel. Counsel could make objections and the judge could rule on them as if Brooke were testifying in the courtroom. Brooke could at no time during questioning see Craig.

Objection to Televised Testimony

Craig objected to the invocation of the procedure on Confrontation Clause grounds. (The Confrontation Clause is found in the Sixth Amendment to the United States Constitution. The clause reads, in pertinent part: "In all criminal prosecutions, the accused shall enjoy the right . . . to be confronted with the witnesses against him. . . .") The trial court overruled Craig's objection, stating that although the procedure precluded a physical confrontation between Craig and Brooke, it adequately preserved the essence of the right of confrontation: to observe, cross-examine, and have the jury see the witness's demeanor. The trial court also adopted the findings of a psychologist regarding the severe emotional strain that would affect the child witnesses should they be required to testify in Craig's presence. The children were found to be competent to testify and were permitted to do so via the one-way closed circuit television presentation. The jury convicted Craig on all counts charged and the Maryland Court of Special Appeals affirmed the convictions.

The Court of Appeals of Maryland reversed the decision of the appellate court and remanded for a new trial. . . .

On appeal . . . the United States Supreme Court . . . addressed the question . . . whether the Sixth Amendment allowed an exception to the right to physical confrontation. After stating that the main goals of the Confrontation Clause were the rights to have adverse witnesses testify under oath, to have an opportunity to cross-examine them, and to have the fact-finder observe their demeanor while on the witness stand, the Court then examined whether the Maryland statutory procedure adequately safeguarded these goals. The Court concluded that the protection of Brooke and the other child witnesses was a compelling state interest that supported the closed circuit television procedure, and that Craig's rights to cross-examine, observe the proceedings, and ensure that the jury observed the witness's demeanor were not abrogated by the procedure. . . .

The Confrontation Clause

The Confrontation Clause has spawned much litigation and commentary. Although its text seems clear, the courts have disagreed over the central concerns embodied in the clause. . . .

Three of the oft-litigated guarantees of the Confrontation Clause [are] physical or face-to-face confrontation, cross-examination, and the exclusion of hearsay testimony.

Physical Confrontation. Physical confrontation is expressly guaranteed by the Confrontation Clause and has often been the focus of the United States Supreme Court. The most recent case that addressed the issue in child abuse cases was *Coy v. Iowa.* In 1988, the United States Supreme Court reiterated the clause's explicit language and held that the Confrontation Clause protected not only the right to cross-examine, but also the guarantee of face-to-face, physical confrontation by the accused of adverse or hostile witnesses. . . .

A Sigh of Relief

Based on the authority of *Maryland v. Craig,* a major ruling on the constitutionality of closed-circuit television, professionals who work with victims of sexual abuse can, at least for now, breathe a sigh of relief. Because of this decision, as well as past decisions, legislatures have been able to construct more constitutionally sound statutes that can protect children from additional abuse by the judicial system.

Wendi K. Cartwright, *Family Violence Bulletin,* Summer 1991.

The Court dissected the term "confront" into its Latin roots and stated that both literal meaning of the word confrontation and the explicit text of the clause demonstrated that it guaranteed face-to-face, physical confrontation with witnesses at trial.

It stated that notions of fairness and justice made physical confrontation an essential step in a criminal prosecution. . . .

The Court expressly reserved the question of whether any exceptions to the right to physical confrontation were proper, but stated that exceptions would be allowed only when indispensable to the furtherance of an important public policy.

Cross-Examination. Cross-examination has also been the subject of much debate in the United States Supreme Court and is regarded as one of the Confrontation Clause's derivative rights. The United States Supreme Court decided *Douglas v. Alabama* on the same day as *Pointer v. Texas* and held that denying the accused the opportunity to cross-examine a hostile witness violated the Confrontation Clause. . . .

The Hearsay Exception. The other oft-litigated issue concerning confrontation is the admissibility of an out-of-court statement of a person not available to testify in court. In *Ohio v. Roberts* [1980], the United States Supreme Court directly addressed this situation. . . .

The . . . Court, per Justice Harry Blackmun, . . . stated that strict adherence to the text of the Confrontation Clause would preclude any out-of-court statement from being admitted, even in cases where there was a reliable showing by the proponent of the statement that the declarant was unavailable. The Court developed a general approach to balance the guarantees of the Confrontation Clause with the rules of hearsay evidence. The Court stated that the Confrontation Clause provided a two-fold restriction on the admission of hearsay. First, the Clause itself required a showing of necessity before physical confrontation would be denied. Normally the demonstrated unavailability of the declarant would suffice. Second, once the declarant's unavailability was demonstrated, the Clause acknowledged only those hearsay statements bearing a high degree of trustworthiness and therefore imposed an "indicia of reliability requirement." The Court further stated that physical confrontation was not an absolute guarantee of the Confrontation Clause, as was the right to cross-examination; in fact, it stated that physical confrontation was only preferred, not mandated. . . .

Balancing Social Goals and Defendants' Rights

Criminal prosecutions for the physical, emotional, or sexual abuse of children in which the child victims testify against the accused pose a difficult task for the courts. They must balance the constitutional rights guaranteed the accused with the physical and psychological well-being of the child victim/witness so that the courts may attain the societal goal of the criminal process: finding the truth. . . .

Justice Sandra Day O'Connor, writing for the majority in

Maryland v. Craig . . . stated that . . . the right to meet face-to-face was not absolute where an exception was necessary to support a significant public policy. The Court in *Craig* answered affirmatively the question reserved in *Coy*: whether any exceptions indeed existed to the right of physical confrontation.

The Court proposed that the fundamental purpose of the Confrontation Clause was to test the reliability of evidence against the accused by subjecting it to thorough scrutiny in an adversarial proceeding before the ultimate trier of fact. A fundamental premise behind the guarantee was the abolition of trial by affidavit. By putting the adverse witness on the stand under oath and subjecting the witness to cross-examination, the judge or jury was allowed to observe the witness's performance and demeanor during testimony. The Court stated that although this manner of physical confrontation increased the accuracy of fact-finding, the face-to-face element was not a mandate of the guarantee. Rather, the Court found that cross-examination was the element that satisfied the Confrontation Clause because cross-examination provided the accused the chance to probe for and discover weaknesses in the witness's testimony. Because cross-examination was considered sufficient to fulfill the guarantees of the Confrontation Clause, the Court stated that the right to physical confrontation could be subordinated, in very limited circumstances, to competing significant interests. . . .

Triggering an Exception

The Court warned, however, that triggering an exception to the preference of physical confrontation was not an easy task and could be accomplished only when necessary to further an important public policy and when the reliability of the testimony already had been established.

The Court then turned to examine the Maryland statutory procedure and determined that it provided for every element of confrontation except the physical aspect. The Court stressed that the procedure required that Brooke be competent to testify and that she be questioned under oath, underscoring in the child's mind the seriousness of the occasion and ensuring the testimony's reliability. Craig was at all times in contact with counsel, who was able to fully examine and cross-examine the witness. Also, the television medium provided the judge and jury with a clear view of Brooke's demeanor under questioning. The Court then concluded that the one-way closed circuit television procedure would not violate the Confrontation Clause if the procedure were used to further an important public policy of the state of Maryland.

Next, the Court had to determine whether Maryland's stated interest in protecting children alleged to be victims of abuse from the trauma of testifying in their alleged abuser's presence was an interest compelling enough to support a procedure which denied Craig her right to physical confrontation with Brooke. The Court balanced the state's interests and Craig's rights and allowed the state's interests to prevail. The Court supported its decision with evidence of similar statutory protective procedures and provisions in other jurisdictions and with documentary evidence of the physical and psychological trauma suffered by children who were forced to testify in court. The Court deferred to the Maryland legislature's determination of the need for such statutory protection of abused children and held that this interest was important enough to create an exception to the Sixth Amendment right to confrontation.

The Court did, however, place strict safeguards around this exception and established a three-part test for determining necessity on a case-by-case basis. First, the trial court must hear evidence on and decide whether the one-way closed circuit television procedure is necessary to protect the testifying child witness. Second, the trial court must find that the child witness would be traumatized by the accused's presence in the courtroom and not simply by the unfamiliar courtroom atmosphere. Third, the distress suffered by the child must be "more than *de minimis*." (The Court defined the requisite level of emotional trauma as something "more than 'mere nervousness or excitement or some reluctance to testify.'") The Court found that the Maryland statute's requirement of a finding of severe emotional distress and communicative incapacitation fulfilled the emotional trauma requirement. . . .

The Purposes of the Confrontation Clause

The scope of the Confrontation Clause has been defined and redefined by both courts and commentators for years. Three main purposes have been generally accepted: 1) to reject trial and conviction by affidavit and thereby ensure truthful testimony; 2) to allow the accused an opportunity to cross-examine her accusers; and 3) to present to the trier of fact the demeanor of the witnesses presented against the accused. The argument to support these purposes is the integrity of the fact-finding process. That flagship rationale must be adhered to, even if certain of the purposes, or derivative rights, flowing from the Confrontation Clause must be somewhat limited. In a child abuse prosecution, the shame, fear, and confusion experienced by a victimized child may be overwhelming on the witness stand in front of the alleged abuser, causing the child to withdraw and be unable to testify about the act allegedly committed. Parents of abused children may also send mixed signals—while trying to protect their children from trauma in the courtroom they may not cooperate with the prosecution. This, too, hinders the fact-finding process and may allow an abuser to go unpunished. . . .

Craig Helps Child Victims Testify Effectively

The legal system must become sensitive to the special developmental characteristics of children and respond in a way which maximizes the likelihood that they will testify effectively. The *Craig* majority took an important step on the road to that goal.

Eugene Arthur Moore, Pamela S. Howitt, and Thomas Grier, *Juvenile & Family Court Journal*, 1991.

In *Craig*, the Maryland statutory procedure gave the respondent every constitutional safeguard provided by the Confrontation Clause. Before allowing invocation of the procedure the judge listened to expert testimony regarding the physical and emotional reactions the children would suffer had they been required to testify in Craig's presence. The individualized findings of fact were made in this case, thus fulfilling the *Coy* prerequisite of case-specific determinations of inability to testify before limiting the accused's right to physical confrontation. The children were then held competent to testify and did so under oath. The closed-circuit television transmission of the children's direct and cross-examination offered Craig, the judge, and the jury a complete view of the examining attorneys and the witnesses, including close-ups to study the physical responses to certain questions. Also, the electronic audio connection between Craig and her attorney while the attorney was in the room with the witnesses gave Craig every opportunity to confer with counsel and discuss lines of questioning or develop strategies. Both the video and audio hookups kept the judge in complete control of the proceedings because objections could be made from the annexed room and ruled upon in the courtroom. Thus, Craig was given a full opportunity to effectively cross-examine witnesses against her in an adversarial proceeding.

Craig Preserved Rights of Victim and Accused

The safeguards to the accused that were provided for in the Maryland statute and required by the trial court in *Craig* preserved Craig's Sixth Amendment right to confrontation. She was able to fully cross-examine the witnesses, who were under oath during their testimony, and the judge and jury were able to view the witness's demeanor during questioning and her reactions via the television transmission. These safeguards—oaths, cross-examination, and observance—were fulfilled completely in *Craig*, although the United States Supreme Court allowed Craig's right to physical confrontation to be subordinated to Maryland's interest in protecting victims of child abuse.

The Court agreed that Maryland's public policy as codified by statute was a compelling state interest based on the serious child abuse problem in the United States and the resulting trauma to child witnesses, not to mention the high percentage of unsuccessful prosecutions for child abuse and child sexual assault. Also, individualized findings regarding the propriety of applying the statute were made before its invocation. The important public policy was upheld in *Craig* with minimal limitation on the rights of the accused. Every constitutional guarantee in the Confrontation Clause was provided, except physical confrontation. Even though Craig was not physically confronting her young accuser, the purposes of physical confrontation were achieved through the elaborate procedures instituted by the trial court. In sum, both the accused's rights and the child victim/witness's physical and emotional well-being were preserved by invocation of the Maryland protective statutory procedure.

"Face-to-face confrontation 'may . . . confound and undo the false accuser, or reveal the child coached by a malevolent adult.'"

Abused Children Should Confront Abusers in Court

Robert H. King Jr.

In the case of *Maryland v. Craig,* the U.S. Supreme Court decided that defendants do not always have the right to directly confront their accusers in court. The Court was wrong, charges Robert H. King Jr. In the following viewpoint, King argues that children who make accusations of abuse must face the accused in court. To allow children to avoid such confrontations threatens the constitutional rights of the accused, King concludes. King is a litigation attorney dealing in commercial and insurance cases in San Francisco.

As you read, consider the following questions:

1. What victims besides molested children does King believe the state might have a special interest in protecting?
2. In the majority opinion in the *Craig* case, what tests did Justice Sandra Day O'Connor say must be met before the right to face-to-face confrontation between accuser and defendant could be denied?
3. According to Justice Antonin Scalia, why was the Supreme Court's debate over the Confrontation Clause inappropriate?

From Robert H. King Jr., "The Molested Child Witness and the Constitution: Should the Bill of Rights Be Transformed into the Bill of Preferences?" *Ohio State Law Journal* 53 (1): 49-99, © 1992 by The Ohio State University. Reprinted with permission.

A divided Supreme Court held in *Maryland v. Craig* [1990] that the Sixth Amendment's unambiguous command that "the accused shall enjoy the right . . . to be confronted with the witnesses against him" reflects a mere "*preference* for face-to-face confrontation at trial" which can be countermanded when "necessary to further an important public policy and . . . where the reliability of the testimony is otherwise assured." The "public policy" identified by the *Craig* Court was the State's interest in "the physical and psychological well-being of child abuse victims." Because this "public policy" was deemed sufficiently important, and because the reliability of testimony taken via one-way closed circuit television was purportedly "otherwise assured," the child could testify outside the presence of the defendant.

The *Craig* decision is a radical departure from the Supreme Court's pronouncement only two years earlier in *Coy v. Iowa* that "the Confrontation Clause *guarantees* the defendant a face-to-face meeting with the witness appearing before the trier of fact." The transformation of the Confrontation Clause's explicit "guarantee" into a mere "preference" in the name of social policy could lead to the virtual elimination of the right to confrontation. Presumably the State has an equally important interest in protecting the traumatized rape victim, the elderly assault victim, or the victim of gang violence. If the Bill of Rights is transformed into the "Bill of Preferences," all of the defendant's "preferences"—from the "preference" for jury trial to the "preference" for counsel—may be ignored if the State's interest is deemed sufficiently "important.". . .

Prosecuting Child Molestation

Child molestation is one of the most difficult crimes to detect and prosecute because often the only witness is the child victim. Studies suggest that a child victimized by abuse is traumatized further when required to testify during the prosecution of the alleged molester. In a 1974 study, eighty-four percent of the judges surveyed believed that children who testified in court in sexual abuse cases were traumatized as a result. Many child abuse cases are not prosecuted "as a result of problems attending the testimony of children who could not deal with the prospect of facing fathers, step-fathers, relatives and strangers in a courtroom setting," according to the ruling in *State v. Sheppard* (N.J., 1984). It has been suggested that requiring the child to confront the alleged molester is particularly frightening, and can produce a condition in which the child simply cannot speak of the incident. In recognition of the ordeal that a trial would entail, many parents simply refuse to prosecute. As of 1986, it had been "estimated that only 24% of all cases [of child molestation] nationwide result[ed] in criminal actions," according to Demetra John McBride.

In response to the rise in reported instances of sexual abuse of children and to the problems associated with the molested child witness, several states enacted laws designed to lessen the effect on children of participation in sexual molestation prosecutions. These laws have taken essentially three forms: use of closed circuit television to take the child's testimony, use of videotape depositions to present the child's testimony, and special child hearsay exceptions which permit parents or doctors to testify as to what they were told by the child. . . .

The constitutionality of some of these procedures was upheld by state courts, while others were struck down as infringing upon the defendant's Sixth Amendment rights. This divergence of view set the stage for the Court's first direct encounter with the molested child witness statutes in *Coy v. Iowa* [1988].

Coy v. Iowa

Coy v. Iowa involved the sexual assault of two thirteen-year-old girls by a man who entered their tent where they had been sleeping. . . . Neither girl ever identified the defendant as her assailant.

Seven days before the trial was to begin, the State filed a motion . . . to have the testimony of the victims taken outside the courtroom and televised by closed circuit television, or alternatively that the defendant be confined behind a screen or mirror that would permit him to see and hear the girls but would not allow the witnesses to see the defendant. The State's motion did not set forth any justification for invoking these procedures. The defense objected, arguing that since the girls were unable to identify the defendant as their assailant, testifying in his presence would not be traumatizing for them. The defense also argued that the proposed screening device implied that the defendant was guilty, infringed on his right to confront witnesses against him, and denied him a fair trial. The trial court overruled defendant's objections, denied the State's request to take the testimony outside the courtroom, but ordered that a one-way screening structure be erected in the courtroom. The defendant was convicted and appealed.

The Iowa Supreme Court held that the use of the screening device did not offend the Confrontation Clause. The court rejected the notion that the purpose of the Confrontation Clause was to require that the defendant be allowed the privilege of idly gazing upon all witnesses. Rather, the court held that the Confrontation Clause serves to insure that (1) witnesses will testify in court in full view of the court and jury so that their demeanor may be judged; (2) the testimony will be under oath to enhance its reliability; and (3) the witnesses will be subject to full cross-examination. Since it was clear that the girls' testimony was given in full view of the court and jury, under oath and subject to cross-examination, the Iowa Supreme Court found no Confrontation Clause violation.

Ben Sargent, © 1990 *Austin American-Statesman*. Reprinted with permission. All rights reserved.

By a vote of 6-2, the Supreme Court reversed. Justice Antonin Scalia, writing for the majority, traced the lineage of the Sixth Amendment's confrontation right "to the beginnings of Western legal culture," although he acknowledged that its language "comes to us on faded parchment." Justice Scalia observed . . . "'simply as a matter of English' [the Clause] confers at least 'a right to meet face to face all those who appear and give evidence at trial.'" "We have never doubted, therefore, that the Confrontation Clause guarantees the defendant a face-to-face meeting with witnesses appearing before the trier of fact."

The Court noted that the Confrontation Clause served "ends related both to appearances and realities." References to and quotations "from antiquity" were contained in the majority's opinion "to convey that there is something deep in human nature that regards face-to-face confrontation between accused and accuser as 'essential to a fair trial in a criminal prosecution.'" That perception of fairness had "much truth to it" because:

> It is always more difficult to tell a lie about a person "to his face" than "behind his back." In the former context, even if the lie is told, it will often be told less convincingly. The Confrontation Clause does not, of course, compel the witness to fix his eyes upon the defendant; he may studiously look elsewhere, but the trier of fact will draw its own conclusions. Thus the right to face-to-face confrontation serves much the same purpose as a less explicit component of the Confrontation Clause that we have had more frequent occasion to discuss—the right to cross-examine the accuser; both "insur[e] the integrity of the fact-finding process.". . .

While acknowledging that face-to-face confrontation "may, unfortunately, upset the truthful rape victim or abused child," Justice Scalia maintained that "it may confound and undo the false accuser, or reveal the child coached by a malevolent adult. It is a truism that constitutional protections have costs.". . .

Left "for another day" was whether "any exceptions exist"; any such exception would "surely be allowed only when necessary to further an important public policy.". . .

Justice Sandra Day O'Connor's concurring opinion . . . emphasized that "the Court has time and again stated that the Clause 'reflects a *preference* for face-to-face confrontation at trial,' and expressly recognized that this preference may be overcome in a particular case if close examination of 'competing interests' so warrants." Justice O'Connor wished "to make clear that nothing in today's decision necessarily dooms such efforts by state legislatures to protect child witnesses." Justice O'Connor . . . noted that . . . "the strictures of the Confrontation Clause may give way to the compelling state interest of protecting child witnesses.". . .

As the first Supreme Court opinion to address a child witness protection statute, the *Coy* decision spawned much scholarly debate. Many feared that the logic of *Coy* doomed such statutes while others saw a glimmer of hope in Justice O'Connor's concurring opinion. State courts struggled with the question left open by *Coy* as to whether any exceptions to the requirement of a face-to-face confrontation were permissible. A mere two years after the Court's decision in *Coy*, an opportunity to answer the question was presented by *Maryland v. Craig*.

Maryland v. Craig

Sandra Ann Craig was indicted in October 1986 for alleged child abuse, first- and second-degree sexual offenses, perverted sexual practice, assault and battery of one of her students over a one and a half-year period. The student in question was seven years old at the time of trial. In addition to calling the alleged victim, the State intended to call other children who had purportedly also been abused by Craig.

Before trial, the State invoked a Maryland statutory procedure that permits a child who is the victim of alleged child abuse to testify outside the presence of the judge, jury and defendant through one-way closed circuit television. Expert testimony was received concerning the difficulty that each child would experience from testifying in front of the defendant. The trial court did not question or observe any of the children.

Closed Circuit Television

Based upon the expert testimony, the court granted the State's motion to employ the one-way closed circuit television, finding that "'the testimony of each of these children in a courtroom will result in each child suffering serious emotional distress . . . such that each of these children cannot reasonably communicate.'" The trial court rejected Craig's Confrontation Clause objection to the procedure, concluding that "although the statute 'take[s] away the right of the defendant to be face to face with his or her accuser,' the defendant retains the 'essence of the right of confrontation,' including the right to observe, cross-examine, and have the jury view the demeanor of the witness."

The implementation of the closed circuit television procedure was far from ideal. The video camera technician was in chambers along with the prosecutor, defense counsel and a court clerk. Craig, an additional defense counsel, an additional prosecutor, the judge and the jury were in the courtroom. The image of the child witness was projected for viewing in the courtroom on two nineteen-inch television monitors. The jury could see only the child witness on the screens; the prosecutor and defense attorneys could be heard, but not seen.

There was concern from the outset about the defendant's ability to speak with her counsel during the testimony. The only way Craig could communicate with her counsel (who was in chambers with the child) was by means of an open phone line. The phone receiver was laid on the table next to defense counsel in chambers. Craig, seated in the jury's view in the courtroom, sat with the phone receiver to her ear and had to speak loudly enough for defense counsel to hear her through the open receiver lying on the table. The acoustics and placement of the microphone for the child witness also made it difficult to hear the testimony in the courtroom. . . .

The jury convicted Craig on all counts and the Maryland Court of Special Appeals affirmed the conviction. The Court of Appeals of Maryland reversed and remanded for a new trial. . . .

The Supreme Court granted certiorari, and in a 5-4 decision vacated the judgment of the court of appeals and remanded the case for further proceedings not inconsistent with its opinion. Although Justice O'Connor, writing for the majority, acknowledged that only two years earlier in *Coy v. Iowa* the Court had recognized that "the Confrontation Clause guarantees the defendant a face-to-face meeting with witnesses appearing before the trier of fact," she countered that "[w]e have never held, however, that the Confrontation Clause guarantees criminal defendants the *absolute* right to a face-to-face meeting with witnesses against them at trial.". . .

Justice O'Connor articulated a two-prong test to determine when face-to-face confrontation may be abrogated: "only where denial of such confrontation is necessary to further an important public policy and only where the reliability of the testimony is otherwise assured."

Justice O'Connor first evaluated the Maryland procedure's compliance with the "reliability" prong of this test. Although invocation of the Maryland statute prevented the child witness from seeing the defendant, "it preserves all of the other elements of the confrontation right": testimony under oath, contemporaneous cross-examination, and the ability of the jury to view the demeanor of the witness. . . .

The "critical inquiry" therefore became "whether use of the procedure is necessary to further an important state interest." Justice O'Connor concluded that "a State's interest in the physical and psychological well-being of child abuse victims may be sufficiently important to outweigh, at least in some cases, a defendant's right" to face-to-face confrontation. . . .

Justice Scalia's Dissent

Justice Scalia authored a blistering dissent. "Seldom has this Court failed so conspicuously to sustain a categorical guarantee of the Constitution against the tide of prevailing current opinion." He challenged the majority's assertion that face-to-face confrontation was not an "indispensable element of the Sixth Amendment's guarantee.". . . "If unconfronted testimony is admissible hearsay when the witness is unable to confront the defendant, then presumably there are other categories of admissible hearsay consisting of unsworn testimony when the witness is unable to risk perjury, uncross-examined testimony when the witness is unable to undergo hostile questioning, etc."

Justice Scalia also challenged the majority's characterization of the State's interest which supposedly outweighed "the explicit text of the Constitution." Justice Scalia did not believe that the Maryland statute was designed to protect child witnesses, because the State always has the prerogative not to call as witnesses children who will be traumatized by the experience. "The State's interest here is in fact no more and no less than what the State's interest always is when it seeks to get a class of evidence admitted in criminal proceedings: more convictions of guilty defendants. That is not an unworthy interest, but it should not be dressed up as a humanitarian one." Justice Scalia observed that the "'special' reasons that exist for suspending one of the usual guarantees of reliability in the case of children's testimony are perhaps matched by 'special' reasons for being particularly insistent upon it in the case of children's testimony [because] [s]ome studies show that children are substantially more vulnerable to suggestion than adults, and often unable to separate recollected fantasy (or suggestion) from reality."

The Impact of Testifying on Child Witnesses

Many observers, conclude intuitively that child victims are further traumatized by their participation in the legal process, particularly testifying at trial. Little is actually known, however, about the impact that testifying has on children.

In the absence of empirical support, it is premature to conclude that child victims' participation in the criminal process will prove particularly traumatizing. That participation in the criminal process can have positive effects on adult victims' psychological functioning is well-accepted, and the same may be true for child victims. Staff from two federally funded demonstration projects for the evaluation and treatment of sexual abuse (the Harborview Medical Center, Seattle, and the Children's Hospital National Medical Center, Washington, DC) have published accounts noting the positive impact that participation in the criminal process can have for child victims.

Randy K. Otto and Gary B. Melton in *Children at Risk*, 1990.

But Justice Scalia felt that this scholarly debate was inappropriate because the value of confrontation need not be defended "because the Court has no authority to question it." Justice Scalia concluded that the Court had engaged in interest-balancing "where the text of the Constitution simply does not permit it. We are not free to conduct a cost-benefit analysis of clear and explicit constitutional guarantees, and then to adjust their meaning to comport with our findings.". . .

Craig represents a significant departure from the Supreme Court's prior interpretations of the Confrontation Clause. To appreciate this, one need only recognize that for the first time in over two hundred years of Supreme Court jurisprudence, a criminal defendant, who neither waived the right to confrontation nor forfeited it by misbehavior, has been denied the right to face a witness who actually appeared and testified at trial. It is important to remember that *Craig* was not a case which required the Court to determine whether a certain type of hearsay testimony could be admitted into evidence without violating the Confrontation Clause; both the majority and dissent assumed that one-way closed circuit testimony was the functional equivalent of "in court" testimony. Instead, the majority concluded that the anticipated (but unproven) reaction of the child to the mere presence of the defendant, who, as far as the Constitution was concerned had done nothing more heinous than be *accused* of a crime, justified the invocation of a procedure that resulted in a loss of her right to face-to-face confrontation.

The Supreme Court Was Wrong

Craig was wrongly decided. The Confrontation Clause does not reflect a mere "preference" for face-to-face confrontation. The Court's conclusion to the contrary is obviously the product of what it perceives to be a logical conundrum created by the fact that the Court has allowed certain forms of hearsay to be admitted despite the Confrontation Clause's admonition. But the very limited exceptions explicitly sanctioned by the Court do not warrant the suspension of face-to-face confrontation of witnesses who actually appear and testify at trial. . . .

A fundamental problem with the Maryland statute is that it does not recognize that there are two reasons that a child might be so emotionally traumatized by testifying in the presence of the defendant that she could not communicate. The first reason is that the defendant has previously harmed her in a particularly offensive manner (and hence is guilty of the crime). But a second possible reason is that the child is afraid of testifying in the defendant's presence because she is lying. Clearly, although the state may have an important interest in protecting the child in the first instance, it has no interest in protecting the child in the latter instance. The statute authorizes use of the one-way closed circuit television procedure in both instances, impacting important constitutional rights, including the presumption of innocence and the due process right to a fair trial.

"By permitting the victim to sue when she discovers the injury and its cause, . . . ultimately there will be a decline in . . . childhood sexual assault."

Child Abuse Cases Should Have Extended Statutes of Limitations

Kristin E. Rodgers

Traditionally, when an injury occurs, a victim has a limited period of time to charge or sue the perpetrator. This period is called the statute of limitations. In the case of child abuse, however, some people do not remember being abused until years after the statute of limitations has run out. In the following viewpoint, Kristin E. Rodgers argues that in child abuse cases, the statute of limitations should begin to run when a victim discovers that he or she was abused, or determines that the abuse has caused damage, even if the discovery occurs decades after the abuse. Rodgers received her law degree from the Catholic University Law School in Washington, D.C.

As you read, consider the following questions:

1. According to Rodgers, what two harms must the court balance when deciding whether to try claims from many years ago?
2. How does the author propose to alleviate the skepticism of those who believe psychotherapists may unduly influence victims' memories of abuse?

From Kristin E. Rodgers, "Childhood Sexual Abuse: Perceptions on Tolling the Statute of Limitations," *The Journal of Contemporary Health Law and Policy* 8 (1): 309-31, © 1992 by The Catholic University of America. Reprinted with permission.

[W]ith the first-born safely submerged and "sleeping" from the age of two, the other Troop members began to evolve one by one and to undergo the abuse for her. The evolution of yet other selves in effect buried the first-born child deeper over the years.

Robert A. Phillips Jr., *The Troops for*
Truddi Chase, When Rabbit Howls

Truddi Chase was sexually abused by her stepfather from the age of two until the age of sixteen. She has not filed a complaint against her abuser, nor does she intend to. Essentially she no longer exists. Truddi Chase's body is a shelter for her inner world of ninety-two personalities that developed over forty years, enabling her to cope with the emotional and physical trauma that arises from sexual abuse.

Like Truddi Chase, many sexually abused children are not aware of their psychological problems until they become adults. While Truddi Chase chose to contribute to the medical profession's understanding and treatment of adult victims of incest, other victims of this abuse decide to sue their abusers in court. However, these lawsuits are often dismissed on procedural grounds and the victims never receive their day in court.

Statutes of Limitations

Statutes of limitations are imposed on both civil and criminal actions to assist the courts in their pursuit of the truth by barring stale claims and to protect potential defendants from the protracted fear of litigation. Numerous courts have addressed policy concerns in limiting the time to bring certain tort claims, namely claims of intentional infliction of emotional harm. These policies: 1) question whether relevant evidence will become stale, lost, or destroyed; 2) recognize the need for judicial economy; 3) address "the possibility of continuing 'blackmail' by potential plaintiffs"; 4) perceive an unfairness to potential defendants who may be required to defend themselves long after the alleged act; and 5) acknowledge the need for "self-reformation by potential defendants," according to James W. Harshaw III. In deciding whether to allow a plaintiff's claim to proceed despite the lapse of the statute of limitations, the court will balance the harm to the plaintiff of being denied a remedy against the harm to the defendant of having to defend against old claims.

Statutes of limitations for torts ordinarily require an action for personal injuries to be brought within a specified period after the cause of action has accrued, usually from one to six years. Traditionally, the cause of action accrues at the time of the injury. (The term "accrue" refers to the date that the damage is sustained and not the date when the causes which ultimately produce injury are set in motion.) However, the term "accrue" is not usually defined in the relevant statute and consequently is subject to judicial interpretation. By neglecting to define accrue, traditional tort statutes of limitations fail to address two problems, according to Susan D. Glimcher: "the medical impossibility of determining the date of injury, even in retrospect . . . [and] the legal impossibility of maintaining an action for an injury inherently incapable of discovery within the limitation period." The response to these problems is a discovery rule whereby the statute of limitations does not commence until a victim discovers or, in the exercise of reasonable diligence, should have discovered the injury.

Some Incest Is Not Discovered Until Adulthood

The preferred rule for the statute of limitations in incest suits would be that the statute began running at the date of discovery of the injury rather than at the date of the actual injury. . . .

Many of the injuries that result from incestuous abuse do not manifest until the victim has reached adulthood. This is true particularly of injuries relating to sexual dysfunction. It is unreasonable to expect an adolescent to "discover" her sexual dysfunction since it is generally thought that emotional maturity is a prerequisite to adult sexuality. Since emotional maturity may not be reached until a woman is in her mid-twenties to mid-thirties, the injury of sexual dysfunction cannot reasonably be believed discoverable until this time.

Jamie M. Moore, *Response*, vol. 9, no. 2, 1986.

An application of this discovery rule to claims of incestuous abuse poses a peculiar problem to victims, courts, and legislatures alike. The circumstances of the abuse and the nature of the related psychological injuries often prevent the victim from recognizing her injuries and their cause until after the occurrence of the last incestuous incident. In such cases, a cause of action might not be filed until well beyond the statutory time limit, requiring the court to dismiss the complaint. To remedy the unfair dismissal of such inherently offensive claims, courts and legislatures must implement the policies underlying statutes of limitations without violating the constitutional rights of potential litigants.

Recently, a number of courts have addressed incestuous abuse claims filed long after the applicable statute of limitations had run. Some jurisdictions construe the statute literally and hold that the action is barred, despite the fact that the victim only recently discovered that the conduct was tortious. Other courts, however, permit such tort actions to overcome the obstacle of time limitations statutes by adopting a delayed discovery rule—a judicially constructed exception to the strict time limitation. Consequently, the disposition of each incestuous abuse complaint rests on how a court construes the statute of limitations in light of the allegations presented, particularly focusing on how and when the cause of action was recognized. The court then takes into account, if applicable, the possibility that professional intervention induced the victim to discover her psychological injury and its most likely cause. . . .

The present method of allowing courts to determine the fate of these suits based on their own sense of justice is not an equitable solution to this social dilemma. As such, a moderate, logical approach to the problem should be presented to all courts of general jurisdiction to allow the adult victim an opportunity to convince a court or jury that there were genuine reasons that she discovered or should have discovered her cause of action after it would otherwise have been foreclosed by the statute of limitations. This date of discovery determination of psychological injuries should logically lie in the hands of a person familiar with the victim's psychological conditions. Because of the nature of the victim's familial background and perhaps her inability to actively participate in a relationship, the person most familiar with the victim is a psychotherapist whom the victim confided in when no one else was available.

A Neutral Third Party

While many scholars may scoff at the weight given to evidence developed during psychotherapy, the nature of these cases provides very little in the way of alternatives. The victim has psychologically repressed traumatic events from her memory; this psychological phenomenon should not preclude her cause of action. To alleviate the skepticism, it is possible for the courts to establish an objective administrative guideline to weigh the credence of the psychiatric expert. Skeptics of psychoanalysis also contemplate the various transformations that separate the historical truth from the psychoanalytic truth, or rather what really happened and what the psychotherapist has interpreted to have happened. Because of the possibility that, in the process of talking with the patient about her memory, the therapist may unintentionally supply a phrase or description which the patient may incorporate into her private experience, the implications of psychoanalysis may be viewed as a construction—rather than a reconstruction—of the past events.

Consequently, it may be necessary to present a neutral third party evaluation of the adult victim's mental condition. In essence, this could be a court appointed neutral expert who is theoretically an "expert on psychological experts," capable of evaluating the long-term clinical treatment of an adult victim of childhood sexual abuse.

Permitting the Adult Victim to Sue

The legislature's role in relieving the potential inter-jurisdictional, as well as possible intra-jurisdictional, discrepancies of these otherwise untimely cases may have a very persuasive impact on the policy arguments of victims of childhood sexual abuse. Since 1989, legislatures across the country have begun to recognize an adult victim's right to bring a civil action against her abuser without regard to the long period of time between the wrongdoing and the suit. This widespread acknowledgment of previously inadequate remedies for childhood sexual assault victims was initially set in motion by Patti Barton, a thirty-five-year-old victim of sexual assault that began when she was five. With the legal assistance of the Seattle-based Northwest Women's Law Center (Law Center), Patti Barton and her husband succeeded in creating the first piece of state legislation in the country to amend the statute of limitations to provide a delayed discovery rule to traumatized victims of childhood sexual abuse.

Agencies and organizations throughout the country have supported legislative efforts as well. A prime example is the efforts outside of Washington by the Law Center and the Bartons' newly formed group, the Legal Rights for Survivors of Childhood Sexual Abuse. Even within the state of Washington, lobbying efforts have afforded these organizations the opportunity to proclaim that "the discovery rule is particularly well-suited to cases involving childhood sexual abuse." Supporters of this discovery rule are seeking to end the unfair protection afforded the abuser and instead force him to face the victim when she is an adult and able to stand up for herself. By permitting the victim to sue when she discovers the injury and its cause, it is more likely that abusers will eventually be held accountable to pay, and ultimately there will be a decline in the incidence of childhood sexual assault.

"Changes in the statutes of limitations . . . open the floodgates for the hysterical false accusers, with tragic consequences."

Child Abuse Cases Should Not Have Extended Statutes of Limitations

Richard A. Gardner

Statutes of limitations, or limits to the amount of time an accused can be prosecuted for a crime, were created to protect the rights of defendants. In the following viewpoint, Richard A. Gardner argues that the hysteria surrounding accusations of long-ago child abuse is an example of a situation in which defendants need such protection. Current legal efforts to extend the statute of limitations for child abuse crimes, he charges, are dangerous erosions of defendants' rights. Gardner, a psychiatrist, is the author of *True and False Accusations of Child Sex Abuse: A Guide for Legal and Mental Health Professionals.*

As you read, consider the following questions:

1. What indicators of false accusations of abuse does Gardner cite?
2. Name two paths offered by the court system to those who believe they have been abused. According to the author, how can one of those paths be used as blackmail for the other path?
3. Protection against hysterical accusations is one reason the author believes the statute of limitations should not be extended. What is the other reason he gives?

From Richard A. Gardner, "Belated Realization of Child Sex Abuse by an Adult," *Issues in Child Abuse Accusations*, Fall 1992. Reprinted with permission.

In recent years we have witnessed a new phenomenon, namely, an adult (usually a woman) claiming that she recently realized—after many years of absolutely no recollection—that she was sexually abused as a child (usually by her father). First, I wish to emphasize that I believe that some of these accusations are indeed true. Child sex abuse is a widespread and ancient phenomenon. Children who are sexually abused grow up and become adults. Children who are sexually abused may repress their memories of such abuse for many years. There is no question, however, that some adults are making false accusations and that it is extremely important to develop guidelines for differentiating between true and false accusations. It is my purpose here to focus on the false accusations, especially with regard to the manifestations that suggest strongly that they are false.

Commonly, the revelation occurs in the office of a therapist who has a reputation for being particularly skilled in bringing such long-repressed memories into conscious awareness. The moment of revelation is considered to be a turning point in the woman's life, and now all unanswered questions about her psychological health are answered. Everything now has "fallen into place." All the years of emotional turmoil, psychiatric treatment (including hospitalizations), wrecked marriages, and other forms of psychological dysfunction are now understood. It was the sex abuse that occurred during childhood that was the cause of all these years of grief. Now that the cause is known, the "healing" process can now *really* begin. (All previous therapies were a waste of time and money.) The treatment may take many years and may involve a significant degree of hardship for the nearest of kin, but it will be worth it. The woman continually extols the brilliance of her new therapist—who saw what others failed to see—and toward whom this woman will have a lifelong debt.

Denouncing the Father

Frequently, the next step is for the woman to remove herself totally from the alleged perpetrator, who is generally a man in declining years. His initial reaction is often one of astonishment and immediate denial, generally supported by his wife. The sessions may extend over days, weeks, months, and sometimes even years. Nothing the father can say will convince his daughter that no sex abuse ever took place. The father—who previously may have had a reasonably good relationship with his daughter—now finds himself totally rejected and isolated. His wife, who supports her husband, is also rejected, as well as anyone else who may support the father's position. The distraught parents feel impotent as every relative whose assistance they wish to enlist is cut off as well and the daughter maintains contact only with those friends and relatives who will support her accusation.

The next step often involves the daughter's appearance on television programs, interviews for newspapers and magazines, and personal presentations to any group willing to listen. One of the purposes here is to help other women (and there are millions out there) "discover" their own childhood molestations in order that they too might now, for the first time, deal properly and effectively with the effects of their childhood exploitations. Whereas most women who are sexually molested traditionally feel some shame over their experiences, both for themselves and their families, these women are just the opposite. If they had the opportunity to appear on "Prime Time" syndicated television, they would seize it. Clubs of such "victims" and "incest survivors" are formed and pressures placed on legislators to provide public funding for the treatment of such women, which, it is predicted, will require many years in order for them to "heal." In some cases, we are told, the trauma has been so formidable that these women may require treatment for the rest of their lives.

Memory Is Not a Camera

Psychologists and lawyers are finding that more and more cases turn on the question of how reliable memory is. . . .

People—not to mention juries—place unwavering trust in the human ability to recall events, especially those that have had a strong emotional impact. But such confidence is often misplaced. "Our memory is not like a camera in which we get an accurate photograph," says psychologist Henry Ellis of the University of New Mexico. . . .

Critics charge that misleading questions as well as the publicity given childhood sexual abuse frequently plant the idea of molestation in the minds of susceptible children and adults, though no abuse has taken place.

Anastasia Toufexis, *Time*, October 28, 1991.

There is no question that child sex abuse is widespread. Obviously, there is also no question that the vast majority of sexually abused children become adults. However, there is no question that most of the women who satisfy the false-accusation criteria described here have never been sexually abused. These cases satisfy many more of the indicators of the false than the true sex-abuse accusation. In fact, I have already mentioned two of the indicators of the false accusation—the strong need to bring the abuse to the attention of the public and the belief that all of one's psychological problems are derivatives of the abuse.

Male Targets of Female Anger

Generally, these are very angry women. When the problems generating anger are not resolved, anger builds up and presses for release. Society always provides targets that facilitate such release, and these change with the times. . . .

In recent years, many women have found that men can serve as useful targets for their hostility. There is no question that women have been terribly subjugated since the beginning of civilization and that the process is still going on in just about every part of the world. There is no question that the women's liberation movement is, overall, a constructive force in human progress. But every movement has its fanatics and zealots, and the women's movement is no exception. Most women have some justification for feeling angry at men in general. However, those who believe that the best way to deal with this is to destroy every man in sight are certainly not making constructive use of their anger. Actually, such women do the women's movement much more harm than good, give it a bad name, and work against its progress. Such utilization of men as scapegoats is a form of bigotry. If scapegoatism is to work, it is important that the scapegoat be close by. And this is an important element in prejudice. One can be intellectually prejudiced against people who live thousands of miles away, but they are not available as targets for the release of anger. Accordingly, one must find a scapegoat close by, even in the next house or neighborhood. Husbands and fathers satisfy this proviso quite well. . . .

People who are angry to the degree described here often want to wreak vengeance on those whom they believe have abused them. Our legal system provides a ready and willing vehicle for gratifying this morbid desire. There are generally two tracks along which such women can operate. On the civil track, they can ask for damages and payment for their "therapy." Because the trauma has been "enormous," the amount of money that can provide compensation is generally an amount equal to the total value of the assets of the father. And because the therapy must be intense and prolonged (no one can predict *how* long—it may be *life*long), then payment for such treatment is also justified. In some cases the blackmail element here is easily seen. I have seen letters written by such women in which their fathers were told that if they did not come forth with the indicated amount of payment, the daughter would consider herself to have no choice but to press criminal charges, with the threat of years of incarceration.

And this brings us to the second track, the criminal track. Here, too, such women will find willing accomplices in the legal apparatus. There is a sea of prosecutors and district attorneys who are quite happy to enhance their images in the public eye by bringing "justice" to these kinds of "perverts." The public media, as well, are happy to provide these individuals with the notoriety (and future promotions and salary increments) that they crave. In most states the punishment for sexual abuse of a child is Draconian, far above and beyond the punishments meted out for most other crimes (including murder). Life sentences for fondling little girls are commonplace, and there are hundreds (and possibly thousands) of individuals who have been convicted of such a crime—some of whom may very well be guilty but many of whom are not. In either case, their punishments are far beyond what was visualized by the Founding Fathers when they framed the U.S. Constitution, which was designed to protect an accused individual from "cruel and unusual punishment.". . .

Sex abuse is big business. There is lots of money to be made by a whole parade of individuals who involve themselves in these cases. Adult women who accuse their fathers of child sex abuse may very well turn to a lawyer for assistance. Considering the fact that in the United States there is approximately one practicing lawyer for every 340 people (1991 figures), it is reasonable to say that there are innumerable hungry lawyers who are happy to take money from any client, no matter how absurd the complaint. I am not claiming that *all* lawyers are this greedy and indiscriminate with regard to whom they take on as a client; I am only claiming that there are enough such types around to make it quite easy for women in this category to obtain legal assistance. . . .

The lawyer, of course, has been enlisted not only to prove in a court of law that the father is guilty but to gain punitive damages and money for the woman's therapy. And the lawyer, obviously, must also be paid for his or her services. This is only "just" because it was the father who caused all this trouble in the first place by his indulging himself in animal behavior with an innocent child who was too tender in years to protect herself. In many of these cases the blackmail element is apparent, especially when the daughter threatens the father that if he does not pay X amount of megabucks, she will press criminal charges and not just keep the case in the civil courts. . . .

Changing the Statutes of Limitations

In the last few years, we have seen yet another development—a development that could almost have been predicted—modifications of statutes of limitations. Traditionally, those who commit criminal acts have enjoyed a certain period beyond which an accuser could no longer gain redress in a court of law. . . . A woman claiming sex abuse 35 years after the alleged crime could not press charges unless there had been some modification of the statutes of limitations.

In many states, recently, such statutes have been changed so that the statute's time frame is not calculated from the actual date of the crime's commission, but from the time the woman first realized she had been abused. Accordingly, if a woman was allegedly abused at age 3 and at the age of 40 (37 years later), while in hypnotherapy uncovers unconscious material that leads her to the conclusion that she was abused at age 3, she could press charges up to the age of 47 (under a seven-year statute of limitations calculated from the day she appreciated she was sexually abused). . . .

Because [the accused] is accused of committing the abominable crime of sex abuse, the statute of limitations (for him) has been extended to 44 years. We see here yet another example of how constitutional safeguards are being ignored in the service of prosecuting individuals who are being accused of sex abuse.

Our founding fathers crafted our Constitution ever mindful of the abominations that those in power have perpetrated upon the weaker and helpless. Constitutional safeguards, more than anything else, were designed to protect individuals from these depravities. Statutes of limitation are an excellent example. Statutes of limitation serve two primary purposes: (1) they protect defendants against irrational and excessive punishments that are likely to be meted out in times of hysteria, and (2) they increase the likelihood that defendants will be able to avail themselves of credible witnesses. In most states, there is a three-year statute of limitation on most misdemeanors and a five-year statute of limitation on felonies.

Preventing an Atmosphere of Hysteria

Adult women who claim they were sexually abused as children are clamoring for changes in these laws, changes that would calculate the beginning of the period of the accused's vulnerability from the time she first realized she had been sexually abused. Some of these women have been sexually abused, and some of them have not. In either case, this change in the statutes would deprive such defendants of a fundamental constitutional right, considered to be one of the cornerstones of the U.S. Constitution. The modification of these laws would deprive sex-abuse defendants of these safeguards in an atmosphere that is exactly of the kind the founding fathers were trying to protect defendants from, namely, an atmosphere of hysteria in which defendants would be deprived of credible witnesses.

Not surprisingly, most lawyers are in favor of these modifications because they would provide more opportunities for lawsuits, lawsuits that the present statutes of limitation would prohibit. Because many (if not most) legislators are lawyers who combine private practice with their legislative obligations, it is likely that these modifications will eventually be instituted in most states. At this point (July 1992), the best information I have is that 21 states have now passed such legislation and many others are in the process of giving serious consideration to these changes. In short, the trend is sweeping the nation at a very rapid rate, and the likelihood of the trend reversing itself in the near future is extremely small. . . .

Murderers today are given shorter prison sentences than sex abusers and are more likely to get out on parole earlier. This is just one example of the hysteria of our times, hysteria that is prevailing over reason and justice. I can appreciate the desire of those who have been genuinely abused to take action against those who have victimized them. However, until we have developed exquisitely sensitive criteria for differentiating between true and false sex-abuse accusations in this category . . ., changes in the statutes of limitations are dangerous. They open the floodgates for the hysterical false accusers, with tragic consequences for the victims of their false accusations.

Periodical Bibliography

The following articles have been selected to supplement the diverse views presented in this chapter.

Mary Avery	"Evaluating the Testimony of a Child," *Criminal Justice Journal* 12 (1990): 115. Available from 2121 San Diego Ave., San Diego, CA 92110.
Richard A. Gardner	"Leading Stimuli, Leading Gestures, and Leading Questions," *Issues in Child Abuse Accusations*, Summer 1992. Available from the Institute for Psychological Therapies, 13200 Cannon City Blvd., Northfield, MN 55057-4405.
Jane O. Hansen	*Suffer the Children*. Special reprint edition of a series of articles on child abuse in Georgia. Atlanta, GA: *The Atlanta Journal-Constitution*, 1989. Available from the Journal-Constitution Marketing Department, telephone (404) 526-5690.
Issues in Child Abuse Accusations	"Confrontation Clause Revisited," special section on *Idaho v. Wright* and *Maryland v. Craig*, Summer 1990.
Eugene Arthur Moore, Pamela S. Howitt, and Thomas Grier	"Child Witness Testimony: Is It Sufficiently Reliable to Justify the Protective Procedures Sanctioned by *Maryland v. Craig*?" *Juvenile & Family Court Journal*, 42 (1990): 1. Available from the National Council of Juvenile and Family Court Judges, University of Nevada, JCB Bldg., Suite 118, Reno, NV 89557.
Lewis Pitts	"Family Values?" *The Nation*, September 21, 1992.
Margaret Reiser	"Recantation in Child Sexual Abuse Cases," *Child Welfare*, November/December 1991.
Sharon Simone and Susan Hammond	"Our Forty-Year Nightmare Is Finally Over," *Redbook*, July 1991.
Peter F. Stevens and Marian Eide	"The First Chapter of Children's Rights," *American Heritage*, July/August 1990.
C. Tamarkin	"The Frailty of Young Accusers Versus the Demands of Justice," interview with John E.B. Myers, *People Weekly*, February 5, 1990.
Carol Tavris	"Can Children's Testimony in Sex Abuse Cases Be Trusted?" *Vogue*, April 1990.
U.S. News & World Report	"The Child Abuse Trial That Left a National Legacy," January 29, 1990.

How Can Child Abuse Be Reduced?

Chapter Preface

Those whom society charges with protecting children from abuse are faced with tough, life-or-death choices. The hardest decision Child Protective Services (CPS) must make is whether to rescue an abused child *from* his or her family—or to try to rescue the family.

Those who favor taking a child from an abusive parent fear that the child may be maimed or even killed if left at home. When a child who has been reported as abused subsequently dies at the hands of his or her abusers, pressure increases on CPS workers to "err on the side of safety" for other abused children. Placing a child in foster care can defuse a dangerous situation; it may give parents a chance to change their abusive behavior and to earn back the right to have their children with them. But there may not always be a safe place for children taken from their homes; there are not enough good foster homes or institutions. Some children are further abused in foster homes, and many, especially older children, spend years being shuttled from home to home, with no permanent caretakers and no contact with their families and friends. Some CPS workers believe a certain level of abuse at home is better than the rootless existence of being a foster child.

Those who favor trying to save the family agree with former U.S. education secretary William Bennett, who points out, "Seldom can a government match or replace the care a parent can offer." Multidisciplinary approaches, with cooperation among welfare, social services, and child protective agencies, are currently favored for keeping families together. If a family becomes homeless, for example, integrated agencies might find housing for the family and help the parents find work. Teaching a young mother with limited parenting skills what to expect from her child at each stage of development and how to discipline him or her without hitting may save mother and child —and the costs of foster care.

Removing the child may destroy the family; not removing him may destroy the child. The authors of the following viewpoints face these hard choices and examine ways to optimize children's chances of living without abuse.

"Respite nurseries should . . . become as socially acceptable and efficient as McDonald's or Radio Shack or K Mart."

Establish More Crisis Intervention Centers

Vincent J. Fontana and Valerie Moolman

The deaths of dozens of abused children in New York City in the early months of 1980 galvanized Vincent J. Fontana, chairman of the Mayor's Task Force on Abuse and Neglect. Many of the parents who were abusing and even killing their children were not monsters, he believed, but overly stressed people without a safety net. In the following viewpoint, Fontana and Valerie Moolman argue that if such parents could just safely ask for help and find a brief respite at times of crisis, children and their families could be saved. The Crisis Nursery at New York Foundling Hospital, which the authors describe in the viewpoint, was set up in April 1982 to offer parents needed resources: money, child care, health care, and other social services. Fontana is medical director and pediatrician in chief at New York Foundling Hospital. Valerie Moolman is an author who lives in Brooklyn, New York.

As you read, consider the following questions:

1. Why did the arrest of the mother who abandoned her daughter in the hospital restroom send the wrong message to parents in trouble, according to the authors?
2. How do Fontana and Moolman deal with the dilemma of those who want child abuse to be abhorred but want parents who are abusing their children to seek help?
3. What problems do the authors see in parents who lack information on child development?

Save the Family, Save the Child: What We Can Do to Help Children at Risk by Vincent J. Fontana and Valerie Moolman. New York: Penguin, 1991. Copyright 1991 by Vincent J. Fontana. Reprinted with permission.

Late one spring night a two-and-a-half-year-old was left in the woman's restroom of King's County Hospital in Brooklyn. Those who found her said she looked cared for and well nourished, although there were some unidentifiable scars on her legs. A note pinned to the child's clothes read:

> To Whom It May Concern:
> I'm an 18-year-old student and I also work. I can't handle the pressure. I sometimes take it out on her. I love her and would not like to hurt. Please find her a good home where she'll get the love she deserves.

The writer signed the note, "Sincerely Desperate."

By the next day, Emmanuelle Jedonne had had second thoughts. She called the hospital.

"How's my baby?" the young mother asked anxiously.

Keisha had already been taken away by child welfare officials, but hospital officials didn't mention that to the mother. They suggested that she come to the hospital.

When she arrived soon afterward with her older brother she asked to get her child back. "I brought her here because I was depressed and didn't have anyone to talk to," she said, and her brother added that she was a loving mother distraught by the breakup of her marriage—or other relationship—to a twenty-nine-year-old man who had since disappeared. Her family had disapproved of the relationship and given her no support. A mother at sixteen, she was a senior in high school and worked as a cocktail waitress after school hours. Her family had immigrated from Haiti about eight years before. Emmanuelle had recently lost her green card and was unable to find a more suitable job without it. She was distressed and remorseful about leaving her baby and wanted to take her home—even though she had no home to go to, because her sister had told her to leave the apartment they had shared. Her life since the child's father had abandoned them both had been a constant struggle to pay the bills and buy food and clothes for herself and her daughter.

Crying Out for Help

This young mother with no support system needed all the help she could get and had obviously been crying out for it. But instead of getting help, she was arrested and taken to the precinct stationhouse, where she was charged with child abandonment and reckless endangerment and jailed awaiting arraignment. . . .

What troubled me about the arrest was precisely that the mother was a classic at-risk case who might easily have done away with her youngster, but didn't. She brought it to a hospital. With a little help and counseling she might well be able to care for her daughter, while prosecuting her as a criminal would put one more young woman in jail and another child in the city's already overstretched foster care system.

The larger picture was the disturbing message that the arrest instantly sent out to young parents in similar situations. . . . Don't you dare come out and ask for help, because you'll be thrown into prison and your baby will be taken away! Stay in your closet and beat up your kid or get rid of her. You'll be safer that way! . . .

What Is a Crisis Nursery?

"Crisis Nursery" sounds like a contradiction in terms. It isn't. Nor is it an intensive care unit for babies. The Crisis Nursery at New York City's Foundling Hospital is an emergency refuge for children at risk of being damaged by their parents—parents desperately in need of relief from stress. The children brought to the Crisis Nursery seldom need much medical care. What they do need is a respite from their troubled parents, just as their parents need a respite from them.

To me, the Crisis Nursery is a metaphor, some might say a mixed one. But I consider it a metaphor for the national crisis in family care, for the breakdown of the American family, and for what can be done on a practical, everyday level to begin to set it right. That is the importance of the Crisis Nursery program: it is part of the solution.

Thousands of parents in trouble do call us, and we do help. . . .

The impetus for the Crisis Nursery program came in the early part of 1980, when fifty children had already died of parental beatings or neglect that year. Then came the single week in which three toddlers were abused to death. . . .

Studying the three cases, I saw certain similarities. None of the parents seemed to be intrinsically bad people. Irresponsible, yes. Lacking in control, pitifully ignorant, and out of their minds with stress, yes. But they were not beyond help, if somebody could have reached them. They should have been helped, and their children should have been saved. . . .

I had a plan for something I was determined we should try at once. . . . Mayor Ed Koch expressed his desire to help and set in motion the slow-grinding bureaucratic wheels that ultimately brought the plan to life. With a budget of $200,000 a year from Special Services for Children, the child protective unit of the city's Human Resources Administration, the Crisis Nursery opened its "island of safety" at the New York Foundling Hospital in April 1982.

A twenty-four-hour-a-day, seven-day-a-week Helpline was instantly made available to parents at the end of their rope—depressed, distressed, and touching bottom. Our public awareness program featured posters displaying our phone number and inviting overburdened people to bring their children to us so that we could help to lift their burden from them.

Not Child Abusers

In the beginning cynics said, "You'll never get *them* to come to you! What're you going to do—advertise?"

Right. That's exactly what we are doing.

"For *child abusers?*"

No. Never for child abusers. For strung-out parents. . . .

And the parents do call. We have found that they are eager to use a program such as ours when they know about it. . . .

Failure to Help in Crisis Is Costly

The human and financial costs of America's failure to support and strengthen families and to provide intensive assistance in times of stress and crisis are high. These costs are measured in the wasted lives of children stranded in foster care, in disintegrating families that could be helped, and in the extraordinary financial burden of sustaining a growing population of children in settings outside their families, sometimes far from their homes.

Beyond Rhetoric: A New American Agenda for Children and Families, Final Report of the National Commission on Children, 1991.

When a mother calls with a problem—and more often than not it is the mother—we may be able to advise her on the telephone, or we may suggest that she and the child come in to see us. Then, after making an assessment of the immediate needs of the whole family, we either admit the child or refer the parent to a variety of support services such as a reputable day care center, a parenting education program, a self-help group such as Parents Anonymous, or specialized medical services. . . .

Helping Families Deeply in Trouble

When the program was set up we anticipated that parents would come in before any abuse or neglect occurred. It hasn't worked out that way. In most cases, some striking out has already started by the time they call. They come in because they're on a roll of anger and they're afraid that it's going to get worse. This came as something of a surprise to us in the beginning, and it points up something that we have had to learn: the fact that many parents cannot bring themselves to reach out for a lifeline until they are already desperately deep in trouble. But it also tells us something else: that even when mothers and fathers are ashamed of what they have done, they *can* ask for help if it is made available in a nonpunitive way in a welcoming place. . . .

Stressed Parents Who Care Are Not Monsters

In a way, child advocates like myself are caught in a dilemma. We have to stigmatize child abuse, to treat it as a major crime against humanity in the hope that it will come to be regarded as the most loathsome of all sins—and we also have to destigmatize volatile acts of striking out so that the mother who raises a hand against her child will not be reluctant to seek help. We talk freely to the parents abut "not being able to cope" or "striking out" at their children, but we are very careful not to use the words "child abuse.". . .

The mothers who feel guilty are not monsters, and the cases we see are not the ones that make headlines. The atypical examples of child abusers and child killers are the ones we read about in our newspapers and see on our TV screens. These are the psychotics, drug addicts, alcoholics, sadists, and religious fanatics who make up only about 1 percent of all maltreating parents. The other 99 percent are people who are simply finding it difficult to cope with the stressful situations of everyday living. They want help but they're afraid to ask for it; they fear the stigma of being known as child abusers and they are terrified that we will take their children away from them. That, incidentally, is something that we ourselves never do and very rarely recommend to the city's child protective unit. Rather, we try to help the child by helping the parent. It is not part of our plan to pry youngsters out of the arms of the family to get shuffled around in the foster care system. Once in a great while we have to, but only as a last resort. . . . What we're in business to do is to help *save* the family, so that all the kids and all the adults in it are safe and continue to be safe.

Lack of Information and Unreasonable Expectations

Picking on a child, and ultimately hitting a child, usually happens when parents don't know enough about parenting to handle their children and don't know enough about life to meet their responsibilities. . . .

Some parents simply lack information on a child's growth and development, and—themselves immature—expect far too much of a baby. Many young parents don't know that a child of a certain age cannot pick up a glass of milk without spilling it, or that children go through a stage in which it seems natural to decorate the walls with crayons or finger paints; or they don't know at what age a child can be potty trained. They whack the child because they think he or she ought to know better or is just being ornery.

231

Or they can't cope with an infant's incessant crying. They don't know if the crying is normal, or if the child is hungry or sick or hurting, or if they themselves are unnaturally depressed or abnormally testy. All they can think of is that the yelling *must stop.*

And a lot of parents have learned only one way to supervise—or discipline—their child, and that is to give it a good smack. Why not? Mother always did it to them. . . .

The Cycle of Abuse

More than half of the parents coming in for help will say that they were battered or neglected in their childhood.

This is our opportunity to go right to work on what they are doing to their children.

Our hope is that if the parent leaves the scapegoat child with us for two or three days and nights, it will not only give the child a break but allow the parent a cooling-off period without having that child around to pick on. At the same time we initiate crisis intervention and longer-term treatment for striking-out parents with the purpose of ending, once and for all, the cycle of abuse that persists from generation to generation.

The parents don't always understand this at first. "Why should I have to get treatment," a mother might say, "when what I really need is help with the bills?". . .

I finally got through to one young mother by telling her that I didn't want to see her grandchildren abused.

"It isn't just a matter of getting you to stop beating your child," I said. "The point is, if you change your behavior, there is a very good chance that your child will not beat up on your grandchildren."

Her eyes widened. After a minute she said "oh," and that's all she said—but she looked as though she might be looking back at her own past or into her children's future; maybe both. . . .

Child Abuse Can Be Prevented

It infuriates me when unthinking people say there is no way we can prevent our children from being damaged by incompetent or callous parents. If we say that something can't be done, *it won't be done.* But child abuse and neglect, and death from child abuse, are being prevented right here, in these rooms, in this Crisis Nursery. This one small, purely local, city-supported effort can be multiplied throughout the country to give parents in every community the bailout they need when they know they are losing control and striking out at their children.

We opened in April 1982. As of November 1990, we have had 27,653 Helpline calls. Nearly 100 percent of these calls resulted in supportive action of some kind; 3,810 children from 2,709

232

families were admitted to the Nursery, and an additional 1,037 children from 504 families were provided with services but not admitted because there was no critical need for their admission.

The Foundling Hospital Crisis Nursery is a model for such centers throughout the country—a front-line, preemptive campaign to help parents in trouble and children in danger.

I see no reason why every large hospital in every major city should not have one of these crisis nurseries. I am sure that many bureaucratic reasons will be presented to me, but I am equally sure they are not valid. Usually they boil down to, "Who's going to pay for the beds?"

Someone Who Cares

One participant [in an intensive intervention research program], responding to the open-ended question, "Please tell me in your own words how the program has worked for you and what it has meant to you," said . . . "They've been so protective. I'm not used to being protected. I'm not used to being cared about. I'm used to being thrown off the side, the black sheep kind of thing. But they've done a lot of caring and gone out of their way to help me and my kids. They don't have to, but they always want to. It's like whenever I'm in trouble I know I can call them, day or night, any time of day or night no matter what my problem is. No matter how small. They care. It really means a lot to me that somebody that isn't part of me cares. The Center gives me a sense of being. The sense I belong. It's like family."

Mary E. Pharis and Victoria S. Levin, *Child Welfare*, May/June 1991.

Respite nurseries should be in welfare hotels and motels, where child abuse and neglect are endemic; they should be in the housing projects; they should be in shopping malls; they should be in community centers. And they should be publicized and run in such a way that they become as socially acceptable and efficient as McDonald's or Radio Shack or K Mart. . . .

But that is another story. Meanwhile, we have to deal with the flaws in the systems we already have.

Emmanuelle Jedonne, the teenager who left her baby in a hospital restroom, was charged and jailed for doing what she felt at the time was the right thing. . . .

I was appalled. With the support of other city medical doctors and child advocates, I held a press conference to let the public know just how inhumane and counterproductive it was to drag the girl into court. . . .

We *want* parents to ask for help! We tell them they will not be punished. We tell them their babies will not be taken away. It is essential that they trust us. Even isolated incidents such as this will drive them underground—and they're going to beat the hell out of their kids without anyone knowing or caring.

Suddenly, the charges were reduced. Emmanuelle's next court appearance was in Family Court. The protective agency abandoned its efforts to place Keisha in a foster home, and the little girl was remanded to her grandmother. The young mother was directed to a family care service called Family Dynamics and found a temporary home with an aunt in New Jersey. She went into counseling and started a series of sessions in infant training. Later she will try to get her general education diploma.

She still has problems—no settled home, no green card, and no job. But she is getting the help she was supposed to have gotten when the system failed in yet another way.

"With family preservation . . . we look for the strengths in people instead of focusing on their weaknesses, as the system always did before."

Create Family Preservation Programs

Mark Sauer

In the early 1990s San Diego County's Child Protective Services was accused of ripping healthy families apart on vague suspicions or unsupported allegations of abuse. A yearlong grand jury investigation indicted the system as being "out of control." In 1992, CPS implemented what Mark Sauer calls "a complete turnaround in philosophy," changing the focus from "When in doubt, remove the child" to "Keep the family together, if at all possible." In the following viewpoint, Sauer examines the beliefs behind the new program and its effects. Sauer is a staff writer for the *San Diego Union-Tribune*.

As you read, consider the following questions:

1. What differences between the Intensive Family Preservation Program and typical social services does Sauer point out?
2. Why did reunification plans often fail to reunify families, according to Sauer?
3. What kinds of help does the new program provide for families that are in trouble, according to the author?

Mark Sauer, "Fixing Families: County Focuses on Changing Behavior," *San Diego Union-Tribune*, December 6, 1992. Reprinted with permission.

Robert's life reads like a sad, twisted road map to oblivion: He started smoking pot at age 8; turned to LSD at 13, the year his parents divorced; and was a full-blown speed freak by age 18, with a felony conviction to prove it.

"IV usage? Yeah, I used to shoot up," Robert admitted. "I was selling a quarter-pound of crystal meth every two days. I was taking in $10,000 almost daily for a while there."

Robert, 26, who insists he's drug-free now, knows he's lucky to be alive. He once pulled a gun on seven El Cajon police officers who'd come to arrest him. In addition to Robert, the cops collected several guns and $50,000 in cash that day. He did time on that one.

All of this would be incidental if not for four children, ages 18 months to 6 years. Robert is their father. His girlfriend, Sheila, is their mother.

Robert and Sheila (whose names have been changed to protect their identities) would have seen their children placed in long-term foster care had it not been for San Diego County's new Intensive Family Preservation Program.

Sheila, who also was seduced for a time by the allure of crystal meth, was asleep with Robert in a back bedroom and could not be roused one day in December 1991 by a social worker who came to the door.

That was it. The children were taken to Hillcrest Receiving Home and then placed in foster care. The charge was neglect—very common in abuse cases. Sheila got the message immediately. Robert eventually did, too.

The Old System Had Strict Conditions

Before family preservation, returning children to couples such as Robert and Sheila would have been an unlikely option for San Diego County social workers.

Typically, Robert and Sheila would have been court-ordered to meet several strict conditions, known as a "reunification plan," over an extended period before returning their children would have even been considered.

Robert and Sheila would have had to test clean for a long time, undergo psychotherapy, attend parenting classes—essentially, demonstrate that they have turned their entire lives around without a slip before the system would entertain the idea of sending their kids back home.

And they would have gotten little assistance in meeting the requirements.

But Robert and Sheila's youngest and oldest children are already back home; the two in the middle, who are visited regularly by their parents, are to return home any day now from foster care. And Sheila is pregnant with the couple's fifth child.

Fran Atwood and John Ramsey, social workers with the county's Intensive Family Preservation Program, took a hard look at Robert and Sheila. They recommended to program director Julie Steidl that they be allowed to work with the family toward reunification with their kids.

The reason the foster-care system is overwhelmed and parents don't get their kids back for months or years is that the social services system placed unrealistic demands on parents in idealistic reunification plans, Steidl said.

"We would say, 'You test dirty, or you fail to attend a parenting class, or don't see a therapist, and you don't get your kid back,'" Steidl said.

"We have cases in this system where we have two children in long-term foster care solely because a parent failed to complete a (reunification) plan—a parent who has two other kids at home who are thriving. It's outrageous."

The key to the system's failure, Steidl said, is unreasonable expectations.

"Our *goal* is for parents to be clean and sober. But we shouldn't expect perfect parents," she said. "In family preservation, we expect that these parents are chronically dysfunctional and that they will have episodic crises that will result in abuse, whether it is neglect or excessive discipline.

"Given that, we make a choice: What is the likelihood that further abuse would result in serious physical or emotional harm to the child? If the answer is 'not very likely,' we accept that case in our program."

How the New System Works

Until now, social services operated on the basis that concerns for the physical and emotional safety of the child took precedence over all other issues.

Family preservation is a behavior-modification model—the idea is to change the destructive behavior within the family, not remove the child.

Whereas San Diego County social workers typically have caseloads of 35 or more abusive families, workers in Steidl's family preservation unit have but five.

Family preservation workers establish an intense, close working relationship with the family for a relatively short period (three months in most cases).

"You almost become part of the family," said Sunny Ariessohn, a probation officer assigned to Steidl's family preservation program.

Like all workers in the program, Ariessohn makes several unannounced visits to her clients each week.

At first, she said, her help may involve finding a new apartment for a family whom few would want as a tenant or neighbor, and requisitioning public funds to cover deposits and first-month's rent.

Next, she might show the parents how to set up a family budget so rent, food, utilities and other essentials will be taken care of out of their Aid to Families with Dependent Children (AFDC) check.

Then she puts together a daily and weekly schedule of chores and responsibilities for each family member, may supply bus tokens for trips to parenting classes or Alcoholics Anonymous meetings, even provide an alarm clock and show them how to use it.

Poor Life Skills

"Some of the most basic things we take for granted in our lives, like getting up and getting dressed and giving the kids breakfast and getting them off to school on time, are things these people have never been able to manage," Ariessohn said.

Children's Best Hope: Their Own Families

For the overwhelming majority of American children, including most of those alleged to be maltreated, there is no child protection without family preservation. Their best hope lies with their own families.

"The state can be a custodian, but not a parent," writes Malcolm Bush. "Children are sustained by the 'illogical' affection of their parents—affection and regard that outsiders would not give to children, particularly when they misbehave or if, by various criteria, they are unattractive. The state can never provide that affection and many surrogate parents cannot maintain it in the face of deviant behavior."

Recall what Dennis Lepak discovered: "*No one* will value and protect another's child as they will their own." If we are serious about erring on the side of the child, we must begin by erring on the side of the family.

Richard Wexler, *Wounded Innocents*, 1990.

"You'd be amazed how bad things are when we start working with some of these families and then how far they come in three months' time."

Ariessohn might teach housekeeping to a former drug abuser, work with a chronically unemployed veteran on a resume and interviewing techniques, show a beleaguered mother how to give a hyperactive child a "time-out" instead of hitting her.

"If the court hadn't intervened, if Sunny hadn't started working with us, my life would have been a heck of a lot worse," said Sandy, a mother of three who was raised mostly in the foster-care system herself.

Sandy, who is typical of those accused of abuse in that she is mired in poverty, is well aware that her children probably would have been in long-term foster care had it not been for the county's change toward family preservation.

"I had to realize that I'm an adult, and if I was going to have my kids with me, I was going to have to change," said Sandy, whose children spent a year in foster care before the family preservation program intervened.

Problems with Drugs

Anne, who has a heart tattooed on the back of her left hand and a gold chain with a pendant reading "No. 1 Mom," said losing her kids "devastated" her but that it wasn't enough, at first, to get her off crystal meth.

"The cops raided our place, and we (she and her husband) were both arrested for manufacturing crystal meth," Anne said, stubbing out a cigarette. "I just fell deeper into addiction for the next couple of years."

She hit rock bottom 15 months ago.

"I made up my mind to do whatever it took to get my kids back," said Anne, who began regularly taking a $4\frac{1}{2}$-hour trip to visit them at an Escondido foster home.

She took parenting classes, completed a 12-step program for drug addicts, sought counseling, submitted to drug tests. And with the help of family preservation social worker Juan Herrera, Anne got her 12-year-old son and 9-year-old daughter back home.

Refusing to Give Up

Her 14-year-old daughter did not want to come home, however; in fact, she wanted nothing to do with her mom and dad (Anne's husband has not shared her resolve and was ordered to County Jail for 20 days after failing to complete a drug program).

But Herrera refuses to give up on vital family relationships. He has made it possible for the oldest daughter to visit with her younger siblings, even though she is not yet ready to meet with her parents. "It's a start," Herrera said.

Anne is circulating her resume now, looking for a job as a clerical worker, a field in which she has considerable experience.

"Anne and her husband both love their kids," Herrera said. "The difference with family preservation is we look for the strengths in people instead of focusing on their weaknesses, as the system always did before.

"Quite a few times I would take children from their homes and drop them at Hillcrest (Receiving Home) and wind up sitting in my car crying," Herrera said. "Taking kids away is so traumatic for everyone.

"No matter what you find when you start working with these families, you have to realize there is a human being in there. It's our job to help these people find ways to help themselves. If we succeed, everybody is better off, especially the children."

"Sexual-abuse education . . . means teaching children that they need not suffer unwanted adult touch without good reason."

Educate Children and Adults About Abuse

Christine Gudorf

Increased awareness of child sexual abuse has led many adults to withdraw physical affection from children and has made some parents overprotective of their offspring, according to Christine Gudorf. In the following viewpoint, she points out that these reactions are harmful and fail to protect children. Sexual abuse education of both adults and children is the key to preventing such abuse, says Gudorf. This education must include giving children control of and responsibility for their own bodies. Gudorf writes on sex education issues and teaches sexual ethics.

As you read, consider the following questions:

1. What overreactions to publicity about child sexual abuse has Gudorf noted?
2. Why does the author feel that children should be allowed to refuse to be greeted by hugs and kisses from relatives and other adults?
3. How does Gudorf distinguish between acceptable and unacceptable touch?

Adapted from Christine Gudorf, "Sexual Abuse: What to Teach Kids About Intimate Touch," *U.S. Catholic*, July 1992. Reprinted by permission of the author and Claretian Publications, 205 W. Monroe St., Chicago, IL 60606.

Child sexual abuse is a serious problem in the United States. One of four girls and one of nine boys is sexually abused. . . .

Child victims of traumatic sexual abuse frequently experience depression, broken relationships, alcohol and drug dependence, self-destructive tendencies, and low self-esteem as adults. Extremely low self-esteem sometimes causes victims to take so little care of themselves that they easily become repeat victims as adults: victims of marital rape and battery, early and unwed pregnancies, and exploitation by pimps and pornographers.

Obviously children should be protected from sexual abuse. But how is this best done?

Overreaction

Some people have overreacted to the publicity about child sexual abuse. It is common knowledge that many teachers, especially day-care personnel, have withdrawn, usually reluctantly, physical affection from their students for fear of accusations of child sexual abuse. Humans have a physical need for affection expressed through touch. Loving touch from parents, relatives, teachers, and adult friends conveys to children that they are valuable and cared for; and this knowledge gives them security and self-confidence. Many studies have demonstrated that children learn better from teachers who express physical affection.

Some parents have completely changed their lifestyles in recent attempts to prevent the sexual victimization of their children. One couple withdrew their children from school and teaches them at home to insure their safety from sexual abuse.

Another couple, learning that a close relative had, unsuspected by the entire family, sexually abused a preschool-age niece for two years, decided that both of them would shift to part-time, at-home work as accountants so that one of them would be with the children at all times. . . .

Other parents develop different alternatives, such as choosing baby-sitters and children's activities from within restricted circles of people, close friends, family, or church, they feel they can trust. Still other parents have worked out elaborate systems for getting child-care personnel so as to weed out potential abusers, sexual and otherwise.

All of these reactions are inadequate, and some introduce more danger than they prevent. The first place to start in dealing with the phenomenon of child sexual abuse is to expand the sexual-abuse education of the general public. . . .

All of us need to become more educated about and alert to cases of sexual abuse among our own children, our nieces and nephews, our neighbors' children, our students, and our patients. The signs of sexual abuse are not only subtle but ambiguous because all of them are frequently present in children facing other nonsexual, even nonphysical trauma.

Signs such as withdrawal from others, listlessness, acting-out behaviors, seductive behaviors, psychosomatic illnesses, fear of adults, and changes in school performance or general mood can be responses to many, many other things in addition to responses to sexual abuse.

Girls without reliable sexual information sometimes respond to menarche with some of these behaviors; and children of both sexes often show many of these signs in the face of disruptive parental divorces, family moves from one place to another, the death of a close friend or relative, or peer problems at school. These signs are indications that *something* is the matter; and they cry out for attention. However, they do not diagnose the *cause* of the child's distress. . . .

Detection of Abuse Is Not Enough

While public education about child sexual abuse is necessary, it is not enough because it deals primarily with detection of abuse and not prevention. As stated earlier, prevention is difficult because the causes of child sexual abuse are not clear. That is, on one hand, we do not know how to define the characteristics or experiences of adults that make them likely child sexual abusers. On the other hand, we do know at least some of the reasons why children are victims. For one thing, children are socially understood as weak, in need of protection, and controlled by adults in a society that regularly eroticizes the domination of the weak by the strong. . . .

Many persons insist that there is no alternative to the understanding of children as weak. Children are simply natural victims of predators of any kind because their smaller stature, lesser physical strength, greater ignorance, lesser experience, and resultant naïveté all make them easily manipulable by adults.

Clearly the situation of children would make a liberal everyone-is-equal-and-looks-out-for-oneself approach to sexual abuse intolerable. Children *do* need to be protected. But to view children as if they were valuable but passive objects around which we must build elaborate security systems is also dangerous to the welfare of children. Children are not objects; nor are they passive. And the very traits that make them vulnerable are, ideally, temporary.

The best method of protecting any child against sexual abuse is the simultaneous education of the child and his or her surrounding adults about child sexual abuse. Ignorance on the part of children is frequently a chief ingredient in child sexual abuse. Although the sexual advances of an adult victimizer are usually experienced as distasteful, even terrifying to the child, unless the child has been socially authorized to reject sexual advances, the victimizer can call upon his or her adult status to legitimatize that touch.

© Filchock/Rothco. Reprinted with permission.

After all, there are other kinds of distasteful, even painful touches that adults force on children: shots at the doctor's, a tooth drilling at the dentist's, sloppy kisses and pinched cheeks from elderly relatives, vigorous face washes, and the pain of removing bubble gum from hair.

Only the prior knowledge that there are adults who will support the child's rejection of sexual advances can empower many children either to resist sexual advances or to defy the abuser's order of silence. Until we understand children—even young preschool children—as able to play a growing role in their own protection, our society will not act to provide the sexual information our children need to be safe.

If we agree that children must be educated to play a role in protecting themselves from sexual abuse, then we must consider the form that education should take. The first step is to let preschool children know that not all adults intend their welfare.

Most parents need to deal with this early on—as we discourage children from approaching strangers in parks and grocery stores and from getting into strange cars. It is usually best not to dwell on the terrible things that can happen to children at the hands of evil adults because some children might react with nightmares of kidnappers and torturers; and others will be curious to experience such thrills. . . .

Sex Education Should Cover Abuse

Once children's sex education begins, general descriptions of sexual abuse should be included. For example, when grade-school children begin asking about how pregnancy begins and are told about the release of ovum in the female and the deposit of sperm by the male, they should be given some instruction about sexual desire and satisfaction.

Children need to know more than the mechanics of lovemaking; they need to know the meaning of the act: a man and a woman who care about each other engage in an act of love in which each takes intense pleasure in giving his or her own body and receiving the body of the other as a gift.

When children know this, then we can help them understand that some adults misuse bodily touch out of greed for the physical feeling of pleasure. These adults want to force others into giving them sexual pleasure without the work of constructing with another adult the loving relationship in which such intimate touch is mutual and reaffirming. They should refuse their bodies to such adults and wait until, as adults, they have a mutual desire to take pleasure in the reciprocal sharing of bodies.

One of the earliest types of distinctions developed for use with young children in preschools is the good-touch/bad-touch distinction. Good touch is ordinary touch that includes everything from good-night kisses from a mother to a friend's touch in "Duck, Duck, Goose!" Good touch is aimed at the hands, back, shoulders, arms, and is sometimes described as touch to any part of the body not covered by a swimsuit.

Most newer programs have abandoned this not-so-subtle teaching that it is sexual touch that is bad, and nonsexual touch that is good. However, many parents still use this approach. In a culture with very ambiguous attitudes toward sexuality, especially in children, the good-touch/bad-touch approach unfortunately appears to many as a common-sense approach to sexual abuse. But parents and teachers must try to understand the later effects on children who learn sexual touch as bad.

Will a wedding suddenly dispel 20 years of learning to fear and disdain sexual touch? Can new husbands and wives who are taught fear and suspicion of sexual touch understand the sexual touch of the other as loving and caring, respectful and generous? . . .

Teaching the Positive Before the Negative

The clearest, most direct method of conveying directions to children is usually the best. But not in the case of child sexual-abuse education. Here we have to do it the hard way. The hard way means beginning with the child as a person and his or her feelings instead of definitions of good and bad, which were designed apart from the child and imposed on his or her experience. Child sexual abuse education should aim not only at protecting children from sexual abuse without traumatic effects on their future sexuality but also at providing positive grounding for children's appreciation of their bodies and their capacity to give and receive bodily pleasure and become bonded to others through that shared pleasure—both genital and nongenital.

One of the dangers in many . . . programs on child sexual-abuse education is that these methods present children with images of and information on sexual abuse before children have learned to see sexuality in a positive light.

This is particularly true for girls, who are often barraged from early childhood on with implicit and explicit warnings about sexuality. Social messages to girls about sexuality often revolve around sexual threats . . . to their chastity, their safety, or both. They are told to avoid sexual self-touch from potty training on, not let boys touch, stay in groups, avoid the dark, be wary of sexual advances on dates, and avoid strange men. . . .

Children's Rights

Beginning sexual-abuse education with a child . . . involves not only teaching children to take their own feelings seriously but also teaching adults to take children's feelings seriously. Put bluntly, it means teaching children that they need not suffer unwanted adult touch without good reason and have the right to challenge the reasons given by adults. Children have a right to insist on the cessation of adult touch that makes them afraid, angry, hurt, embarrassed, or confused until the necessity for such touch is validated by other adult authorities.

We as adults have become accustomed to the exercise of such rights over our bodies. Without our permission, no one touches us with impunity. There are various laws that protect adults from the unauthorized touch by others. But children have not been recognized with the similar rights of their own bodies.

It is a painful fact that in our society the child who conforms to the traditional social ideal for children is more likely to be molested than the nonconforming child. The socially ideal child is obedient to parents, defers to greater adult authority, and doesn't question adult power. Children whose experience includes responding to the unexplained orders of parents, teachers, and other adults are unlikely to question the orders or explanations of sexual abusers. Therefore, children whose obedience to adults is normally coerced through fear of punishment will be more easily coerced into silence about their abuse. . . .

The greater freedom for children to physically express their feelings also reinforces children's control and responsibility for their bodies. Children who do not want to be kissed, hugged, or pinched should be allowed to express greetings or affection in other ways. . . . Parents need to insist that children make such substitutions as courteously as possible, inflicting the least possible hurt, but should never insist that children suffer unwanted touch in order to benefit adults—"You'll hurt Aunt Beth's feelings if you don't let her kiss you!"

It is a important that as children grow they should be able to have a growing role in decisions that affect their bodies, such as whether they will play on a sports team, how they want their hair cut, whether or not they want to bother having this birthmark removed. And when parents really look at their interaction with children, they often find that children are seldom consulted about the decisions made about their bodies.

I am not advocating that children be understood as the sole arbiters of whether they need surgery or glasses or exercise or vegetables in their diet or thousands of dollars of acne treatment, but all of us need to do a lot more consulting with our children. We need to allow them to have a voice in basic decisions about their bodies if we expect them to learn to claim ownership of those bodies against potentially abusive adults.

Loving Touch

In addition to making our relationships with our children more mutual and consultative, we need to teach them, beginning very early on, about loving touch by example. We need to demonstrate to our children that we take, as they do, a great deal of pleasure in our physical closeness and intimacy with them. But they need to understand that our pleasure in touching them is dependent upon our touch being pleasurable for them. We do not feel—and should not feel—pleasure in a hug that we force on an angry daughter or son. . . .

However, sometimes we have to touch children coercively to hold them still for shots, clear runny noses, prevent their running into streets, and prevent their hitting others in tantrums. But we need to make it very clear to children that our coercive touch of them is only justified by its necessity for their welfare, not ours, and that such coercive touch is never pleasurable for us. It would be wrong of us to take pleasure from our physical coercion of them.

Stop Abuse Before It Starts

Children need to know that their bodies belong to them and no one has the right to touch them without permission. Children have traditionally been taught to comply with adults' requests, but they need to know that, regarding touching, they have the right to say NO, even if the touch seems accidental or even if the person touching is a relative or trusted adult.

National Committee for Prevention of Child Abuse, *Scared Silent*, 1992.

All unnecessary touch should be pleasurable. Pleasurable touch does not make demands on us; it is an invitation and gift. While receiving gifts often inspires us to giftgiving ourselves, the initial gift should free us, not constrain us in any way. And so sexual touch is a powerful good that is misused when it demands response, seeks to use or control others, presents an agenda not shared with the person touched—in short, does not pleasure the person touched.

And sexual touch does not pleasure children; it scares them not only because they are not ready for it but because children intuitively sense that adults who touch them sexually are not interested in them as persons but have rather objectified them to use them for the adult's personal sexual gratification. . . .

This May Be Inconvenient

The real challenge in educating our children about child sexual abuse is to live up to our message that touch should be mutually pleasurable and that touch that is not mutually pleasurable should be terminated until openly and expressly validated by other trusted adults. We all need to prepare for the fact that if we teach this well to children, there will be children who will challenge us for touching them in less than mutually pleasurable ways. . . .

Children who learn to disallow nonpleasurable touch will occasionally embarrass and inconvenience us. For example, one of my sons once held off more than 20 doctors making grand rounds in a major teaching hospital after he had reconstructive urinary surgery. It took some keen diplomacy on my part to mediate the issue.

My son wanted to know why he was supposed to allow his

doctor to expose and touch his genitals in front of 20 strangers. The doctor, a major reconstructive surgeon, thought that my son should do as his doctor told him; and when the child refused, the doctor called me so that I would "order" my son to comply. The surgeon was flabbergasted when I suggested that he should answer my son's questions: "Why should I do this? What is the good involved?"

The idea that a child (a child *patient* at that) should be able to demand explanations of adult experts was mindboggling for the doctor. But the converse is dangerous to children: what is convenient for parents, doctors, teachers, and other adults who work with children—that children trust and comply with their adult orders—is also convenient for sexual abusers.

Accept Your Limits

After we exercise responsible judgment about the persons to whom we entrust our children, and after we educate our children about refusing or reporting disturbing and unwanted touch by others, then we also need to acknowledge that there is no completely reliable way to protect our children from harm—whether that harm is child sexual abuse, meningitis, or drunk drivers. There is a certain degree of inescapable randomness in the evils of this world; and in the face of such randomness, parents are powerless. . . .

Child sexual abuse is a complex social issue. The delusion that it can be avoided through the exercise of caution is dangerous in the extreme. It sets parents up for horrible guilt if they should fail to protect their child; it sets children up to blame their parents for not protecting them. And sexual abuse prevents families from effectively supporting those families in which child sexual abuse has occurred. . . .

We must do our best to protect our children, to combat the social structures and attitudes that put children at risk, and hand the rest to God—not expecting God to erect Plexiglas shields around our children but trusting that God's presence will support us through whatever evil and suffering come our way. Relinquishing power we really do not have can be a tremendous relief, lifting a huge burden of responsibility from our shoulders. It can often give us the license to enjoy much more thoroughly the joyful gifts that our children are to us.

=====

"You should never hit your children."

=====

Discourage Corporal Punishment

Katherine Schlaerth

Many American parents use spanking and other forms of corporal punishment to discipline their children. In the following viewpoint, Katherine Schlaerth argues that the use of physical force as discipline teaches violence and eventually becomes ineffective. Even when used as a last resort, hitting should be avoided, for that is when it is most likely to cross the line into abuse. Schlaerth is assistant professor of family medicine and clinical pediatrics at the University of Southern California in Los Angeles.

As you read, consider the following questions:

1. What effect have Piaget, Spock, and Brazelton had on ideas about child discipline, according to Schlaerth?
2. Why does the author believe a parent should not spank a small child even after the parent has calmed down?
3. What negative consequences does Schlaerth believe result from the use of physical punishment?

Adapted from Katherine Schlaerth, "Adults Should Never Hit Kids," *U.S. Catholic*, January 1993. Reprinted by permission of the author and Claretian Publications, 205 W. Monroe St., Chicago, IL 60606.

He was a weathered, old Scotsman cast upon the shores of America long ago. He seemed reluctant to talk about his years in this country. And it was obvious that his transplantation here hadn't brought him much good fortune. Sensing his bitterness at the path his life had taken, I threw in some questions about his upbringing while taking his medical history. It turned out that he came from the middle of a large working-class family living in a Scottish industrial town. He considered himself intelligent, but his educational opportunities had been painfully restricted. Most of what he knew was self-taught over many years. His childhood memories seemed full of intense animosity.

"Did Your Parents Hit You?"

One question I sometimes ask patients when attempting to get a feel for their emotional upbringing is how they were disciplined as youngsters. With a Scotsman, the direct approach is generally best: "Did your parents hit you when you were a child?"

He stared at me for a second or two before answering, clearly incredulous that someone as presumably well educated as a family physician would need to ask such a question. Then he slowly and deliberately replied in his inimitable Scottish burr, "Of course they did. And what did ye expect? After all, I was a boy, ye know. They beat me all the time."

In this elderly gentleman's class and culture, a good beating, or at least a spanking, was not only an accepted type of discipline but was almost a reinforcement of his own masculinity. (His sisters weren't disciplined with the same ferocity his parents reserved for their boys.)

I believe that this routine use of physical discipline is lazy parenting—a quick fix.

Children today are no longer considered miniature adults, as they were before the 20th century. Jean Piaget, Benjamin McLane Spock, Thomas Berry Brazelton, and countless other experts have outlined for us the thought processes and intellectual development of infants and children and in doing so have given those responsible for children the tools to discipline more effectively and less violently.

To discipline means to teach. The need to discipline usually arises in a social situation when a child is learning how his or her own rights and autonomy relate with the rights of others. He or she must be taught how to amicably negotiate solutions to everyday problems—such as sharing a toy—and to follow the laws and traditions each society evolves so that everyday life flows smoothly. (An example would be taking turns at the playground.)

Considering the reasoning behind discipline, physically striking out at a child who is not doing what he or she has been told to do will actually give that child a message that is opposite the lesson a parent or teacher is trying to get across. Let's take the example of a $2\frac{1}{2}$-year-old, with an emerging sense of self, who sees a toy airplane he just has to have. Unfortunately this airplane is in the paw of his 2-year-old, next-door neighbor. (Neither child has reached the developmental stage where interactive play and rules have meaning.) To the horror and embarrassment of the older child's mother, her son grabs the airplane and simultaneously shoves the previous possessor into nearby bushes and renders the child momentarily unable to muster a defense. If this mother grabs the toy and slaps or spanks her child, the message she sends her child is: "Kid, you got that airplane by force; and now because I'm bigger, I'm going to do the same thing to you"—a perfect example of might makes right.

Respect the Child's Feelings

The mother in this situation should take into account the developmental stage and personality of her child: a $2\frac{1}{2}$-year-old child can recognize emotions and feelings in others; his or her sense of group cooperation is rudimentary but evolving; and he or she has an emerging need to demonstrate his or her own individuality.

This mother should pick the younger child out of the bushes and ask whether she's okay, point out to her own child that his friend is sad, take the airplane and return it (a little tugging may be necessary here), and talk to her son about how he would feel were the situation reversed. He now has a time-out to contemplate what she's said.

We all know this scenario may not play out exactly as described because time-outs are notoriously difficult to enforce, especially in the type of child who is bold enough to grab another child's toy right under Mother's nose. But it is important that mothers and fathers respect their children's autonomy, teach their children about another's feelings, and enlarge their children's knowledge base. Chances are that after another 10 or 50 repetitions of the above episode, the child will finally get Mom's message. However, if a child is spanked another 10 or 50 times, he or she will incorporate a message of violence instead.

Authoritarian parents are most likely to use physical force to discipline. These parents usually produce children less able to creatively handle new situations. Children routinely disciplined through physical force have less of a sense of the options they can use to attain a goal. The only way they know to get someone to do what they want is to use force because that's what's been done to them. They haven't been taught the art of negotiation, which is an integral part of effective verbal discipline. Nor do they understand cause and effect as they would have if "consequences discipline" had been employed by their parents.

"Who says violence has to *solve* anything?"

From *The Wall Street Journal*—Permission, Cartoon Features Syndicate.

There's another subtle problem with the routine use of physical force to discipline little ones: it loses its effectiveness. However, if physical force is not routine discipline, the instant in which force is used will have a significant effect on a child. And the only time a swift whack on the behind is justified is when there is a serious risk to life or limb. The child about to run unknowingly into the path of an oncoming truck will probably remember to stop at the curb next time if this is the only occasion in his or her life when a spanking is administered.

Physical Discipline Can Become Physical Abuse

You should never hit your children, even when you've reached the end of your rope because that's exactly when you are the least in control of yourself. Lines can blur and a hitting can turn into real, if unintentional, child abuse. I vividly remember a child, perhaps a 1-year-old, with golden curls and a cherubic face. She lay still in the hospital ward, her bandages hiding a head full of fluid that developed after her stepfather, quite a wealthy and intelligent man, let his disciplining of her childish crying get out of hand. She would never cry again.

Even after a parent has cooled down a bit he or she should never administer physical punishment. Chances are a 2- or 3-year-old's attention span is much shorter than a parent's, and a child will have forgotten the offense by the time the parent calms down. The spanking won't be associated with the infraction, and the child will be bewildered and frightened rather than chastised.

A father or mother must put himself or herself in a child's place. Think about how it would feel to be hit on the backside, or worse, slapped across the face. Even little children have a sense of their own dignity, and one can well imagine the shame and embarrassment that is attached to such a demeaning physical violation. Is every little mistake a child makes deserving of such long-lasting bruises?

How Much Can It Hurt?

"Sure it sounds all right in principle not to spank your child," you may say, "but get real. It seems to stop the bad behavior. And how much can a light slap on the backside hurt anyway? My parents did it to me all the time, and I turned out okay." Or, "If your child or another child is beating up one of your children, what else can you do?"

Good discipline takes time and thoughtfulness. Good discipline should be individualized to the needs and understanding of the child. Hitting is discipline by formula and doesn't promote healthy emotional growth—it takes more time to figure out exactly what motivates your child and to use that information in disciplining him or her. But the outcome of this type of parenting will be much better overall.

In a study of almost 300 children from healthy, intact, large families, almost all the parents found nonphysical interventions more effective than physical ones. One mother had her daughter write out reasons why her behavior wasn't good by considering its impact on others. In another family, poor hearing was found to be the root cause for a young child's persistent failure to follow instructions. Imagine how awful his parents would've felt if they had hit him every time he didn't do what he was told.

Yes, the Bible does suggest, "Spare the rod and spoil the child." But this message is from the Old Testament. In the New Testament Jesus tells us to love one another. And what's a better way to start loving one another than by making the discipline of our children loving and nonviolent?

"Research now confirms what our ancestors knew, that touch can heal."

Teach Parents Infant Massage Therapy

Noel Heiser

A lack of bonding between parents and children is a major risk factor for child abuse, according to Noel Heiser. Bonding is often difficult for parents who abuse drugs, especially if their babies are also born addicted. Massage has proven to calm such babies. In the following viewpoint, Heiser suggests that teaching parents to massage their infants can be a low-cost, effective way to prevent child abuse and help addicts become effective parents. Heiser, a licensed massage therapist in Albuquerque, New Mexico, is a certified infant massage instructor.

As you read, consider the following questions:

1. How does a lack of caring touch lead to escapist behaviors, according to Heiser?
2. What characteristics of addicted infants does the author mention that make bonding difficult for caregivers?
3. List some of the benefits of infant massage that the author gives.

Noel Heiser, "Therapeutic Touch," *Creation Spirituality*, July/August 1992. Reprinted with permission.

The most powerful things in life are often very subtle. In their quietness they have the power to be catalysts for great change, but in our complicated, technical society, these gifts are often overlooked because of their simplicity. Simple human touch has the potential to bring wholeness and healing to other human beings. By allowing them to feel accepted for who they are, supported and nurtured, an awakening of inner power can take place, lighting the way to the healing of the self. In his book, *Birth Without Violence*, Fredrick Leboyer describes the impact touch has on the newborn child:

> A word about the hands holding the newborn child. It is through our hands that we speak to the child, that we communicate. Touching is the primary language, "understanding" comes long after "feeling". . . . Immediately we sense how important such a contact is, just how important is the way we hold a child. . . . The newborn baby's skin has an intelligence, a sensitivity that we can only begin to imagine. It is through its skin that the unborn child once knew its entire world.

So it is through touch that children first experience the world, the community, and who they are. If they are touched with acceptance, with love, they learn to accept themselves and others. If they are often left isolated, held rigidly, or held with anger and impatience, they will probably begin to build walls around themselves to keep from feeling the pain of not being wanted or accepted. These feelings, if left unresolved, are some of the underlying causes of a person's inability to function in society in a healthy way. Drug and alcohol abuse, physical violence, sexual dysfunctions, and denial of emotions are some ways often used to escape from these feelings of isolation. These behaviors have been passed down from generation to generation. In the book *Touch Starvation in America*, author Denny Johnson states:

> It is estimated that one in eight Americans will have a mental breakdown requiring hospitalization within his or her lifetime. It is also estimated that 25% of all families produce incestuous relationships and that 50% of all children will at some time be abused. Our hospitals are full, our prisons are overflowing. Technology and money cannot solve the problems because they are not treating the cause. The answer lies buried in our hearts and hidden behind a wall of fear: millions of people are suffering mentally and physically because they cannot give and receive touch.

It is time for us all to look within ourselves, within our families and communities, to look at our priorities and where they are leading us as a society. Are they leading us to separation or unity? What actions can we take to support the growth of healthy, creative individuals? Many changes need to be made in our lifestyles, and in the larger government structures before we will see a decrease in family violence, crime, poverty, and experience a cleaner, healthier Earth.

Lao Tzu said centuries ago, "The journey of a thousand miles begins with one step." So although touch alone will not heal all of society's problems, it is a simple step that we can take on our journey here together. It is a beginning ready to unfold. We have the power to weave a harmonious world with our hands.

Lack of Bonding Leads to Abuse

A major factor in children being at high risk for abuse is lack of bonding between parents and their children. Professionals are seeing an increase in child abuse which they feel is related to the steady rise in the use of drugs, i.e., cocaine, crack, heroin, alcohol, and an increase in the number of infants born addicted to these drugs. Low self-esteem, difficulties in forming intimate relationships, and a low tolerance for stress are common characteristics in addicts and in adults who abuse their children. Infants who are born addicted to drugs have difficulties bonding, are not as responsive to being held, and often cry for long periods of time. So it is easy to see why an "on edge" adult, with unhealthy coping skills, might become frustrated, and the child is at high risk of being abused.

Our Primary Language

Touch is our primary language. It is the first sense we develop in the womb and our most reliable form of communication in the first years of life. . . .

Touch doesn't simply feel good, it is essential to our survival: In European orphanages during WWI, there were no-touch policies to prevent the spread of infection. In nine out of ten institutions studied, every baby under the age of two died, despite adequate food and shelter. By the 1940's at Bellevue Hospital in New York City, every baby was picked up and held several times a day. The infant mortality rate was less than 10 percent.

Glamour, March 1992.

Showing parents and caregivers ways to begin the bonding process with these children and supporting them in their own relearning of touch, communication, and self acceptance are essential to stop the cycle of abuse and addiction that creates a dysfunctional society. "Cocaine is having a devastating impact on the lives of a booming generation of babies born to addicted women. The number of cocaine-exposed babies is growing explosively, doubling each year in many major cities; estimates put the number in the U.S. as high as 200,000," says Andrew Revkin. These infants will soon become adults having their own children and it is overwhelming to think how that could affect our society. It is important to educate women about choices made before and during pregnancy, and support them in letting go of their addictions so that their babies can be born healthy and drug free. But for the babies already here and the other ones to come, it is essential to understand the different ways drugs can affect infants so that we can be more sensitive to their special needs. These babies may be premature and exhibit respiratory, circulatory, glandular, and lymphatic malfunctions, which can lead to frequent and possible long term hospitalization. Other common characteristics are hypersensitivity, tremors, vomiting, diarrhea, irregular breathing, a weak suck, and mottled skin. The nervous system is also affected and these babies often spend their time either in a deep sleep or crying. The crying is frequently extremely high pitched and hypertonia is common, making it difficult to hold and comfort them. They tend to shun intimate contact and will close their eyes or turn away when eye contact is made. It can be very frustrating for a caretaker because often nothing seems to soothe these babies, and feelings in the caretakers of rejection, irritation, and incompetence are common. Lorretta Finnegan, a research neonatologist, supports the fact of difficulties in dealing with the situation: "An explosive situation is bound to develop when a difficult baby is placed in the care of a woman on cocaine. It's not too good to have a child in front of you when you're irritable or depressed and you have a drive for cocaine. What are you going to do with that baby? Certainly not what you're supposed to," says Revkin. Targeting high-risk families from the beginning and training staff in hospitals, shelters, and other institutions to help begin the healing process in these infants by using massage are ways to help prevent child abuse. Researchers have begun to conclude that bonding can be re-created by the use of focused, nurturing touch such as swaddling and infant massage. The use of these simple tools could be the catalyst for shifting the cycle of violence in the family.

A Simple But Effective Skill

Teaching parents how to massage their children is a simple yet effective way to deal with the bonding difficulties that addicted parents and infants often face. Massage helps to increase circulation, calm and soothe the nervous system, relieve gas (often a problem for many drug babies because of weak or underdeveloped digestive systems), and promote bonding and self awareness. Special ways of caring for drug addicted infants can reduce and often prevent the periods of intense, frantic crying and other behaviors which can be so stressful for a caregiver. Some examples are:

• Massaging the baby 10 to 15 minutes in the morning and afternoon about one hour before the crying period usually begins (these often occur nightly around the same time in "colicky babies") can reduce the intensity and the length of crying time.

• Frequent warm baths help to relieve gas discomfort and soothe and relax the baby's nerves.

• Swaddling the baby, using sheepskin and baby packs can help soothe the child's nerves, and help the infant feel safe and contained, like being in the womb.

• Keeping the child protected from bright lights, loud noises, and sudden movements prevents the child from being startled, which can trigger the frantic crying.

• Using a soft voice, firm, gentle touch and allowing the child to direct the interaction, so that it is moving at its own pace, can prevent the child from becoming overstimulated and encourage the baby to gain trust in the relationship.

Benefits of Massage

Regular consistent massage brings about many positive changes such as increased eye contact, reduction of tremors, and increased responsiveness to being held and talked to. Confidence in parenting skills is often increased because of positive responses in the infant and the parent's increasing ability to read the child's body language, making it easier to respond to the baby's needs. Both parent and child can learn that hands can touch to nurture and that touch can be nonsexual, something often confused in our society. Trust and the joy of constantly "rediscovering" each other and oneself are just some of the many benefits of massage. Fathers especially can benefit. Unable physically to give birth or breastfeed and often not sure what to do with a tiny baby, it is a way for fathers to spend intimate, one-on-one time and actively take part in nurturing their children. Many parents however have never learned to give or receive touch. Often abused or neglected in their own childhoods, it is possible that nurturing touch has never been a part of their lives. It is important for parents to experience "healthy touch" so that they can begin to understand the powerful effect it can have in their child's life. Exercises for parents to overcome fears of touch and learn new communication skills can be integrated into programs. Massaging a child allows parents or caregivers to discover slowly the beauty in that child and within themselves. With the opening of a flower, every day a new petal unfolds—so it is with a child. As you watch the expression on the child's face while you massage her or him and look into the eyes, you begin to see the real beauty of this child. Your hands feel the lifeforce radiating from deep within. Massage can bring about the realization that this child is one of a kind, bringing special gifts to the world. As the hands feel the rhythm of that special soul, the heart opens and the bonding begins.

Attachment Process Is Crucial

The first months of a child's life are critical to well-being—more so than science ever imagined. For it's in those early months that children build their first emotional and psychological bridges to the outside world, with the critical help of a nurturing care-giver—mother, father or someone else. The quality of their lives will depend on the strength of those bridges.

The early part of the attachment process works like this: Babies get hungry or wet their diapers. They cry and scream, kick their legs and wave their arms, and tension builds until a parent answers. The child is given a breast and cradled, or the diaper is changed, and the mother sings to baby softly. The mother and the child come down from the stressful peak together, relaxing and comforting each other. . . .

But if emotionally crippled parents respond to children's crying with neglect or violence, the children can begin to "numb out," to actually stop feeling pain and to stop expressing needs, both physical and emotional. They never develop basic skills for bonding and cannot bond in a healthy way to others.

Jim Robbins, *Los Angeles Times Magazine*, January 19, 1992.

It is essential that we integrate our "primary language" of touch into programs in hospitals, family centers, etc., as a tool for the prevention and rehabilitation of infants born addicted to drugs, abused children and their parents. Overdependence on technology, fears of being accused of child abuse, and disbelief in the effectiveness of this type of therapy are just a few of the reasons that people hesitate to use touch as a treatment for abuse and drug related problems in infants. But high technology is not working for these babies and their families. We need to slow down and acknowledge that often the simplest, least costly ways of healing can also be the most effective. Research now confirms what our ancestors knew, that touch can heal. Since many "cocaine babies" are born prematurely and premature babies are at high risk for abuse, massage would be especially beneficial for these babies.

Hospitals in some states are beginning to teach staff to massage infants on a daily basis, to teach parents swaddling and massage skills, and to encourage family involvement in the child's care so that the child can learn from the beginning to receive touch and bond with family and caregivers. This simple addition to hospital care and other programs for families in the community could prevent a lifetime of pain and abuse for a child. Jules Older, Ph.D., from New Zealand, sums up how valuable touch may be in treating abuse:

> Child abuse may be viewed as a disorder of touch. The disorder may be expressed in terms of quantity, quality or strength. Insufficient touch is a major component of neglect. Incest is touch of the wrong sort. Battering is a form of touch at the wrong strength. The literature of child abuse clearly recognizes that it is a frequently transmitted phenomenon, parents who neglect or seduce or beat their children are often those who were themselves badly touched as children. Yet this same literature strangely ignores what might seems an obvious conclusion, that is, if touch was the damaging modality, it may also be a source of restoration.

Teaching people how to help themselves and their families can be very powerful medicine. Through the use of nurturing touch, we can communicate to our children and the generations to come that they are wanted, so that they can grow to accept themselves and others, to become all that they can be. It is a gentle wind that blows a seed to the Earth, allowing it to find a safe place for roots to grow. And years from that time a beautiful tree, abundant with fruit to share, stands because its seed was once nurtured by a gentle wind. One touch can make a difference in a life and then like a gentle wind, plant another seed.

VIEWPOINT

"We have but one choice: Call them monsters and isolate them."

Imprison Chronic Sexual Sadists for Life

Andrew Vachss

A failure of socialization—perhaps because they were abused as children—keeps sociopaths from feeling empathy, according to Andrew Vachss. In the following viewpoint, Vachss asserts that for those sociopaths who become chronic sexual predators, including those who prey on children, rehabilitation is impossible. If these criminals are released, the author says, they will attack again. Vachss argues for permanent incarceration for chronic sexual sadists. Vachss, author and juvenile justice advocate, is an attorney in New York City.

As you read, consider the following questions:

1. Why does Vachss find the death penalty an unacceptable solution to the problem of chronic child molesters?
2. What, according to the author, causes the failure of mandated therapy programs?
3. What possible problems does Vachss see in the Washington State law that permits indefinite confinement of sex offenders?

Westley Allan Dodd was scheduled to be hanged at 12:01 A.M. Tuesday, January 5, 1993, at the Washington State Penitentiary in Walla Walla. Sentenced to execution for the torture-murder of three boys, Mr. Dodd refused all efforts to appeal his case. He may not have exhausted his legal remedies, but he certainly exhausted society's efforts at "rehabilitation."

A chronic, calcified sexual sadist, Mr. Dodd stated in a court brief, "If I do escape, I promise you I will kill and rape again, and I will enjoy every minute of it."

How Shall We Deal with Monsters?

Mr. Dodd's threat demands a response because we know he is not unique. There can be no dispute that monsters live among us. The only question is what to do with them once they become known to us.

The death penalty is not a response. Racially and economically biased and endlessly protracted, it returns little for its enormous economic and social costs. Though it is effective—the killer will not strike again—the death penalty is limited to murderers; it will not protect us from rapists and child molesters who are virtually assured of release and who are almost certain to commit their crimes again.

If we do not intend to execute sex criminals, does our hope lie in killing their destructive impulses? Mr. Dodd and his ilk are sociopaths. They are characterized by a fundamental lack of empathy. All children are born pure egoists. They perceive their needs to the exclusion of all others. Only through socialization do they learn that some forms of gratification must be deferred and others denied. When a child's development is incomplete or perverted—and child abuse is the most dominant cause in that equation—he or she tends not to develop empathy. There's a missing card, one that cannot be put back in the deck once the personality is fully formed.

Evil Is a Choice

While early childhood experiences may impel, they do not compel. In the end, evil is a matter of choice. Sociopaths can learn to project a veneer of civilization—for predators, it is part of their camouflage—but they will always lack the ability to feel any pain but their own, pursuing only *self*-gratification. Not all sociopaths choose sexual violence. For some, the outlet can be political or economic skulduggery. But those for whom blood or pain is the stimulus act no less efficiently and at a terrible and unacceptable cost.

Some predatory sociopaths can be deterred. None can be rehabilitated, since they cannot return to a state that never existed. The concept of coercive therapy is a contradiction; successful psychiatric treatment requires participants, not mere recipients. What makes sexual predators so intractable and dangerous is that, as Mr. Dodd candidly acknowledged, they like what they do and intend to keep dong it.

The obsession of sexual predators is typified in the case of Donald Chapman, a New Jersey rapist who was released in November 1992 after serving 12 years, the maximum for his crime. He underwent continual therapy in prison, and was utterly unaffected by it. He vows to continue to attack women—a threat that reflects his total absorption with sexual torture. As a result of his threat, he sits in his house in Wyckoff, N.J., surrounded by a 24-hour police guard.

Psychiatric Treatment May Hurt More than It Helps

A 1992 study of 767 rapists and child molesters in Minnesota found those who completed psychiatric treatment were arrested more often for new sex crimes than those who had not been treated at all. A Canadian survey that tracked released child molesters for 20 years revealed a 43 percent recidivism rate regardless of the therapy. The difference between those simply incarcerated and those subjected to a full range of treatments appears statistically negligible. And the more violent and sadistic the offense, the more likely it is to be repeated.

Another factor that thwarts rehabilitation is the need for offenders to seek higher and higher levels of stimulation. There is no observable waning of their desires over time: sexual predators do not outgrow their behavior. Thus, while most sadistic sex offenders are not first arrested for homicide, they may well try to murder someone in the future.

What about a traditional self-help program? Should we concentrate on raising their self-esteem? Imprisoned predators receive as much fan mail as rock stars. They are courted by the news media, studied by devoted sociologists, their every word treasured as though profound. Their paintings are collected, their poetry published. Trading cards celebrate their bloody passage among us.

I received a letter from a young woman who gushed that, after a long exchange of letters, she was "granted visiting privileges" with Mr. Dodd and subsequently appeared on "Sally Jessy Raphael" "due to my relationship" with "Wes," who she believes is "sincere." So do I. We simply disagree about the object of his sincerity.

Sexual Predators Have Contempt for Society

Sexual predators are already narcissistic; they laugh behind their masks at our attempts to understand and rehabilitate them. We have earned their contempt by our belief that they can change—by our confusion of "crazy" with "dangerous," and "sick" with "sickening."

If we don't intend to execute sexual predators, and we have no treatment, what is our final line of defense? Washington State has a so-called sexual predator law permitting indefinite confinement of sex offenders deemed to be dangerous if released. The law's critics argue that psychiatry has been a woefully inadequate forecaster. Others cite the constitutional problems of imprisonment based on prospective conduct.

Even Castration Will Not Work

Recently there has been much discussion of voluntary castration. Such a "remedy" ignores reality. Sexual violence is not sex gone too far, it is violence with sex as its instrument. Rage, sadism and a desire to control or debase others are the driving forces. Castration can be reversed chemically with black-market hormones, and sex murders have been committed by physically castrated rapists. People have been raped by blunt objects. And how do you castrate female offenders?

There Are No Cures

The world's most advanced nation, as it enters the 21st century, appears to be helpless in stopping its citizens from destroying their children. . . .

An official of the Oregon State Hospital, a primary treatment center for sex offenders, stated, "There are no cures in this business. About the only thing we haven't tried is Magnum therapy—blowing their brains out with a bullet.". . .

Most child abusers . . . don't really want to stop, since it is the only way for them to be sexually gratified.

As author John Crewdson [*By Silence Betrayed*] observes: "The longer the compulsion to have sex with children goes on, the stronger it becomes, and by the time a pedophile has had four or five victims, it's usually too late."

V. Doner, *Child Protection Guide*, 1992.

Our response to sexual predators must balance the extent and intensity of the possible behavior with the probability of its occurrence. An ex-prisoner likely to expose himself on a crowded subway may be a risk we are willing to assume. A prisoner with even a moderate probability of sexual torture and murder is not. Such violence is like a rock dropped into a calm pool—the concentric circles spread even after the rock has sunk. More and more victims will be affected.

When it comes to sexual violence, the sum of our social and psychiatric knowledge adds up to this: Behavior is the truth.

They Can't Change—and Don't Want To

Chronic sexual predators have crossed an osmotic membrane. They can't step back to the other side—our side. And they don't want to. If we don't kill or release them, we have but one choice: Call them monsters and isolate them.

When it comes to the sexual sadist, psychiatric diagnoses won't protect us. Appeasement endangers us. Rehabilitation is a joke.

I've spoken to many predators over the years. They always exhibit amazement that we do not hunt them. And that when we capture them, we eventually let them go. Our attitude is a deliberate interference with Darwinism—an endangerment of our species.

A proper experiment produces answers. Experiments with sexual sadists have produced only victims. Washington State's sexual predator law will surely be challenged in the courts and it may take years before constitutional and criminological criteria are established to incarcerate a criminal beyond his or her sentence.

A Straightforward Solution

Perhaps no-parole life sentences for certain sex crimes would be a more straightforward answer. In any event, such laws offer our only hope against an epidemic of sexual violence that threatens to pollute our society beyond the possibility of its own rehabilitation.

Periodical Bibliography

The following articles have been selected to supplement the diverse views presented in this chapter.

American Bar Association	"The Probation Response to Child Sexual Abuse Offenders: How Is It Working?" 1990. Executive Summary available free from American Bar Association, National Center on Children and the Law Pubs., 1800 M St. NW, 2d Floor South Lobby, Washington, DC 20036-5886.
Douglas J. Besharov and Andrew Vachss	"Sex Offenders: Is Castration an Acceptable Punishment?" *ABA Journal*, July 1992. Available from 750 N. Lake Shore Dr., Chicago, IL 60611.
Peg McCartt Hess and Gail Folaron	"Ambivalences: A Challenge to Permanency for Children," *Child Welfare*, July/August 1991.
David A. Kaplan	"The Incorrigibles," *Newsweek*, January 18, 1993.
James J. Krivacska	"Child Sexual Abuse Prevention Programs," *SIECUS Report*, August/September 1991. Available from Sex Information and Education Council of the U.S., 130 W. 42d St., Suite 2500, New York, NY 10036.
Leroy H. Pelton	"Resolving the Crisis in Child Welfare: Simply Expanding the System Is Not Enough," *Public Welfare*, Fall 1990.
Mary E. Pharis and Victoria A. Levin	" 'A Person to Talk to Who Really Cared': High-Risk Mothers' Evaluations of Services in an Intensive Intervention Research Program," *Child Welfare*, May/June 1991.
Corrine Scheuneman	"Prevention and Rehabilitation: Communities' Best Defense Against Child Sexual Abuse," paper presented to the American Psychological Association, August 16, 1992. Available from Family Violence & Sexual Assault Institute, 1310 Clinic Dr., Tyler, TX 75701.
Mark D. Simms and Barbara J. Bolden	"The Family Reunification Project: Facilitating Regular Contact Among Foster Children, Biological Families, and Foster Families," *Child Welfare*, November/December 1991.

For Further Discussion

Chapter 1

1. The Family Research Council and Douglas J. Besharov suggest in their viewpoints that educational, emotional, and physical neglect of children are problems that do not require "urgent, emergency attention." Why do the authors believe this? How does David Finkelhor rebut this argument in his viewpoint?

2. David Finkelhor is codirector of the Family Research Laboratory, which receives financial support from government grants and private foundations. Douglas J. Besharov is a legal scholar for the American Enterprise Institute for Public Policy Research, a private research group that seeks to limit government. Explain how these affiliations are reflected in their viewpoints and in the conclusions they draw. Use examples from the viewpoints to illustrate your answer.

3. Robert Sheridan charges in his viewpoint that child advocates illogically use contradictory facts to prove that child abuse occurred; for example, both confessions and denials by the accused can be considered proof that abuse occurred. Examine Sheridan's arguments, then respond to them from the point of view expressed by Meredith Sherman Fahn.

4. The viewpoints of Ellen Bass and Laura Davis and of Richard Ofshe and Ethan Watters both address the ways in which the mind can repress—and later recall—memories. How do the authors support their assertions? Which viewpoint is more compelling? Why?

Chapter 2

1. Some statistics show that as many as sixteen million Americans use illegal drugs every year. While many of these people will not abuse or neglect their children, parental drug abuse has been strongly linked to child abuse. The viewpoint by Ron Harris contains the stories of several families damaged by drug abuse and child abuse. What do addicted parents say about abusing their children? How are the children affected?

2. Vincent J. Fontana and Valerie Moolman begin their viewpoint with "People say 'Eliminate poverty, and you'll eliminate child abuse!' I wish it were true." They conclude that it would not cure child abuse. Brian H. McNeill, however, asserts that poverty contributes significantly to the incidence

of child abuse and that reducing poverty would reduce child abuse. In what ways are the arguments in these two viewpoints similar and in what ways are they different?

3. Authors Vincent J. Fontana and Valerie Moolman argue that humanity's long history of war and domestic violence led straight to the domestic violence that permeates American society today. What are some concrete ways the authors suggest to reduce this violence, especially violence against children?

4. In the viewpoint entitled "A Lack of Community Ties Causes Child Abuse," Richard Farson discusses how isolation from extended family and community can cause families to feel lonely and alienated. These feelings, Farson argues, can push parents to abuse their children. Author Elaine Landau also touches on loneliness and social isolation in her viewpoint but goes on to discuss a variety of factors that she believes can lead to abuse. Compare and contrast these two authors' discussions about isolation as a cause of abuse.

Chapter 3

1. Carl A. Raschke believes satanic cults and conspiracies are flourishing. Kenneth V. Lanning thinks it is unlikely that such conspiracies could remain secret for long. Yet Raschke and Lanning agree on several points about child molesters. What are they?

2. How are the molesters discussed by Lanning and Raschke different from priests and scout leaders who molest children? How are they alike?

3. Would the techniques to prevent child sexual abuse taught by the Boy Scouts work for very young children? Would they work for children molested by people who claimed to be satanists? Why or why not?

Chapter 4

1. The Sixth Amendment to the U.S. Constitution reads in part, "In all criminal prosecutions, the accused shall enjoy the right . . . to be confronted with the witnesses against him." When this amendment was written, children were not allowed to testify in court and closed-circuit television had not been invented. Should these changes affect the interpretation of the Sixth Amendment to allow children to testify without having to physically face those they accuse? Explain your reasoning.

2. In considering the question of witness confrontation, what values do Katherine A. Francis and Robert H. King Jr. believe should be paramount? Explain which values you believe should be given the most weight and why.

3. Robert H. King Jr. cites several technical problems with the use of closed-circuit television in the *Craig* case. Do you think such problems are an integral part of the argument about the constitutionality of the procedure? Why or why not?

Chapter 5

1. You hear your neighbor's ten-year-old child scream—apparently her father is beating her again. This has happened three or four times since he lost his job six months ago. If you report him, he may be forced to move out, or the child may be put into a foster home. Consider the chapters authors' suggestions for reducing abuse; then determine how you would deal with this specific situation.

2. Abused children taken from their parents may remain in foster care for many months, or even years, and may be moved to several different homes. Many complain of being abused in their foster homes. Some are never reunited with their parents. What solutions to the foster care system do the authors in the chapter propose? Evaluate the possible effectiveness of these solutions and propose some of your own.

3. Present an argument for each side of this issue: Teachers should be allowed to spank unruly students.

4. Consider the solution for reducing child abuse proposed by Vincent J. Fontana and Valerie Moolman in light of the viewpoints of Douglas Besharov and David Finkelhor in the first chapter. How would Besharov and Finkelhor each respond to Fontana and Moolman's proposal?

Organizations to Contact

The editors have compiled the following list of organizations that are concerned with the issues debated in this book. All of them have publications or information available for interested readers. For best results, allow as much time as possible for the organizations to respond. The descriptions below are derived from materials provided by the organizations. This list was compiled upon the date of publication. Names, addresses, and phone numbers of organizations are subject to change.

American Academy of Child and Adolescent Psychiatry (AACAP)
3615 Wisconsin Ave. NW
Washington, DC 20016
(202) 966-7300

AACAP is an association of psychiatrists with additional training in child and adolescent psychiatry. In addition to professional publications, it publishes *Facts for Families*, information sheets on psychiatric disorders affecting children and adolescents. Titles include "Child Sexual Abuse" and "Child Abuse—the Hidden Bruises."

American Bar Association (ABA) Center on Children and the Law
1800 M St. NW, Suite 200
Washington, DC 20036
(202) 331-2250

The ABA Center aims to improve the quality of life for children through advances in law and public policy. It publishes the monthly *ABA Juvenile and Child Welfare Law Reporter* and specializes in providing information on legal matters related to the protection of children.

American Humane Association (AHA)
Children's Division
63 Inverness Dr. East
Englewood, CO 80112-5117
(303) 792-9900

AHA's children's division works to protect children and strengthen families through education, advocacy, and policy-making—especially policies encouraging the development of community-based systems of care for children and families. It publishes books, working papers, fact sheets, and a quarterly magazine, *Protecting Children*.

American Professional Society on the Abuse of Children (APSAC)
332 S. Michigan Ave., Suite 1600
Chicago, IL 60604
(312) 554-0166

APSAC is dedicated to improving the coordination of services in the fields of child abuse prevention, treatment, and research. It publishes a quarterly newsletter, *The Advisor*, and the *Journal of Interpersonal Violence.*

Child Abuse & Disabled Project (CADP)
The Lexington Center
30th Ave. at 75th St.
Jackson Heights, NY 11370
(718) 899-8800

CADP works to protect children who are especially vulnerable to abuse because of disabilities and addresses the challenges in intervention with such children. It offers reprints of articles on these subjects and lists of professionals and organizations active in these areas.

Child Assault Prevention Project
National Assault Prevention Center
PO Box 02005
Columbus, OH 43202
(614) 291-2540

The National Assault Prevention Center (NAPC) was founded to prevent violence through curriculum development, research, and education. Its Child Assault Prevention (CAP) Project, provides abuse prevention services to children of all ages, children with special needs, parents, teachers, and professionals. NAPC and CAP publish brochures, videos, booklets, and books such as *New Strategies for Free Children*, a manual for running a CAP project.

Child Protection Program Foundation
7441 Marvin D. Love Freeway, Suite 200
Dallas, TX 75237
(214) 709-0300

The foundation was created to help prevent the criminal neglect and physical, emotional, and sexual abuse of children in America. Its advocacy efforts include distribution of educational materials, including the *Child Protection Guide* and *Victim Resources Manual*.

Children's Healthcare Is a Legal Duty (CHILD)
PO Box 2604
Sioux City, IA 51106
(712) 948-3500

CHILD works to prevent medical neglect and abuse of children due to religious beliefs. It offers a list of references on the subject and a booklet, *Cry, the Beloved Children*, about children who have died or been permanently harmed by the withholding of medical care for religious reasons. It reports on such cases in its quarterly newsletter.

Child Welfare League of America (CWLA)
440 First St. NW, Suite 310
Washington, DC 20001-2085
(202) 638-2952

The goal of the CWLA is to ensure the welfare of all children. It publishes a wide variety of books, booklets, videos, and bibliographies for professionals, parents, and the public, including the book *Tender Mercies: Inside the World of a Child Abuse Investigator*, the quarterly magazine *Children's Voice*, and the bimonthly journal *Child Welfare*.

Clearinghouse on Child Abuse and Neglect Information
PO Box 1182
Washington, DC 20013-1182
(800) 394-3366

The clearinghouse provides free information from the U.S. government on child abuse and neglect, including the *Catalog of Child Abuse and Neglect Publications* and a child abuse and neglect information packet.

Committee for Mother and Child Rights, Inc.
Rt. 1, Box 256A
Clear Brook, VA 22624
(703) 722-3652

The committee offers emotional support and guidance for mothers with child custody problems. It is concerned with the mental, physical, and sexual abuse often associated with contested custody decisions. The committee publishes a fact sheet on contested custody problems.

End Violence Against the Next Generation, Inc. (EVANG)
977 Keeler Ave.
Berkeley, CA 94708-1498
(415) 527-0454

EVANG seeks to end the use of corporal punishment in schools. It publishes a quarterly newsletter and booklets such as *1001 Alternatives to Corporal Punishment*, vols. 1 and 2, and *The Influence of Corporal Punishment on Crime*.

False Memory Syndrome Foundation
3508 Market St., Suite 128
Philadelphia, PA 19104
(215) 387-1865

The foundation believes that many "delayed memories" of sexual abuse are the result of false memory syndrome (FMS). In FMS, patients in therapy "recall" childhood abuse that never occurred. The foundation seeks to discover reasons for the spread of FMS, works for the prevention of new cases, and aids FMS victims, including those falsely accused of abuse. The foundation publishes a newsletter and various working papers and distributes articles and information on FMS.

Family Research Council (FRC)
700 13th St. NW, Suite 500
Washington, DC 20005
(202) 393-2100

FRC is a consulting and lobbying organization that applies traditional values to current problems. Its interests include strengthening the family to avoid the formation of abusive patterns, encouraging private alternatives to public child protection agencies, and reforming the child protection system. It publishes the monthly newsletter *Washington Watch*; the bimonthly publication *Family Policy*; and the book *Free to Be Family*.

Family Research Laboratory (FRL)
University of New Hampshire
Durham, NH 03824-3586
(603) 862-1888

FRL is an independent research unit devoted to the study of the causes and consequences of family violence, including physical and sexual abuse of children, and the connections between family violence and other social problems. A bibliography of works on these subjects, produced by staff members under the sponsorship of the University of New Hampshire, is available from FRL.

Family Violence & Sexual Assault Institute (FVSAI)
1310 Clinic Dr.
Tyler, TX 75701
(903) 595-6799

FVSAI networks among people and agencies involved in studying, treating, protecting, or otherwise dealing with violent or abusive families. FVSAI maintains a computerized database that includes unpublished or difficult-to-find articles and papers that are available for copying and postage charges. Publications include the bibliographies *Sexual Abuse/Incest Survivors* and *Child Physical Abuse/Neglect* and the quarterly *Family Violence & Sexual Assault Bulletin*.

Federation on Child Abuse and Neglect
134 S. Swan St.
Albany, NY 12210
(518) 445-1273

The federation is dedicated to preventing all types of child abuse by raising public awareness about the causes and prevention of abuse and to advocating legislation and programs to protect children from abuse. It offers brochures such as *What Kids Should Know About Child Abuse and Neglect*, booklets such as *Child Sexual Abuse Guidelines for Health Professionals*, fact sheets, and reprinted articles.

Focus on the Family
420 N. Cascade Ave.
Colorado Springs, CO 80903
(719) 531-3400

Focus on the Family believes that reestablishing the traditional two-parent family will end many social problems. Its resource list, *Information on Abuse*, lists books, audio tapes, and information sheets.

For Kids Sake, Inc.
31676 Railroad Canyon Rd.
Canyon Lake, CA 92380
(714) 244-9001

For Kids Sake, dedicated to the prevention of child abuse through education and intervention, maintains a large research library on this subject. It believes that the problems of parenting are best solved by the community. For Kids Sake offers brochures on parenting and child safety; molestation-prevention programs and curricula; and educational materials for medical, law enforcement, and teaching personnel.

Incest Resources, Inc. (IR)
Cambridge Women's Center
46 Pleasant St.
Cambridge, MA 02139
(617) 354-8807

IR provides educational and resource materials for incest survivors. The IR legal packet is a series of articles and resource listings related to civil prosecution of incest offenders. A self-addressed, stamped envelope (two first-class stamps) must accompany requests for information.

Incest Survivors Resource Network International (ISRNI)
PO Box 7375
Las Cruces, NM 88006-7375
(505) 521-4260

ISRNI stresses awareness of male incest victims of female abusers and of the concept of emotional incest. It offers bibliographies and networking information that enables survivors of child sexual abuse to contact similar organizations throughout the United States.

Kempe National Center for the Prevention and Treatment of Child Abuse and Neglect
1205 Oneida St.
Denver, CO 80220
(303) 321-3963

The Kempe Center, a clinically based resource for research in all forms of child abuse and neglect, is committed to multidisciplinary approaches to improve the recognition, treatment, and prevention of abuse. The Kempe Center Resource Library offers a catalog of books, booklets, information packets, and articles on these issues.

National Center for Missing & Exploited Children (NCMEC)
2101 Wilson Blvd., Suite 550
Arlington, VA 22201-3052
(703) 235-3900

NCMEC serves as a clearinghouse of information on missing and exploited children and coordinates child protection efforts with the private sector. A number of publications on these issues are available, including guidelines for parents whose children are testifying in court; help for abused children; and booklets such as *Children Traumatized in Sex Rings* and *Child Molesters: A Behavioral Analysis.*

National Center for Prosecution of Child Abuse
American Prosecutors Research Institute
99 Canal Center Plaza, Suite 510
Alexandria, VA 22314
(703) 739-0321

The center seeks to improve the investigation and prosecution of child abuse cases. A clearinghouse on child abuse laws and court reforms, the center supports research on reducing courtroom trauma for child victims and publishes a monthly newsletter, *Update,* as well as monographs, bibliographies, special reports, and a manual for prosecutors, *Investigation and Prosecution of Child Abuse.*

National Center for Study of Corporal Punishment & Alternatives in Schools
Temple University
253 Ritter Annex
Philadelphia, PA 19122
(215) 787-6091

The center offers literature on various child abuse issues, including corporal punishment and alternatives to physical discipline.

National Coalition Against Domestic Violence (NCADV)
Child Advocacy Task Force
PO Box 18749
Denver, CO 80218-0749
(303) 839-1852

NCADV represents organizations and individuals that assist battered women and their children. The Child Advocacy Task Force deals with issues affecting children who witness violence at home or are themselves abused. It publishes the quarterly newsletter *The Bulletin.*

National Coalition to Abolish Corporal Punishment in Schools
Ohio Center for More Effective Discipline
155 W. Main St., Suite 100-B
Columbus, OH 43215
(614) 221-8829

The coalition works to eliminate corporal punishment in schools. The center offers information on alternative forms of discipline. The coalition and center share offices and resources; they publish information on the effects of corporal punishment and on alternatives to its use.

National Committee for Prevention of Child Abuse (NCPCA)
332 S. Michigan Ave.
Chicago, IL 60604-4357
(312) 663-3520

NCPCA's mission is to prevent child abuse in all its forms. NCPCA distributes and publishes materials on a variety of topics, including child abuse and child abuse prevention. A free catalog is available from NCPCA Publications Dept., PO Box 94283, Chicago, IL 60690.

National Institute of Justice (NIJ)
U.S. Department of Justice
National Criminal Justice Reference Service
Box 6000
Rockville, MD 20850
(800) 851-3420

NIJ is the research and development agency of the U.S. Department of Justice established to prevent and reduce crime and to improve the criminal justice system. Among its publications is the report *When the Victim Is a Child*, which reviews new research on the consequences of child sexual abuse, and the capabilities of children as witnesses.

National Resource Center on Child Abuse and Neglect (NRCCAN)
63 Inverness Dr. East
Englewood, CO 80112-5117
(800) 227-5242

NRCCAN identifies and organizes resources on child abuse and neglect, disseminates information, and coordinates with the National Resource Center on Child Sexual Abuse and the National Clearinghouse on Child Abuse and Neglect Information. It responds to requests for information, makes referrals to other agencies as appropriate, and tracks requests for information to identify emerging issues and developmental needs in the field of child protection.

National Resource Center on Child Sexual Abuse
106 Lincoln St.
Huntsville, AL 35801
(800) 543-7006

The center is funded by the National Center on Child Abuse and Neglect of the U.S. Department of Health and Human Services and is operated by the National Children's Advocacy Center. In addition to its toll-free information line, the center publishes a newsletter, information papers, monographs, and bibliographies free or for a small charge.

National Victims Resource Center (NVRC)
Box 6000
Rockville, MD 20850
(800) 627-6872

NVRC is a primary source of information on crime victims, and of research and statistics on child abuse. It distributes a child abuse information package and documents such as *Child Sexual Abuse Victims and Their Treatment,* and *Police and Child Abuse.*

NOW Legal Defense and Education Fund
99 Hudson St., 12th Floor
New York, NY 10013
(212) 925-6635

This arm of the National Organization for Women (NOW), an organization that seeks to end discrimination against women, offers a select publications list on incest and sexual abuse and a legal resources kit on incest and child sexual abuse.

Parents and Teachers Against Violence in Education (PTAVE)
PO Box 1033
Alamo, CA 94507-7033
(510) 831-1661

PTAVE's mission is to promote universal acceptance of the belief that every child has the right to grow and learn in an environment that is violence-free. It distributes the booklet *Plain Talk About Spanking.*

The Safer Society Program
RR 1, Box 24-B
Orwell, VT 05760
(802) 897-7541

The Safer Society Program, a project of the New York State Council of Churches, is a national research, advocacy, and referral center for the prevention of sexual abuse of children and adults. The Safer Society Press publishes, studies, and books on treatment for sexual victims and offenders and on the prevention of sexual abuse.

Sex Information and Education Council of the U.S. (SIECUS)
130 W. 42d St., Suite 2500
New York, NY 10036
(212) 819-9770

SIECUS is a clearinghouse for information on sexuality, with a special interest in sex education. It publishes sex education curricula, the bimonthly newsletter *SIECUS Report*, and fact sheets on sex education issues. Its articles, bibliographies, and book reviews often address the role of education in identifying, reducing, and preventing sexual abuse.

United Fathers of America, Inc. (UFA)
595 The City Dr., Suite 202
Orange, CA 92668
(714) 385-1002

UFA believes that protecting children should not come at the expense of the emotional and psychological trauma caused when vindictive parents falsely charge ex-spouses with sexual abuse of their children. Primarily a support group, UFA answers specific questions and suggests articles and studies that illustrate its position.

VOCAL/National Association of State VOCAL Organizations (NASVO)
PO Box 1314
Orangevale, CA 95662
(916) 863-7470; (800) 745-8778

VOCAL (Victims of Child Abuse Laws) provides information, research data, referrals, and emotional support for those who have been falsely accused of child abuse. NASVO maintains a library of research on child abuse and neglect issues, focusing on legal, mental health, social, and medical issues, and will provide photocopies of articles for a fee. It publishes the bimonthly newsletter *NASVO News*.

VOICES In Action, Inc.
PO Box 148309
Chicago, IL 60614
(312) 327-1500

Victims Of Incest Can Emerge Survivors (VOICES) provides assistance to victims of incest and child sexual abuse and awakens public awareness about the prevalence of incest. It publishes a bibliography and the newsletter *The Chorus*, and offers reprints of papers and articles such as "Myths of Male Sexual Abuse: Factors in Underreporting."

Women Against Rape (WAR)/Child Watch
PO Box 346
Collingswood, NJ 08108
(609) 858-7800

The WAR/Child Watch offices handle requests for information for Society's League Against Molestation (SLAM), an organization that researches social, psychological, and legal aspects of molestation; monitors court cases; and suggests legislation to prevent abuse. WAR/Child Watch's publications include brochures such as *Incest/Molestation* and statistics on sexual assault.

Bibliography of Books

Robert T. Ammerman and Michel Hersen, eds.
Children at Risk: An Evaluation of Factors Contributing to Child Abuse and Neglect. New York: Plenum Press, 1990.

Keith Barnhart with Lila Wold Shelburne
Guilty Until Proven Innocent. Hannibal, MO: Hannibal Books, 1990.

Ellen Bass and Laura Davis
The Courage to Heal: A Guide for Women Survivors of Child Sexual Abuse. rev. ed. New York: HarperCollins, 1992.

Jason Berry
Lead Us Not into Temptation: Catholic Priests and the Sexual Abuse of Children. New York: Doubleday, 1992.

Douglas J. Besharov
Recognizing Child Abuse: A Guide for the Concerned. New York: Free Press, 1990.

Douglas J. Besharov, ed.
Family Violence: Research and Family Policy Issues. Washington, DC: AEI Press, 1990.

Frank G. Bolton, Larry A. Morris, and Ann E. MacEachron
Males at Risk: The Other Side of Child Sexual Abuse. Newbury Park, CA: Sage, 1989.

John Crewdson
By Silence Betrayed: Sexual Abuse of Children in America. Boston: Little, Brown, 1988.

John Doris, ed.
The Suggestibility of Children's Recollections: Implications for Eyewitness Testimony. Washington, DC: American Psychological Association, 1991.

Billie Wright Dziech and Charles B. Schudson
On Trial: America's Courts and Their Treatment of Sexually Abused Children. Boston: Beacon Press, 1991.

David Finkelhor and Linda Meyer Williams with Nancy Burns
Nursery Crimes: Sexual Abuse in Day Care. Newbury Park, CA: Sage, 1988.

Vincent J. Fontana and Valerie Moolman
Save the Family, Save the Child. New York: Mentor, 1991.

Vera Gallagher
Becoming Whole Again: Help for Women Survivors of Childhood Sexual Abuse. Blue Ridge Summit, PA: TAB Books, 1991.

Richard J. Gelles and Jane B. Lancaster, eds.
Child Abuse and Neglect: Biosocial Dimensions. Hawthorne, NY: Aldine de Gruyter, 1987.

Neil Gilbert, Jill Duerr Berrick, Nicole Le Prohn, and Nina Nyman
Protecting Young Children from Sexual Abuse: Does Preschool Training Work? Lexington, MA: Lexington Books, 1989.

Seth L. Goldstein   *The Sexual Exploitation of Children: A Practical Guide to Assessment, Investigation, and Intervention*. New York: Elsevier, 1987.

Philip Greven   *Spare the Child: The Religious Roots of Punishment and the Psychological Impact of Physical Abuse*. New York: Random House, Vintage Books, 1991.

Lorraine Fox Harding   *Perspectives in Child Care Policy*. New York: Longman, 1991.

David Hechler   *The Battle and the Backlash: The Child Sexual Abuse War.* Lexington, MA: D.C. Heath, 1988.

Sylvia Ann Hewlett   *When the Bough Breaks: The Cost of Neglecting Our Children*. New York: Basic Books, 1991.

Dean D. Knudsen   *Child Maltreatment: Emerging Perspectives*. Dix Hills, NY: General Hall, 1992.

Elaine Landau   *Child Abuse: An American Epidemic*. Englewood Cliffs, NJ: Julian Messner, 1990.

Kenneth V. Lanning   *Child Sex Rings: A Behavioral Analysis*. Arlington, VA: National Center for Missing & Exploited Children, in cooperation with the Federal Bureau of Investigation, 1992.

Richard Layman   *Current Issues*, vol. 1, *Child Abuse.* Detroit: Omnigraphics, Inc., 1990.

Murray Levine and Adeline Levine   *Helping Children: A Social History*. New York: Oxford University Press, 1992.

Elizabeth Loftus and Katherine Ketcham   *Witness for the Defense: The Accused, the Eyewitness, and the Expert Who Puts Memory on Trial*. New York: St. Martin's Press, 1991.

Arthur Lyons   *Satan Wants You: The Cult of Devil Worship in America*. New York: The Mysterious Press, 1988.

Susan Mufson and Rachel Kranz   *Straight Talk About Child Abuse*. New York: Facts On File, 1991.

John E.B. Myers   *Legal Issues in Child Abuse and Neglect.* Newbury Park, CA: Sage, 1992.

National Commission on Children   *Beyond Rhetoric: A New American Agenda for Children and Families*. Final Report, 1991. Available from the National Commission on Children, 1111 18th St. NW, Suite 810, Washington, DC 20036.

Michael Quinn Patton, ed.   *Family Sexual Abuse: Frontline Research and Evaluation.* Newbury Park, CA: Sage, 1991.

Leroy H. Pelton   *For Reasons of Poverty: A Critical Analysis of the Public Child Welfare System in the United States.* New York: Praeger, 1989.

Nancy Walker Perry and Lawrence S. Wrightsman   *The Child Witness: Legal Issues and Dilemmas.* Newbury Park, CA: Sage, 1991.

Practising Law Institute   *Child Abuse, Neglect, and the Foster Care System 1991.* Criminal Law and Urban Problems Course Handbook Series, no. 158. New York: Practising Law Institute, 1991.

Carl A. Raschke   *Painted Black: From Drug Killings to Heavy Metal—The Alarming True Story of How Satanism Is Terrorizing Our Communities.* New York: Harper & Row, 1990.

James T. Richardson, Joel Best, and David G. Bromley, eds.   *The Satanism Scare.* Hawthorne, NY: Aldine de Gruyter, 1991.

Dean Tong   *Don't Blame Me, Daddy: False Accusations of Child Sexual Abuse.* Norfolk, VA: Hampton Roads, 1992.

Cynthia Crosson Tower   *How Schools Can Help Combat Child Abuse and Neglect.* 2d ed. Washington, DC: NEA Professional Library, n.d.

U.S. Senate Committee on the Judiciary   *Hearing on the Treatment of Child Abuse Allegations and Victims in the Judicial and Victims Services System,* May 16, 1989. Serial No. J-101-16. S. Hrg. 101-761. Washington, DC: U.S. Government Printing Office, 1990.

The Violence Against Children Study Group   *Taking Child Abuse Seriously: Contemporary Issues in Child Protection Theory and Practice.* London: Unwin Hyman, 1990.

Michael S. Wald, J.M. Carlsmith, and P.H. Leiderman   *Protecting Abused and Neglected Children.* Stanford, CA: Stanford University Press, 1988.

Jill Waterman, Robert J. Kelly, Mary Kay Oliveri, and Jane McCord   *Beyond the Playground Walls: Sexual Abuse in Preschools.* New York: Guilford Press, 1993.

Richard Wexler   *Wounded Innocents: The Real Victims of the War Against Child Abuse.* Buffalo: Prometheus Books, 1990.

Debra Whitcomb   *When the Victim Is a Child.* 2d ed. Washington, DC: National Institute of Justice, 1992.

Index

285

287